Dealignment
A New Foreign Policy Perspective

Dealignment
A New Foreign Policy Perspective

Edited by

Mary Kaldor and Richard Falk
with the assistance of Gerard Holden

UNITED NATIONS UNIVERSITY
Basil Blackwell

First published 1987

Basil Blackwell Ltd
108 Cowley Road, Oxford, OX4 1JF, UK

Basil Blackwell Inc.
432 Park Avenue South, Suite 1503
New York, NY 10016, USA

British Library Cataloguing in Publication Data

Dealignment : A New Foreign Policy Perspective.
1. North Atlantic Treaty Organization
2. World politics – 1985–1995
I. Kaldor, Mary II. Falk, Richard
III. Holden, Gerard
327.0917′7 D849

ISBN 0-631-15594-5

Library of Congress Cataloging in Publication Data

Dealignment : A New Foreign Policy Perspective

Includes index.
1. Europe—Nonalignment—Congresses. 2. North Atlantic Treaty Organization—Congresses. I. Kaldor, Mary. II. Falk, Richard A. III. Holden, Gerard.
JX1393.N54D42 1987 341.7′2′094 86–32723
ISBN 0-631-15594-5

Typeset in 10 on 12 pt Baskerville
by Alan Sutton Publishing Ltd, Gloucester
Printed in Great Britain by
Billing & Sons Ltd, Worcester

Contents

Contributors

HANNE-MARGRET BIRCKENBACH works for the Hamburg Institute for Peace Research and Security Policy. She was formerly armament information officer for the Green Party and participated in the study group on West European Peace Politics at the Free University of Berlin.

RICHARD FALK is Albert G. Milbank Professor of International Law and Practice at Princeton University, New Jersey. His books include *Indefensible Weapons* (with Robert Jay Lifron) and *The End of World Order*.

SHIRLEY HUNE is an Associate Professor in the Department of Educational Foundations at Hunter College of the City University of New York. Her books include *Namibian Independence* and *Non-alignment in an Age of Alignments* co-authored with A.W. Singham.

MARY KALDOR is a Senior Fellow at the Science Policy Research Unit, University of Sussex, and a Fellow of the Transnational Institute, Amsterdam. Her books include *The Disintegrating West* and *The Baroque Arsenal*.

BEN LOWE is a freelance writer and researcher. He has recently published *La Cara Oculta de la OTAN*.

ROBIN LUCKHAM is a Fellow of the Institute of Development Studies, University of Sussex. His books include *The Nigerian Military*.

GIAN GIACOMO MIGONE is Professor of History at the University of Turin and editor of *L'Indice*.

CHRISTIANE RIX works for the Hamburg Institute for Peace Research and Security Policy. She formerly participated in the study group on West European Peace Politics at the Free University of Berlin.

A.W. SINGHAM is Professor of Political Science at Brooklyn College of the City University of New York. His most recent books include *Namibian Independence* and *Non-alignment in an Age of Alignments* co-authored with Shirley Hune.

ALBERT STATZ is Assistant Professor of International Relations at the Free University of Berlin and was a member of the former study group on West European Peace Politics.

RAIMO VÄYRYNEN is Professor of Political Science at the University of Helsinki, and in 1986–7 is Visiting Professor of War and Peace Studies at Princeton University, New Jersey.

CHRISTIAN WELLMANN is a senior researcher at the Department of International Relations at the Free University of Berlin and was a member of the former study group on West European Peace Politics.

ALAN WOLFE teaches at the City University of New York. His recent books include *The Rise and Fall of the Soviet Threat* and *America's Impasse*.

Acknowledgements

This book resulted from a conference on the subject 'Dealignment for Western Europe?', which was held at the Transnational Institute in Amsterdam in November 1983. We are grateful both to the Transnational Institute and the Peace and Global Transformation Subprogramme of the United Nations University, which sponsored the conference.

We would also like to thank all the participants at the conference for a stimulating discussion which led to the ideas put forward in this book. In particular, Richard Barnet, John Palmer, Pedro Vilanova and Judith Winther wrote papers which made an important contribution to our thinking. The conference and the book could not have happened without the invaluable assistance of June Garson, Maureen Kelly, Caroline ter Braak and Claire Trevelyan in typing and administration.

Mary Kaldor
Richard Falk

1

Introduction

RICHARD FALK AND MARY KALDOR

Perhaps for the first time since 1945, there is ferment and uncertainty surrounding the place of Europe in the world political order. A new plural process of questioning has begun in recent years that controversially touches timeworn fundamentals, especially the future relationship of the two superpowers – the United States and the Soviet Union – to European security. In essence, Europeans from East and West alike are wondering aloud whether there is not some regional solution to their twin torments – repressive dominance by outsiders and the infernal risk of nuclear incineration or a devastating near-nuclear regional war.

What is new in all this is the emerging awareness that there is *one* problem and *one* solution, not two or more. Earlier, struggles for human rights and democracy, largely in the East, were regarded almost exclusively as encounters with the Soviet Union during which no substantial help could be expected from the West, particularly from Washington. Underneath, however, was the political reflex reaction – a pro-NATO disposition embodying the view that the enemy of my enemy is my friend.

Similarly, anxiety in the West about a limited nuclear war that might reduce Europe to ashes was overwhelmingly expressed as a challenge to NATO doctrines and deployment patterns, and especially addressed to fears about American militaristic leadership of the Western alliance. To challenge Soviet hegemony, or even policies, in Eastern Europe was regarded as added fuel to the Cold War, red-baiting, and generally inconsistent with the serious quest for peace. The Soviet Union chortled from the sidelines as the United States squirmed.

Of course, these distinctions were never quite this neat, but almost. In recent years, oppositional tendencies in both East and West have led each to redefine their political situation in a rather dramatic manner. For one thing, there is a regional sense of shared destiny. The somewhat differing agendas of East and West have been understood more and more as mutually linked and dependent. In this regard, the imagery of Europe as physically and psychologically occupied has started to catch on.[1] To achieve either a more peaceful prospect in the West or a more humane prospect to the East, requires an end to this occupation, that is, a finish to the unnaturally prolonged conditions that became ultra-stabilized in the decades following World War II. The presence of each superpower obtains a degree of legitimacy through the presence of the other. And the reverse, too, would seem likely to hold. Interestingly, just as the two parts of Europe can mutually reinforce a shift away from the status quo, the two superpowers mutually reinforce the rationale for the status quo by mounting hostility against one another.

Further, Europeans are realizing that their respective agendas are also more intertwined and convergent than they had previously understood. Activists in Eastern Europe realize that they, too, would be engulfed by nuclear war and that pressure on Moscow in the form of the first-use missiles produces counter-moves and rigidity on the Soviet side. At the same time, peace movement leaders in Western Europe have become aware of erosions of their own sovereign rights through the delegation to Washington of authority to wage war, and that denials of human rights and political democracy in the East help validate the basic argument that only the military strength of NATO keeps the Soviet Union from marching westwards.

This European questioning is being reinforced, admittedly in as yet a tentative and speculative manner, by some developments within the superpower nations. Americans of varying political persuasions are raising doubts as to whether Europe is worth the cost and risk (especially of being drawn once more into a Europen war) of persevering with the postwar arrangement. Leaders are muttering to the effect that it does not make sense to invest so heavily in Europe when the main arena of geopolitical rivalry is increasingly centred in the Pacific Basin. In the background is also the decadence argument. If Europe is worth saving, by which is meant Western Europe in these formulations, then the Europeans should shoulder their share of the defence burden. Alleged burden-shirking is taken as a ground for reducing the American commitment.

In contrast, the Soviet doubts are said, and here we rely on conjecture and hearsay, to centre on their anxiety about a breakdown of regional deterrence given the hardware that is now being deployed on the continent, as well as the expense and failure of their effort to establish a zone of sympathetic subordination in Eastern Europe. Recurrent Soviet intervention since the early 1950s makes it evident to anyone but a hardened Stalinist that socialism – Soviet style – has not taken hold, that the political arrangements imposed after World War II can be preserved only as an incident of a continuing occupation, and that this embarrassing circumstance is transparent to all. The last shred of ambiguity was removed by the massive Solidarity movement and the Moscow-abetted crackdown by Polish party hardliners. Besides, the economic relationship has moved from one of benefit to Moscow to one of growing burden. Is it totally unrealistic to imagine that a more opportunistic Soviet leadership might be receptive to some gradual process of mutual withdrawal from the continent by both superpowers? There is a caveat, however. Such a relaxation of the Soviet grip on Eastern Europe must not be regarded as an invitation to let escape the genie of German reunification or, analogously, to draw into question the territorial delimitation ratified by the Helsinki Final Act of August 1975.

It is against this background that we present this volume of essays, carrying on the interrogation, so to speak, from a variety of angles. The superpowers and the European governments are reluctant, for an array of differing, somewhat contrasting, reasons, to let go of the rigid postwar alliance arrangements. But refusing to let go is assuredly worse. This book, then, is about learning to let go, gradually at the start, more dramatically as confidence grows. We call this process 'dealignment', and specify some of its main dimensions and perspectives in the remainder of this introductory chapter.

The book focuses on the transatlantic relationship. Interest in dealignment emerged from the debate about nuclear weapons in Western Europe over the past few years. What began as a campaign against a new round of the arms race developed into a deeper understanding of the political nature of the relationship between the United States and Western Europe. The campaign revealed a fundamental breakdown in the consensus that legitimized the American military presence in Western Europe both between the United States and West European nations and domestically in Western Europe. Dealignment offers a way out of the current impasse. It is to be hoped that the analysis put forward here could also be applied to other regions, especially Eastern Europe.

THE BREAKDOWN IN TRANSATLANTIC CONSENSUS

In one of the essays in this book, NATO is described as a mechanism for building a consensus among the Western powers.[2] It is a way of arriving at a set of common positions. The NATO Council is in permanent session.

The NATO ambassadors meet three or four times a week to discuss a wide range of political, economic and social issues. The term 'Western bloc' means much more than a military alliance; it tends to mean a shared perspective on economic policy or global affairs, an appreciation of each others' domestic problems on the part of the American and West European establishments, and a common set of assumptions about the virtues of 'Western civilization'.

Seen in a global context, it means a united stance on the part of the advanced capitalist world, a way of sustaining its predominant influence on economic, political and cultural affairs. This consensus is said to be anchored on the US security guarantee, especially the American commitment to defend Western Europe with nuclear weapons, if necessary. The security guarantee implies American willingness to risk millions of American lives for the sake of Western Europe and European willingness to entrust the ultimate responsibility for millions of West European lives to the government of the United States. It expresses a distinctive arrangement of indefinite duration and unknown scope. It is this security guarantee that is variously described as the 'glue' or 'cement' that binds the Atlantic alliance.

After several years of intense debate about the Euromissiles, hardly anyone, on the Left or Right, retains much confidence in the security guarantee. On the Right it is argued that the emergence of nuclear parity means that the security guarantee has lost its credibility. Some, like the neo-conservative Irving Kristol, argue that what the Europeans 'have always fancied is a conflict between the Soviet Union and the United States in which the nuclear missiles fly high over their heads and spare Western Europe. But being an American I don't fancy it one bit, and I don't think the American people are going to continue to expose themselves to nuclear war and nuclear annihilation . . . '.[3] On the Left, in Western Europe, the opposite is feared – namely, that the presence of nuclear weapons in Europe could mean that Europe becomes the nuclear battlefield of the superpowers who, probably wrongly, might believe that their own territory could be spared. These fears have been fuelled by President Reagan's Strategic Defense Initiative, more accurately known as Star Wars, which promises, at least in theory, to create an astrodome over American territory; and by the attack on Libya, in which West Europeans were implicated with or without their complicity, and even their assent.

All the same, it would be wrong to attribute these arguments against the security guarantee to any specific development in technology or strategy. From the moment, in the late 1950s, when the Soviet Union acquired the capability to hit American territory, it was difficult to believe, as de Gaulle put it, that the United States would risk New York for Paris. It is true that nuclear weapons have become much more accurate and that the limited nuclear war rhetoric of those associated with the Reagan administration is deeply disturbing. Nevertheless, it was always the case that nuclear weapons in Europe were targeted against military targets and from the first introduction of tactical nuclear weapons into Europe military experts like Lord Mountbatten were warning of the irrationality of nuclear war-fighting doctrines.

So why, after so many years of apparent unconcern, is the security guarantee being so publicly called into question? What has happened to undermine the generally accepted assumptions of at least a generation? A large part of the answer has to lie in the increasingly divergent interests of the United States and Western Europe; the fact that there is no longer a consensus even on the need for consensus. On a whole range of issues, it is harder and harder to find a set of common positions. Article after article, from Henry Kissinger to Lawrence Eagleburger, from Helmut Schmidt to Michael Howard, has detailed these growing disagreements: on economic issues such as protectionist moves on both sides of the Atlantic, high technology sharing, energy prices, American interest rates; on Third World conflicts, including the European condemnation of the American invasion of Grenada, their less than enthusiastic support for Israel, their publicly expressed support for the Sandinistas in Nicaragua, their opposition to the policy of military reprisals against Libya; and on detente policy, from which the West Europeans have gained much more than the United States. It was, after all, only fifteen or so years ago that West European governments supported the American war in Vietnam, that exchange rates were stable and tied to the dollar, and that the United States, without explicit resistance from Europe, determined how the West would relate to the East.

Out of this breakdown in consensus has come a plethora of proposals for restructuring the Euro-American relationship. Those that emanate from the establishment both in the United States and Western Europe focus on the defence of Western Europe. The idea is that, in one form or another, a new consensus can be built around military strategy.

One set of proposals that emanates from committed Atlanticists emphasizes the conventional component of NATO strategy. The idea is that fears may be damped by reducing reliance on nuclear weapons in the defence of Western Europe. Some of these proposals are quite radical in that they would abandon the strategy of using nuclear weapons first in the event of a Warsaw Pact conventional attack on Western Europe.[4] Others like the proposals put forward by the Supreme Allied Commander Europe (SACEUR), General Bernard Rogers, would leave NATO's nuclear doctrine intact but would raise the so-called nuclear threshold, i.e. the moment when NATO would resort to nuclear weapons, by strengthening NATO's conventional capabilities,[5] thereby presuming to avoid pressure for so-called 'early use' of nuclear weapons.

All these proposals emphasize the need to increase NATO's offensive conventional capabilities, i.e. the ability to hit targets deep in Warsaw Pact territory with conventional weapons. Some of the weapons proposed are said to have the same destructive effect as small nuclear warheads. They appear to be linked with the new US Army doctrine, AirLand Battle, now enshrined in US Army manuals.[6] This doctrine, which is intended for Europe and the Third World and puts great emphasis on manoeuvre and on 'deep strike' or 'deep attack', represents the first effort to integrate nuclear, conventional and chemical war-fighting. Congress has called on the US administration to implement AirLand Battle in Europe: AirLand Battle exercises involving American and West German units have already taken place in Europe.

The conventional deep strike proposals tend to be espoused by what one might describe as the liberal or European Atlanticists. These are the successors to the Trilateralists who believe in a more equal sharing of power in the Atlantic role. They include a range of opinion from West European social democrats, through American moderates like Robert McNamara, through to the NATO establishment, including SACEUR General Rogers and Lord Carrington, the Secretary General. Because the US role in Europe is symbolized by the nuclear guarantee, any increase in conventional weapons is supposed to give Europe a more significant political role in the alliance.

These proposals have, however, been overshadowed by President Reagan's Strategic Defense Initiative. Although more global in scope, it has captured the public imagination in a way that conventional deep strike has not. President Reagan has been much more successful than General Rogers in coopting the language of the peace movements – he talks about the prospects for future generations, the end of deterrence and so on.

As far as Europe is concerned, the strategic consequence of Star Wars is much the same as the new war-fighting doctrines embodied in the deployment of Euromissiles. For Star Wars offers to insulate, at least in theory, the United States from mutual deterrence and hence leaves an American president free to fight a war in Europe without risking American territory.

Star Wars might be described as American unilateralism, an attempt to reimpose a dominant American role in the alliance, to replace Atlantic consensus with American coercion. Caspar Weinberger has said that Star Wars takes us back to the situation of the 1950s when the United States was the only nuclear power. Because attacks on European territory can no longer threaten to embroil American territory, Europeans are dependent on the military whims of the American administration.

American unilateralists feel that American postwar policy was aimed at the good of the world and not enough at the good of America. Atlanticists like General Rogers put the common European–American or Atlantic interest before the American interest. To quote Irving Kristol again:

> The era of liberal internationalism, extending from World War II until 1980, has pretty much petered out. The old liberal Establishment that ran American foreign policy and that basically agreed with the European view of the world has lost, to a large degree, its credibility, its authority and its political influence. . . . The United States is becoming a much more nationalistic country, a country much more concerned with its national interests and more willing to act unilaterally if necessary to pursue its national interest.[7]

In answer to European criticisms that Star Wars offers unequal levels of security, protecting American territory and not European territory, President Reagan has generously offered to extend the shield to Europe. The European Defense Initiative (EDI) is a proposal to develop an anti-tactical ballistic missile to defend Western Europe from Soviet missiles. The proposal has been embraced by Chancellor Kohl in West Germany.

Both Star Wars and conventional deep strike are technological visions. They depend on mobilizing new electronics technologies for so-called battle management, as well as the development of new types of weapons and sensors. In both cases, the technologies are to be mainly American, but some kind of technology sharing has been offered as bait.

Another set of proposals comes from what one might describe as the Euro-Gaullists. They favour the pursuit of the West European interests as opposed to the Atlantic interest. They favour greater West European unity, greater economic protection from the United States and an increasing capability to pursue independent interests in the rest of the world.

Euro-Gaullism finds an echo in isolationist sentiment in the United States. US Senators like Sam Nunn advocate the withdrawal of American troops from Western Europe in order to administer the kind of shock treatment needed to prod the Europeans into greater military efforts. Henry Kissinger, in an article which caused a great stir, also proposed that the Supreme Allied Commander in Europe should be a European, so that Europeans would feel more responsible for their own defence.[8]

The European Gaullists talk about a political union and a Europe-wide defence alliance. This kind of thinking has been most pronounced in France where it has been linked to ideas about the renaissance of European culture. Fernand Braudel, the historian and honorary Professor of the College de France, said, in an interview with *Le Monde*, that it is necessary 'to reinvent the United States of Europe with the aim of saving European culture . . . Europe cannot really be rebuilt culturally . . . if there is no common European defence'.[9] The Nouvels Philosophes, many of whom emerged out of the student movement of 1968, have been associated with this kind of thinking. André Glucksmann and Cornelius Castoriadis took part in a colloquium in Paris in February 1983, organized by the Mouvement Européen, on the theme 'Towards European Defense for Europe'.

In fact, European Gaullism represents a fundamental shift from the original Gaullism. De Gaulle always emphasized the importance of having the national freedom to opt out of the mutual defence commitment and the theory of the force de frappe was the 'sanctuary' theory, namely the protection of France in the event of an East–West conflict. However, a new French consensus has emerged, shared by both Mitterand and Giscard d'Estaing, on the need for a new European alliance to substitute for NATO. The Giscardian concept of 'extended sanctuarization' is merely a verbal sop to the Gaullists. This new European alliance, centred on the Franco–German relationship, would be nuclear as well as conventional. Giscard envisaged 'a situation in which the French nuclear umbrella would protect both sides of the Rhine in exactly the same way, and in which the French and German peoples' perception of the nuclear threat and nuclear protection would gradually converge to become those of neighbours with common views'.[10] French defence experts, echoed by socialist deputies in the National Assembly, have been proposing that the new French tactical missile HADES should be dual-key and should be deployed in West Germany. (In fact, their range is too short to reach the Soviet Union from France.)

Some of these ideas have been taken up in West Germany, especially among the ruling CDU–CSU coalition. In particular, the German defence minister, Manfred Woerner, has been enthusiastic about Franco–German defence cooperation. There is even talk of an integrated European nuclear force, combining British and French nuclear weapons with a joint European decision-making process. It is pointed out that the number of French, and possibly British strategic nuclear warheads is likely to increase considerably in the 1990s. This idea has been strongly promoted by David Owen, leader of the SDP in Britain.

The idea of European defence cooperation is frequently raised in the European Parliament. A recent report of the political committee, for example, envisages an integrated European defence as the final goal of European political cooperation. More significant, perhaps, has been the attempt by France to revitalize the Western European Union (WEU). The

WEU was founded in 1954 after a failed attempt to create a European defence community, in order to contain the rearmament of Germany. (Many regard the formation of the Warsaw Pact in 1955 as a response to this event.) It includes seven West European states — France, Britain, West Germany, Italy, Belgium, Luxembourg and Holland, and excludes some of the more troublesome members of NATO like Greece and Denmark. The WEU has a much stronger mutual defence commitment to use armed force in the event of an attack on another party. Moreover, unlike the North Atlantic Treaty, the defence commitment is not confined to Europe and some argue that the WEU could be used to support 'out of area' operations — such as intervention in the Third World — by West European countries. So far, the revival of the WEU has involved the lifting of many of the restrictions on West German arms production that were imposed in 1954, and a meeting of foreign and defence ministers in Rome in October 1984, which ended with a rather innocuous statement about 'strengthening the European pillar of NATO'.

In all these discussions, a good deal of emphasis has been placed on technology. If NATO is a market for American technology with some gestures towards technology sharing, then proposals for European defence cooperation, within the European Parliament, the WEU or even NATO's Eurogroup, have a lot to do with the pressure from the European defence industry for a large protected market. It is characteristic that the French answer to Star Wars is a technology project known as Eureka. In theory, the project is civil but the technologies to be encouraged seem likely to be those suitable for space-based defence for nuclear war-fighting. As one German defence official put it: 'For the European defense industry to grow and remain viable will require biting the bullet and excluding US involvement and technology in favor of cooperative programs in Europe'.[11]

Despite the grand pronouncements, however, the project of European defence cooperation is far from being realized. It may be fair to say that the project of building a West European consensus is as difficult as it is to maintain the present Atlantic consensus. If it is difficult to reach agreement about a common agricultural policy, then how much more difficult to reach agreement about a common defence policy. The West European project does not have the advantage that NATO enjoys of a single dominant partner. Even now cooperative technology ventures are fraught with disagreements about worksharing, technology transfer, financial participation, conflicting military requirements. Even if a consensus can be reached at a governmental level, can it acquire popular support? Already, the West European peace movement is vociferously opposing trends towards a new European military bloc. One of the progressive elements of NATO could be said to have been the way it diluted European nationalism. British jingoism and French chauvinism do flare up from time to time, though this is much less true of the other West European countries. Moreover, it is reasonable to ask how many Europeans, apart from some French intellectuals, feel a sense of West European as opposed to French, British or German identity.

All the proposals, the Atlanticist technological fix and the Gaullist Europeanization, are based on the assumption that the Atlantic consensus was required for collective defence against a Soviet threat. In a sense, discussions about alternative defence postures are surrogates for deeper discussions about political relationships. These proposals are all designed, in different ways, to sustain an East–West confrontation. In this book, we start from a different assumption – namely, that the Atlanticist consensus was and is required for internal cohesion among Western capitalist countries. The Soviet threat came afterwards. The East–West confrontation is a consequence as much as a cause of collective defence.

Internal cohesion could serve several purposes. First, and perhaps most important, the Atlantic consensus provided a way in which centrist governments, especially in Western Europe, obtained political support from each other in the face of strong domestic challenges, especially from the Left. As some of the chapters in this book show, the alliance, particularly in the early years, provided a mechanism for neutralizing radical policies. It was not only important in Western Europe; it played a role in American domestic policies as well. In a sense the alliance developed a kind of Atlanticist philosophy, which for most of the period was shared by all the major political parties in the Atlantic region – a commitment to managed capitalism, to some redistribution, to collective security, parliamentary democracy etc.

Secondly, the Atlantic consensus made possible the international economic cooperation referred to explicitly in Article 2 of the Treaty, so as to avoid the disastrous tendencies towards economic nationalism displayed by the capitalist world in the 1930s. The Bretton Woods system of basing the international economy on the dollar, the gradual dismantling of tariff barriers, GATT (the General Agreement on Tariffs and Trade), OECD (Organization for Economic Cooperation and Development), the World Bank, were all underpinned by this consensus between the major industrial powers of the world, as well as by the prudent exercise of US hegemony, especially in diplomatic, economic and cultural spheres.

And thirdly, the Atlantic consensus disciplined global relationships, particularly North–South relations. Pax Americana was only possible in the context of a unified policy on the part of the advanced industrial countries. Although the Soviet Union could and did challenge American power through the provision of arms and military aid, its capacity for economic penetration was limited and this, as well as the revelations of Stalinist repression, ultimately constrained its political role in the Third World. It was Western Europe and later Japan that represented the real potential competitors in the Third World. NATO, which was limited to Europe and North America initially, enabled the United States to take over many of the hegemonic roles of the European powers in large parts of the Third World and later provided for a common North position – the super imperialism predicted by classical Marxist writers like Bukharin – which limited the possibilities for independent action on the part of Southern elites. The reluctance of West Europeans to provide sufficient material assistance to the Sandinistas in Nicaragua is an ongoing example of this Atlantic discipline.

The Atlantic consensus could be said to have provided a framework for the postwar economic boom and political stability. This is no longer the case, and this is a major reason for its breakdown. Central to its success was the fact that the American policy-makers identified the Atlantic interest as the American interest. With the relative economic and political decline of the United States *vis-à-vis* Western Europe, this attitude changed. For West Europeans, it appeared as though successive American administrations were imposing the American interest on the Atlantic region, shifting from Atlantic consensus to American coercion. This was evident in new protectionist moves, in high interest rates, the determination to push through the Euromissile deployment rather than finding a face-saving formula through talks and cosmetic arms control with the Soviet Union, the Strategic Defense Initiative and, more recently, the US-led counter-terrorist campaign, highlighted to date by the 15 April 1986 air attack on Libya. The new coercion undermines what remains of the Atlantic consensus.

If this argument is right and the Soviet threat is mainly a way of legitimizing internal cohesion, then the breakdown of consensus is very dangerous. Once the role of the alliance is perceived through the prism of the Soviet threat, any internal dissension is attributed to external interference. Renewed consensus is achieved through ever more shrill denouncements of the Soviet Union. Indeed the Soviet Union *has* to be expansionist and oppressive in order to justify consensus. As long as we cling to the consensus, divergent interests between Western Europe and the United States are necessarily transmogrified into Cold War rhetoric, whatever the Soviet Union does, and no matter what the genuine interplay of interests and values.

But the New Cold War, as it is often described, is less convincing than the old Cold War. Perhaps it could be described as a phoney Cold War. On the one hand, the alliance has been consolidated over the last several years with the deployment of the missiles, the Star Wars initiative, the new emphasis on conventional and chemical defence, the defeat of the Spanish peace movement in the referendum on NATO. On the other hand, there is more questioning of alliance policies than ever before within the European establishment, taking the form of critiques of Star Wars and unwillingness to increase defence budgets; with renewed pressure for arms control, especially a comprehensive test ban and an agreement on medium range missiles in Europe, following the Gorbachev proposals and the Rejkyavik mini-summit; with the new nuclear-free status of Greece and Spain; and with continued civil disobedience against cruise and Pershing missiles; and with European dismay at the global unilateralism displayed by the United States.

In the 1950s, Europeans were afraid of a repetition of World War II; the Cold War succeeded in marginalizing radical policies and in creating a domestic and international consensus. Today, when there is much to gain – economically, culturally, scientifically – from East–West exchange, confrontational military policies are no longer seen as deterrents to war but as dangerous and expensive provocations. Such policies do not underwrite consensus; rather they polarize society and stimulate radical consciousness. There is a real risk that the very failure of external confrontation could lead to more and more 'remedies' – remedies that entail increased internal repression and the possibility of proving the reality of Cold War through a real war. But, at the same time, failure of those policies also reflects a new scepticism on the part of public opinion towards the traditional remedies. It is a healthy scepticism that could mean a new receptivity towards alternative approaches. It is in such paradoxical contradictory situations that political creativity can often flourish.

In this respect, the growth and evolution of the peace movement, especially in Western Europe, over the past few years has been profoundly important. For the peace movement could act as an agent of transformation, offering a way out of the cul-de-sac established by government policies. The peace movement could be said to represent a new phenomenon in political life, appropriate to the stage of evolution of West European society. The insistence on independence both from political parties and state institutions, and the notion that policies are changed not through capturing positions of power but through changing relations of power, are original concepts. It would not be exaggerated to compare the rapid recent growth of the peace movements with the emergence of the labour movement at the end of the nineteenth century. If the historic role of the labour movement was to challenge relations of economic power, then the historic role of the peace movement could be to challenge relations of political power, and conceivably cultural power as well.

Up to now, the peace movement has been primarily an anti-nuclear movement. But that is by no means the same thing as a single issue movement. Nuclear weapons are an encompassing issue. Their very possession and development for use is a hideous irrationality suggesting something profoundly wrong with the power structures that produced them. The unwillingness to recognize this irrationality, indeed the complicity of many well meaning citizens that follows from the long-standing consensus about nuclear weapons, is a kind of blindness akin to the refusal to believe Cassandra's prophesies about the fall of Troy, which eventually resulted in her death for telling the truth.[12] Challenging the existence of nuclear weapons necessarily involves challenging the structures within which political power is currently exercised.

The recognition by the peace movement of the link between nuclear weapons and global power structures has brought the movement closer to other social movements that are challenging power structures in their own societies. Human rights movements in Eastern Europe, or movements arising from economic and ecological devastation in the Third World, have also come to recognize a similar link between their struggles and the current international state system. 'Dealignment' in Western Europe represents a possible opening for political transformation.

THE CONCEPT OF 'DEALIGNMENT'

Atlantic technical fixes or new Gaullist institutional arrangements seek a new consensus within an Atlantic or West European framework, predicated on a New Cold War. The alternative is to seek a consensus about dissensus. Internal cohesion is no longer a strength but a constraint. If we are to seek alternative approaches to economic and social problems, or to restructure relations with the Third World, then we need to create space for new political forces in Europe.

This is what we mean by 'dealignment'. In essence, we are aiming for diversity while diminishing polarization and conflict. This means that the military elements in relations between states need to be reduced so that economic and social change does not threaten to engulf us all in war. It means finding new democratic ways of managing international disagreements. If the Atlantic alliance is about internal cohesion and not about the Soviet threat, then the first priority is to reconsider internal cohesion. Dealignment would mean gradually moving away from the necessity for common positions – building a new consensus around respect for pluralism and tolerance for a variety of social experiments. It is on this pluralistic basis that West Europeans can restructure East–West and North–South relations.

How to deal with the Soviet threat becomes a matter of analysis of the nature of the East–West conflict. It follows from our assumptions about the nature of the Atlantic alliance that the Soviet military build-up is not necessarily intended for expansionist purposes, though this does not mean that the Soviet Union is benign. It could be a response to the Western military build-up or it could be about internal cohesion within the Warsaw Pact. If this is the case, a lessening of the Western military build-up could directly lessen the Soviet military threat or indirectly do so by weakening the external legitimation for internal Warsaw Pact cohesion. 'Dealignment' could be a concept and approach with attractions for East Europeans as well.

'Dealignment' differs from non-alignment and neutrality in that it is a policy of *beyond the blocs* rather than *between the blocs*. Neutral countries simply try to stay out of the blocs, although this may mean paradoxically that they have an interest in preserving a stable bloc system. Some Swiss and Swedish military experts consider that their neutrality depends on a military balance between East and West. Non-alignment is, in general, a Third World concept but it has some parallels with dealignment in that non-aligned countries aim to increase their international freedom of manoeuvre, the space for domestic self-determination. Nevertheless, non-aligned countries regard themselves as outside the blocs and may protect their non-aligned status militarily. Dealignment is a positive effort to unravel the blocs and, in this, it has more in common with the Swedish concept of positive neutrality.

'Dealignment' does not necessarily mean withdrawing from or dismantling the formal structures of the alliances. But it does mean changing the *content* of the alliance. It means an abstention from and an erosion of alliance culture. It means an eventual military disengagement from the alliances and a willingness to dissent from the alliance consensus. In this sense, countries like Denmark or Greece may be more dealigned than a country like France which has formally withdrawn from NATO's integrated command structure. In particular, if alliance consensus is symbolized in the US security guarantee, then strategies for nuclear disarmament *are* strategies of dealignment.

Dealignment is a process rather than a goal or an objective. The aim is to reduce the alliance system to marginality. The formal structures of the alliances might never be dissolved; rather, they could become relics of the current epoch. Without influence on economic and social relationships, whatever survives in the form of treaties or even the occasional get-together of foreign ministers would be merely reminders of a time when politics was held in thrall to the fear of nuclear war.

In practice, this process has already begun. Already, there are varieties of status within the Western alliance. Denmark, Norway and Canada are non-nuclear members of NATO. Greece and Spain have declared their intention to follow the non-nuclear example. France and Spain, after the referendum, do not belong to the military structure of NATO. Dissent also has become admissible. Greece and Denmark did not consent to the deployment of cruise and Pershing missiles. Norway, Denmark, Holland, France and Greece have all refused to participate in President Reagan's Star Wars project; indeed, only Britain, West Germany and Italy have so far been prepared to sign an agreement about participation.

To a much lesser degree, one can observe the same kind of diplomatic pluralism in the Warsaw Pact as well. Romania has a rather independent foreign policy. Hungary, and on occasion the GDR, have sometimes nuanced their support for Soviet military policies. In a sense, we are describing a blurring of the meaning of alliance membership. If the process continues, it may eventually become irrelevant to distinguish alliance members from neutral states.

In effect, we are seeking a political formula for transforming power relations within the Atlantic region. 'Dealignment' is a concept and policy which could help to develop such a formula, although it may be applicable to other regions as well. It involves a shift in orientation, and it is the orientation that seems especially important. It means, on the one hand, a more cooperative relationship between the superpowers, and it also means that all countries must or should seek a more independent pursuit of security, from their own national perspectives, and on the basis of their individual situations. In a European context it seems to us that dealignment means taking sovereign rights more seriously, and in a sense this is a very conservative argument. It is not really a nationalistic argument, it is a constitutional argument. It asserts that, in the first instance, the leadership of any particular country is responsible to and for the people of that country, and that the government cannot properly relinquish that responsibility by transferring it to other external centres of power. That kind of transfer of responsibility entails an entirely unacceptable delegation of authority, especially to the extent that it is not truly appreciated by the public and possibly not even by the leaders. It is one of several factors that confines and stifles the role of parliamentary democracy under present conditions.

The debate about Euromissiles illustrates the point. The fact that deployment began in Britain, Italy and West Germany at the end of 1983, despite vociferous and articulate public opposition, and despite the fact that the polls indicated that a majority of the population opposed deployment in all five deployment countries, seemed to call into question the proper functioning of democracy. In Holland in November 1985 the decision to deploy went ahead despite a constitutional petition to Parliament that contained 3.7 million signatures. It was argued that, having taken the decision to deploy in December 1979, NATO had to carry out the decision in order to display to the Soviet Union its collective ability to implement decisions. In other words, it was an argument that alliance cohesion comes before accountability to public opinion on the political priorities of governments.

To elaborate what dealignment means in concrete terms, it seems useful to specify five dimensions of the concept that would together amount to a process of loosening ties within the alliance system. The first dimension is *denuclearization*. Denuclearization has a particular significance in the transatlantic context, because of the role that fear of nuclear war combined with American nuclear protection has played in forming the alliance consensus, in delineating the framework for US–European agreement.

It is possible that nuclear weapons could come to play a similar role in Eastern Europe. When the Soviet Union announced the deployment of SS-21 and SS-22 missiles in Czechoslovakia and East Germany, allegedly in response to the deployment of cruise and Pershing II in Western Europe, it was the first time that the Soviet Union had publicly announced the presence of nuclear weapons in Eastern Europe. Formally, the cohesion of the Warsaw Pact was maintained in circumstances of extreme challenge through direct military force, as in Czechoslovakia in 1968 or Hungary in 1956. The imposition of martial law in Poland in December 1981, may have betokened, among other things, a growing disutility of, or at least reluctance to depend upon, direct Soviet military intervention. The ideology of imminent nuclear war could represent an alternative mechanism to sustain Soviet hegemony in the face of mounting discontent.

Because of the role of the US nuclear guarantee, we have emphasized strategies of denuclearization as a prime element in the process of dealignment. It is not so much that such proposals lessen the risk of nuclear war by reducing the number of nuclear weapons around or by rejecting nuclear war-fighting strategies. After all, whatever Europe does, it has to be recognized that no part of the planet could escape a global nuclear war. Rather, it is that such proposals represent a repudiation of the notion that power is represented by nuclear warheads and that European countries in particular face a permanent confrontation only held in check through combined alliance determination. By refusing nuclear weapons on foreign territory, by freeing particular geographical regions of nuclear weapons, and by rejecting particular nuclear strategies, these assumptions about the nature of international politics are eroded if not undermined.

Three proposals for denuclearization are prominent in the discussions about dealignment. One is the proposal for a no-first-use declaration by NATO, discussed in chapter 6. Such a declaration has already been made in unconditional form by the Soviet Union. Of course, a comparable declaration by NATO would have far greater significance because NATO strategy is currently based on the doctrine that, in the event of a Warsaw Pact conventional attack that NATO failed to repel, NATO reserves the option to resort to the use of nuclear weapons. A declaration of no-first-use ought, therefore, to involve a drastic shift of strategy and weapons deployment. It ought to mean the removal of potential first-use weapons; this would include cruise and Pershing as well as other weapons with a deep strike role such as the F-111 or Tornado. At present, NATO planners appear to regard a deep strike against selected targets in the Warsaw Pact the most likely form of first use. However, battlefield nuclear weapons – short range missiles, ground attack aircraft, mines – are also likely to be used at an early stage of any battle and, in the past, were considered a probable trigger mechanism for all-out escalation.

Of course, it is possible that a no-first-use declaration could be a cosmetic measure, allowing for a redefinition of roles around the concept of deterrence without altering the pattern of deployment. A chemical weapons no-first-use agreement has been in force since 1925 without ending the threat of chemical warfare. The modernization of NATO's chemical warfare capability proceeds in any event, being justified on the ground of like-with-like deterrence.

The no-first-use proposal is interesting in part because it represents a possible compromise strategy between the liberal Atlanticists and the peace movement. It does appear to reduce the provocation of NATO's posture towards the East and hence allows for a defusion of the confrontation and an opening for further measures. To ensure that the declaration is not merely cosmetic, it is important to reinforce the proposals with other measures of denuclearization.

A second denuclearization proposal is 'freeze and withdraw'. This proposal emerged from joint discussions between the American and West European peace movements in the context of their joint campaign against the deployment of Euromissiles in the autumn of 1983. It was seen as a way of taking that experience a step further and building a common global platform within which local, regional and national initiatives could be pursued. The proposal included a global freeze on development and production of new nuclear weapons combined with the withdrawal of all nuclear weapons on foreign territory. The two demands represent a concept for denuclearization as much as an arms control proposal, even if a treaty might be the result. The demands are multilateral in the sense that they apply to all countries but they are most likely to be achieved through unilateral or independent initiatives. Nevertheless, it is interesting to note that the Soviet Union has adopted the proposal as a negotiating stance; freeze and withdraw is the centrepiece of stage two of Mr Gorbachev's proposals for eliminating nuclear weapons by the year 2000.[13]

The demand for withdrawal of nuclear weapons from foreign territory is a way of reasserting the sovereign rights of countries. No nuclear-weapons state has the right to risk the territory of a non-nuclear-weapons state. The presence of foreign nuclear weapons, even dual-key systems, represents a serious limitation of national sovereignty. At the same time, the concept of sovereignty is not identified with military strength. Rather, it is linked to self-determination and is, in this sense, an essential component of dealignment.

The freeze demand differs from the proposal of the American peace movement in that it is world-wide: it includes Britain, France and China as well as the United States and the Soviet Union. And the withdrawal demand differs from the European peace movement's demand for a European nuclear-free zone, which envisages the roll-back of nuclear weapons to the territories of the superpowers, in that it is also world-wide and links the situation in Europe to the situation in the Pacific and the Third World.

Contained in the concept of dealignment is the notion of replacing coercion by states with popular cooperation. As emphasized in chapter 4, dealignment in Europe should be implemented in such a way as to avoid encouraging isolationist or aggressive tendencies in the United States. Unless there are powerful domestic political constraints in the United States, dealignment could provoke confrontation. 'Freeze and withdraw' offers a proposal around which popular cooperation could once again coalesce. As the official Atlantic alliance is increasingly discredited with missile convoys, barbed wire, police and paratroopers, an alternative alliance needs to emerge, based on the ideals of friendship, cooperation and common interest instead of fear.

The third proposal for denuclearization is nuclear-free zones.[14] Nuclear-free zones have been central to the demands of the European peace movement, and assume a variety of distinct symbolic and substantive moves. They include local and municipal nuclear-free zones that represent a political declaration by local government — declarations of responsibility for foreign policy. They include regional and sub-regional nuclear-free zones. Especially important, at present, are the campaigns for nuclear-free zones in the Nordic areas, the Balkans, the Iberian peninsula and Central Europe, especially the so-called 'Palme corridor' that would separate the two Germanies.

A principal purpose of a nuclear-free zone is to increase political rather than military security. It is true that if a zone is created, some nuclear targets will be removed. But bomb depots and launching pads are not the only targets. On the military priority lists of important areas to be destroyed are also command posts, listening devices, airfields, traffic junctions and so on. Furthermore, it is not very realistic to suppose that any region would remain unaffected as an isolated island during a nuclear war between the superpowers, whether or not it is nuclear-free, although in a small-scale nuclear exchange, significant differences in damage would certainly result.

To expect security against nuclear attack during a war is illusory. It is based on the same kind of thinking as traditional defence strategies; i.e. what is important is to save our own country and our own region no matter what happens to the rest of the world. But this attitude is impossible today. With the existence of nuclear weapons the security of any country is decisively linked to the security of all other countries. This position was taken in the report of the Palme commission.[15]

We live in a world where mistrust is one of the main dispositions in international relations, and we must be aware of the fact that nuclear-free zones mean a radical break with attitudes that have been built up during centuries of Western culture. Again, it is a way of separating the concept of sovereignty from the belief in military power. To most people, it seems improbable to imagine that coexistence between nations could be managed mainly through agreements, treaties and international laws. War has always existed and it will go on existing, they say. As proof they can point to our historical experience and the number of treaties which have been broken – always to the detriment of those who have been naive enough to uphold them – as well as to persisting structures of conflict.

But whether or not treaties are broken depends significantly on the extent to which an environment is created in which a treaty can be fulfilled. It is the institutions of NATO that made the Atlantic Treaty such an enduring arrangement. A nuclear-free zone would also have to establish measures and institutions that regulate everyday communication and intercourse between the parties involved. The aim would be not only to translate the nuclear-free zone concept into a working reality but also to further its development through cooperation with surrounding societies.

Denuclearization should not be undertaken in such a way as to produce a supposedly compensatory build-up of conventional armaments. Hence, the second dimension of dealignment that follows closely from the first is *demilitarization.* It is the presence of Soviet and American troops and weapons in Europe, periodic hostile manoeuvres and the integration of the armed forces of individual national armed forces into the alliance military structures that fundamentally expresses the content of alignment. The process of dealignment has to aim, first and foremost, for military disengagement – the withdrawal of American and Soviet troops from the continent of Europe, the stabilization and eventual reduction of European military capabilities and the phased disintegration of alliance command structures. In Eastern Europe it is demilitarization in general that is most important rather than denuclearization; it was tanks that were used in Budapest and Prague, not the psychological fear of nuclear war, although the nuclear dimension appears to be becoming more relevant, especially after Chernobyl. In Western Europe, NATO's new proposals for conventional war-fighting strategies, as well as new proposals for Europeanization, upgrade the significance of conventional weapons so that they can come to play a psychological role similar to that previously performed by nuclear weapons. New conventional weapons are extremely destructive and can be used to attack targets deep inside Warsaw Pact territory. Combined with Reaganite talk of 'rolling back' Europe, they represent a profound and dangerous provocation, a way of sustaining the military confrontation, even without nuclear weapons.

Proposals for alternative non-nuclear, non-provocative defence policies are, therefore, an important element of a strategy of dealignment. Such policies eschew *both* nuclear weapons *and* offensive conventional weapons. The idea is to provide protection without provocation, thus providing opportunities for alternative ways of overcoming the East–West confrontation. Applied in Europe, alternative non-provocative defence policies would mean eliminating American, Soviet, British and French nuclear weapons, deep strike weapons and excessive numbers of tanks. The aim is to make it practicably impossible to attack the other side's territory while maintaining a reasonably effective defence of one's own territory. There are a range of alternative defence strategies currently under discussion in military, academic and political circles, especially in Britain and West Germany. It is interesting to note that the WTO (Warsaw Treaty Organization) statement of June 11, 1986, dealing with proposals for conventional force reductions, also proposed a shift of strategies towards defensive postures on both sides.

Of course, even a claim of protection can be provocative, as has become abundantly clear in President Reagan's Star Wars programme. Alternative non-provocative defence policies ought to be accompanied by constraints on the overall size of military budgets and, above all, grounded in an alternative East–West policy.

This is why the third dimension of dealignment, *depolarization*, is so important. Depolarization means lessening the influence of bipolarity. Depolarization means that individual European countries demarcate for themselves possibilities for independent action both with respect to domestic affairs and with respect to North–South relations. In effect, depolarization is an ongoing process. Already, West European domestic policies – the welfare state, civil Keynesianism – diverge from the Atlantic consensus, although they are threatened by austerity policies. Over the past ten to twenty years, some West Europeans have begun to restructure relations with the Third World so as to widen the space for defining Third World problems outside the arena of East–West conflict. Dutch and Norwegian support for the Sandinistas in Nicaragua is one example. It is worth noting that this process affects East European countries as well. The recently elected international secretary of the Hungarian Communist Party has argued for adapting new models of socialism to national characteristics. He has pointed out the 'serious danger' of 'mechanical adoption of the experience of other countries, mere copying' and the need to recognize the 'dialectic of identity for substance and variety of forms, of the national and the international . . . not only in the various areas of the socialist work of construction but also in socialist foreign policy'.[16] Depolarization is about reducing tensions and finding space; it is a shift away from the overwhelming role of East–West conflict in determining domestic and global affairs.

Depolarization should not be confused with multipolarity, a concept favoured by President Nixon and, more recently, President Mitterand. The creation of a West European bloc simply means the creation of a new pole of political and military influence. Depolarization means an overall weakening of coercive international relationships. Depolarization includes detente, in the sense of a more cooperative relationship between the superpowers and their respective allies. But it means more than detente. It means both increased cooperation and a lessening of the social division between East and West; it means less identification between each superpower and its allies; it means a blurring of the distinction between East and West. It involves both increased autonomy and increased cooperation. In the language of the peace movement, depolarization encompasses both official detente, or detente from above, and citizens' detente or detente from below. Official detente did not actually entail and was not expected to entail an erosion of the bloc system, the definition of East and West, although there were elements in the Helsinki Accords, especially Basket III human rights concerns, that had the inevitable secondary effect in Eastern Europe of questioning bloc cohesion. On the contrary, it was mainly seen as a different way of managing East–West relations. In practice, official detente could not contain citizens' detente – new forms of East–West communication, cooperation and exchange, increased space for autonomous activities – because the discipline of external confrontation was less. And this was one reason why official detente was foreclosed. Depolarization deliberately fosters both official detente and citizens' detente.

The fourth dimension is *democratization*, which obviously follows from depolarization. Democratization is self-evidently an essential element of dealignment for Eastern Europe. But as became clear, in the campaign against the Euromissiles, it is crucial for Western Europe as well. It involves, in particular, popular control over security policy. It challenges the domination over security that has been instituted by the state and which has established for its purposes a permanent condition of emergency. The whole foundation of democratic theory rests on the normalcy of peace as an underlying condition; it is premised on the rare exceptionality of war, during which the institutional procedures embodying democracy are not expected to function adequately. We are aware of the abridgements of liberties associated with wartime. We know about the kind of voluntary and involuntary censorship that restricts the flow of information to citizens in wartime. We realize the ease with which the rights of suspect citizens can be overridden by wartime claims of national security. The complicity of national institutions, including the US Supreme Court, with the 'relocation' of West Coast Japanese citizens during World War II is one prominent instance. We know less well that the period since World War II, as a result of a constant state of prewar mobilization, has provided a structure of habitual justification for special claims on behalf of national security. This circumstance has all the political effects of a perpetual war condition for the civic order, for the society and for the state. The state is always claiming a war footing because it is then entitled to have a full range of emergency prerogatives at its disposal according to the tradition, including the control of public information and the management of defence and the curtailment of opposition. This massive change has been managed so gradually as to be virtually invisible to the citizen, and is virtually unnoticed even by the peace movement. It constitutes a kind of huge unseen encroachment on the sovereign power of the people; the state, as the supposed repository of delegated power, has become extraordinarily autonomous, especially in the national security area. The people, the citizens, have become subjects and are consequently very passive, and expected to be passive. The knowledge needed for democratic judgement is either secret or expert or both, and therefore there is said to be, by definition, very little room for citizen participation. To the extent that the professional community is concerned with arms control, negotiations have also operated within the context of this expert discourse, and they have also reinforced a sense of impotence on the part of the citizenry.

It is not just that the normalcy of peace is a condition for the proper functioning of democracy. It is also that democracy – public debate, open government, public accountability – represents a condition for a depolarized and denuclearized world. If new forms of democratic relationship are to be established among states, replacing more coercive relationships, these have to be overseen, as it were, by a responsible, alert and politically effective citizenry.

The fifth and last dimension is *development*. This is the least elaborated of our five dimensions and yet could conceivably turn out to be the most important. Development is an imperative for all societies, not just those in the Third World seeking to mobilize their resources, to overcome mass poverty and to build up an economic strategy that can satisfy internal needs without producing dependency. Several of the richer industrialized societies face a crisis of cultural underdevelopment, the mounting consequences of having neglected the needs of the poor, of the environment, of cities. This cultural underdevelopment is directly related to the postwar alliance framework. This is not just in the direct sense that heavy military spending has represented a drain on resources and dictated technological priorities, although this is by no means unimportant. But there is also the broader sense in which the Atlantic framework provided a consensus about the direction of development, as will be discussed in chapters 6 and 7. It was a framework for managing economic conflicts between elites that simply did not take into account those social, ecological and cultural problems that emerged in the 1960s and 1970s. Energy conservation, alternative renewable sources of energy, pollution control, for example, were literally outside the discourse of governments either because they were not foreseen, or because they had no political constituency at the time. Other problems, like the re-emergence of mass unemployment, cannot be solved within the Atlantic consensus because of the changed economic relationship between the United States and Western Europe. The adoption of diverse local, national or even sub-regional approaches to development in the fullest sense both requires and contributes to the erosion of Atlantic consensus. In particular, conversion, the attempt to develop plans for socially useful production as an alternative to military production or unemployment, offers to transform the passive role of the labour movement, its complicity in militarization, and its political marginalization.

Just as the Atlantic consensus had to do with the direction of the Atlantic economy, so Soviet coercion had to do with the imposition of

Soviet-style socialist systems. The East–West confrontation did eventually involve a redefinition of capitalism and socialism as relatively homogeneous identifiable models, based on the American and Soviet experience respectively. They were models which were, so to speak, 'blind' with respect to problems outside their own social definition, such as environment, welfare or Third World poverty in the West or democracy in the East. Dealignment has to mean, therefore, pluralism in development, in social and economic trajectories, so that socioeconomic systems can no longer be rigidly categorized into one or the other type.

The campaign against Euromissiles raised the issues of denuclearization and democratization. The campaign increased consciousness about the effects of war, about constraints on democracy and about the nature of the East–West conflict. But the issue of development, especially in an East–West context, was hardly touched.

The emerging campaign against Star Wars has begun to raise this issue. Star Wars is a research programme; its main immediate effect is on the direction of new technologies, especially information technology. Who decides what kind of technologies should be developed, and for what purpose, are integral questions within the broader discussion about the arms race and the Cold War. Thinking about alternative technologies is thus part of any attempt to halt the Star Wars programme.

These five dimensions provide a framework to encourage an overall rethinking of West–West and East–West relations. This framework also helps to illuminate the complex kinds of tensions and contradictions that derive from specific undertakings, for instance, a no-first-use proposal in Europe.

The framework is not, of course, complete unless it is applied to East–East relations as well. This book has focused on the West–West relationship as enacted in Europe. But there has emerged from our work a sense that, at least conceptually, the problems faced by East Europeans can be presented in a similar way. It does seem as though the concatenation of circumstances in Europe – the intensification of ostensible external confrontation, combined with growing cooperation, the relative economic power of Europe combined with passivity in the face of apparent military power of the superpowers – gives rise to confusing and diverging perceptions of what is happening. A clear-sighted insight may be what is needed to produce change in Europe – change which could have far-reaching implications for the way the world is organized.

We are, of course, aware that the European focus of the book may appear to misstate Europe's role in global affairs. During the period we describe, it is probably true to say that a geo-political shift has been taking place from Europe to the Pacific. Atlantic rivalries, American political, economic and military rivalries, cannot be properly described without taking into account the role of Japan as an economic superpower, the complex relations between China, the Soviet Union, Japan, and Australasia, the rise of newly industrializing countries like South Korea and Taiwan, the wars in Indo China and so on. Nevertheless, Europe, we believe, still retains a pivotal psychological importance as a theatre of war and a source of ideological conflict. And we believe that some of the analytical concepts developed in this book are relevant to the Pacific area. The increasing dominance of East–West relations, Japan's assent to the Strategic Defense Initiative, New Zealand's practical example of dealignment have parallels and resonance in Europe.

Chapters 2 and 3 of this book set the European context. The contributions by Falk and Migone, in different ways, explore the notion of Europe as an occupied continent. They provide an alternative to the orthodox interpretation of NATO (or the Warsaw Pact) as an instrument for collective defence against an external threat. The concept of dealignment, or beyond bipolarity as Migone describes it, emerges from their analysis of the nature of the Cold War as a means to legitimize the military presence of the superpowers and their command of European politics.

Chapters 4 and 5 look at the role of the Atlantic alliance in domestic politics. Both develop the argument that dealignment makes possible, and is only made possible through, a changed constellation of domestic political forces. Wolfe's contribution, which may strike Europeans as surprising, shows the importance of NATO in creating a domestic political consensus in the United States in the early postwar period. Precisely because Europe has been so important for domestic American politics, it is crucial to build an alternative alliance between the peace movements in the US and Western Europe as a basis for dealignment. Dealignment has to be a policy for the US as well. Otherwise a kind of European Gaullism could provoke dangerous tendencies of militarist confrontational isolationism within the United States, already prefigured by the unilateral character of President Reagan's military attack on Libya despite European objections.

Ben Lowe, in chapter 5, vividly describes the way in which the Cold War constrained the political Left in Britain, Italy and West Germany in the postwar years, and inhibited the proper functioning of democracy. He sees the right-wing conservatism of Western Europe and the Stalinism of Eastern Europe in the 1950s as parallel components of the Cold War. Detente allowed for a re-emergence of radical politics in Western Europe, while increasingly repressive measures adopted recently by West European states are associated with the reappearance of the Cold War. Lowe also analyses the difficulties faced by socialist and social democrat parties in a Cold War setting. In Britain, the fact that the Right dominated the foreign policy of the first postwar Labour government constrained the domestic policies of the Left.

Chapters 6 and 7 are about the economic dimension of the transatlantic relationship. Chapter 6 explores the link between the Reaganite military policies and monetarism, or austerity policy, as the West German authors prefer to call it. They develop the 'compensation' thesis, on the use by Reagan and others of military policies to compensate for economic decline. Policies of dealignment are a necessary condition for alternative economic approaches. Mary Kaldor, in chapter 7, argues that NATO, from the beginning, has profoundly influenced the technological development of Western Europe. The myth of superior American technology is an element of the psychological occupation of Western Europe. Dealignment has to mean technological dealignment, in the sense that Europeans have to abandon the conviction that military technology is 'advanced' and must be mindlessly emulated.

The next two chapters explore the concepts of neutrality and non-alignment and examine the global context. There is an evident difference between neutrality, which largely applies to Europe, and non-alignment, which is primarily a Third World concept. Neutrality, as described by Väyrynen, is primarily a security concept, a means of avoiding war. Neutral countries are radical about East–West relations but, by and large, remain content with the current international economic order. Non-alignment, as described by Singham and Hune, a natural outgrowth of the movement for decolonization, aims at much more fundamental structural transformation; in particular, non-alignment makes the connection between peace and self-determination. Unlike neutrality and non-alignment, dealignment does not have to mean formal withdrawal from alliances, but it is closer to non-alignment than neutrality because it does imply structural transformation. Peace and self-determination are also encompassed by the concept of dealignment. Dealignment is about phasing out international relationships of military dependence that limit sovereignty, just as decolonization was about phasing out colonial relationships that denied sovereignty.

The opportunities for restructuring North–South relationships, the complementarity between dealignment and non-alignment, are the subject of the last chapter. Luckham details NATO's relationships with the Third World and explodes the myth that NATO is a purely regional alliance. Transforming NATO would also transform North–South military connections since arms sales, military strategies, intervention etc. are all integrated in varying ways with NATO's military structure. It is, indeed, even doubtful whether, without NATO, an independent Euro-imperialism could be sustained in the post-colonial era. Challenging the bloc system in Europe is thus connected, in quite concrete ways, to the challenge mounted by the world's dispossessed to global power structures.

NOTES

1 See Mient Jan Faber and Mary Kaldor, 'Ending the Occupation of Europe: The Only Way to Save Detente', paper presented to the END Convention in Perugia, July 1984, and 'Occupation Revisited', paper presented to the END Convention in Amsterdam, July 1985.

2 See chapter 6.

3 'Should We Stay in NATO?' *Harpers*, 16 May 1984.

4 McGeorge Bundy, George F. Kennan, Robert S. McNamara and Gerard Smith, 'Nuclear Weapons and the Atlantic Alliance', *Foreign Affairs* (Spring 1982); Frank Blackaby, Jozef Goldblat and Sverre Lodgaard *No-First-Use* (SIPRI; London and Philadelphia: Taylor and Francis, 1984); *No-First-Use: A Report by the Union of Concerned Scientists*, (Cambridge, Mass.: Union of Concerned Scientists, 1983).

5 Bernard Rogers, 'Sword and Shield: ACE Attack of Warsaw Pact Follow-on Forces', *NATO's Sixteen Nations* (Feb–March, 1983).

6 US Army Field Manual, *FM–100–5* (Washington, DC, 1982).

7 'What's Wrong with NATO?', *New York Times Magazine*, 25 September 1983.

8 'A Plan to Reshape NATO', *Time*, 5 March 1984.

9 *Le Monde*, 13 December 1983.

10 Quoted in Michel de Perrot, 'Commercial Fast Breeders: Towards an Integrated European Nuclear Force?', in Michel de Perrot (ed.), *European Security: Nuclear or Conventional Defense?* Proceedings of the IVth International Symposium, organized by the Groupe de Bellerive, Geneva 8–10 December 1983 (Oxford: Pergamon Press, 1984).

11 *Aviation Week and Space Technology*, 21 May 1984.

12 See Christa Wolf, *Cassandra* (London: Virago, 1984).

13 'Statement by Mikhail Gorbachev', *Soviet News*, 22 January 1986.

14 This section is drawn from a paper by Judith Winther on nuclear-free zones presented at the UNU/TNI Conference on 'Dealignment for Western Europe?' November 1983.

15 *Common Security: A Programme for Disarmament*, Report of the Independent Commission on Disarmament and Security Affairs under the Chairmanship of Olof Palme (Palme Report) (London: Pan Books, 1982).

16 Matyas Szuros, 'Interaction of the national and the international in Hungarian policy', *New Hungarian Quarterly*, 25 (Spring 1984).

2

Superseding Yalta: A Plea for Regional Self-determination in Europe

RICHARD FALK

It is possible that we are poised at one of those rare and opportune moments in history that provide leaders and citizens with a chance to enhance the prospects of peace and justice in a dramatic fashion. A series of developments is converging in such a way as to create the possibility of shaping the future of Europe in a more positive direction. There is a great risk that this historic moment will pass if not soon acted upon in a constructive spirit. In this event, yet another generation of Europeans will be condemned to live on the front line of the strategic nuclear stand-off and to endure a variety of cruel encroachments upon their autonomy arising from the ambitions and insecurities of the superpowers.

The stakes are exceedingly high. There are pitfalls, as well as openings. Primary responsibility continues to reside in Moscow and Washington. The superpowers have left their imprint on Europe in terms of its enduring occupation and partition now an incredible forty years after the guns of World War II have fallen silent. Can they now take the initiatives needed to remove their military forces in a mutually reassuring manner and in a political environment that encourages both European unity, improving state/society relations in the various countries, especially those in Eastern Europe, and above all, avoiding a costly and dangerous regional arms race?

This is not a time for ideological posturing, or the pursuit of one-sided policies. It is appropriate to emphasize the mutual benefits associated with compromise and moderation on all sides. Seeking too much could result in nothing, or worse; not seeking enough could also lead to a disillusioning reinforcement of the status quo.

I

Whether it is a conversation with the noted Hungarian novelist George Konrad, a discourse on East–West relations by a prominent Reaganite official, or conjecture about the future of the European peace movement by one of its leaders, there is a notable tendency to anchor observations about the contemporary scene on the continent in a particular view of the Yalta conference and its outcome. That dramatic wartime meeting on the shores of the Crimean Sea in the closing months of World War II is widely assumed to have set the course of the postwar world, including especially the division of Europe into Eastern and Western spheres, leading directly to the breakdown of the anti-Fascist alliance and its displacement by bipolarity, Cold War, a nuclear arms race and a vicious rivalry for influence and paramountcy throughout the Third World.

This resonance attached to Yalta contains fascinating insight into the sorts of dialogues that have dominated political thinking during the past several decades. For some Western conservatives, Yalta is synonymous with betrayal, almost treason; the fatuity of liberalism that can be excused, if at all, only by the exhausted condition of Europe, especially the decline of the British Empire, after five and a half years of devastating warfare.[1] In this view, only Churchill of the Western democratic leaders knew what he was doing at Yalta, but had no choice, given the battlefield dependence of both East and West on continuing military cooperation up to the very end, as well as the westward movement of Soviet armies, Stalin's insistence upon an East European buffer and a persisting effort by the United States to extend the anti-Fascist alliance into the postwar world. Often conservatives, especially neo-conservatives in the United States, place the onus on a sickly, sentimental Franklin Roosevelt, who failed to diagnose the Soviet threat to Western interests and, astoundingly, was reapplying the disastrous diplomacy of Munich appeasement to abet the geopolitical ambition of Kremlin ideologues. In this regard, the Yalta cession remains to this day as an indecent capitulation by wimpy Americans willing to sacrifice the destinies of the East European peoples to single-minded Soviet diplomacy, and sustained over the intervening decades by an unimaginative and weak foreign policy. From such a perspective, rearticulated in different ways in recent years by such seemingly diverse commentators as George Shultz and Zbigniew Brzezinski, it is still not too late to repudiate the dark legacy of Yalta. The policy question these revisionists ask is one of tactics: What is the best way at this stage to push the Russians out of Europe?

Significantly, progressive European voices are suggesting a new course that seems strikingly similar, but upon reflection, is fundamentally different.

For one thing, the Left attack on Yalta is not only on outcomes, but also on method. Konrad or Charter 77 in Czechoslovakia, emphasize that the essential sin of Yalta was secret superpower diplomacy determining the lives of peoples denied a voice in their own future. From these origins they find the extension of military rule and the rise of military blocs in Europe an inevitable sequel to a style of diplomacy not essentially different from that used by the colonial powers in the previous century to carve up the African continent. In this regard, the United States gained its own foothold in Europe through the wider dynamic of Yalta. From this perspective, then, two spheres of influence, not one, were created by the Yalta solution. From this perspective, the key to undoing the dark deeds of Yalta lies in the belated assertion of what might be a novel claim in international relations, namely, that of *regional self-determination.* What Europeans, both East and West, seek at this stage is to control their own assertion of control and responsibility. To be effective, such an historic assertion needs to build on what exists, yet move to a sustainable alternative set of arrangements that does not altogether neglect either the sensitivities or the interests of the superpowers. To combine all these considerations in a viable strategy will test severely the capacities of European statespeople.

Some opinion leaders in the West continue to believe that detente from above remains the highest priority in the nuclear age. In this spirit, they believe it is dangerous and futile to mount any kind of challenge against Soviet hegemony in Eastern Europe. They regard the 1975 Helsinki Accords as a beneficial step in the direction of stabilizing inter-European relations by validating postwar boundary adjustments, but regard any more extensive role for European diplomacy as an impediment to the overriding quest for world peace that can only be effectively waged at an inter-governmental level.

II

This renewal of concern about postwar arrangements in Europe discloses two important sets of circumstances that transcend partisan debate: the postwar adjustments reached at Yalta cannot yet be translated, even forty years later, into a *de facto* peace treaty that establishes a generally acceptable political order for Europe; and, shifts in the setting and its perception have created a conviction from various ideological standpoints that the situation has become fluid enough to consider alternatives.

It needs to be recalled that in 1945 Yalta was generally perceived by the American public as a natural culmination of World War II. Rather than as a betrayal by the victors, it was accepted as a realistic bargain that took apt account of the play of forces and the historical experiences then alive in the political consciousness of the victorious powers. Stalin had just endured a war that had cost an estimated 20 million Soviet lives on the battlefield alone, or more than the whole of Europe had lost in the prior 2,000 years of warfare! The Soviet Union for the third time in modern history had been invaded through Poland from the West. Soviet armies were in secure control of Eastern Europe, and could not be dislodged without the virtually unthinkable commitment on the part of the Western powers to redefine the war, initiating an anti-Communist phase as if the real struggle had been anti-totalitarian rather than anti-Fascist. At the time, only a small, rightist sector of public opinion among the allies, and that excluded from leadership, would have countenanced such a dramatic conversion of wartime goals that might have enabled the Western liberation of Eastern Europe, and then, with great military uncertainties as to costs and consequences.

With varying degrees of subtlety and sophistication, Western leaders accepted the notion that the European phase of World War II must be concluded amicably as an anti-Fascist enterprise, even if agreement among the victors on a permanent peace settlement could not be soon negotiated. For the sake of postwar stability and as an acknowledgement of the disproportionate sacrifice endured by the Soviet Union, was it really unreasonable to concede what could not have been prevented in any event? Besides, the overall Yalta bargain was more reciprocal than is generally appreciated. It included a willingness by the Soviet Union to circumscribe its veto power in the United Nations considerably beyond its earlier stated policy and to enter the Far Eastern war against the Japanese in a context in which considerable further fighting was then foreseen. These commitments were important to the West at the time, perhaps, harsh as it is to admit, more so than the political fate of the East Europeans, especially given the relative remoteness of the region and the realization that there was nothing that in any event could have been done to dislodge the Red Army. As John Gittings observed quite recently in the *Guardian,* Yalta can still be seen as 'the benchmark for great power cooperation on equal terms from which post-war American policy has since tried to exclude them'.[2] In this image Yalta, despite its unfortunate side-effects, is a kind of model for superpower cooperation, a definite alternative to the Cold War; diplomacy seeking a moderate international order based on a series of mutual bargains. Its main drawback is that lesser peoples and nations are sacrificed to foster such cooperation, and that the region itself did not participate in settling its own future.

It is, of course, striking that World War II produced neither a peace treaty nor World War III. Instead it produced the Cold War, intense military preparations on both sides, a menacing nuclear arms race, offsetting alliances that relocated vital sovereign rights in the two superpower capitals, and seemingly permanent heavy military presences on the European continent by both the United States and the Soviet Union. Despite the dangers of general war associated with the Berlin Crises of 1948 and 1961, the division of Europe did produce militarization and tension, but also a mutual awareness that it was vital to keep the peace at all costs. For several decades, despite the vagaries of the European balance, the general wisdom has been that any attempt to alter the status quo in Europe by military means would clearly result in a kind of ultimate destruction of European civilization and would, in all likelihood, bring about a wider arc of devastation that included both superpowers in the course of strategic nuclear war. It is this overall awareness that has contributed to a sense of stability with respect to the postwar arrangements, even if their normative effects at a societal level are bitterly resented.

This stability has other dimensions as well. Yalta helped produce the Cold War, which in turn assures the long-term, if not permanent, division of Germany, a result that undoubtedly serves the interests and expresses the preferences of many West Europeans. Yet, as with other 'geopolitical solutions', such an outcome can only be praised by policy-makers in private. The postwar division of Germany undoubtedly violates principles of national self-determination as applicable to the German people. The division creates the sort of tensions that are symbolized by the divided and artificial status of the city of Berlin, epitomized since 1961 by the existence of the Berlin Wall. Yet this division, by reducing the relative weight of Germany *vis-à-vis* the rest of Europe and towards the Soviet Union, is seen on many sides as some assurance that German revisionist diplomacy will not get out of hand once again. Specifically, Soviet concerns about the revival of German militarism are to some extent alleviated by the continued presence of American troops in West Germany. These concerns may be derided in the West as 'irrational', but given the Russian historical experience there exists a plausible basis for seeking reassurance by way of encroachments upon German sovereign rights.

These considerations that explain, and even help us appreciate, the wider effects of Yalta do not imply an endorsement of its overall results. There is a tendency of geopolitical solutions to express immediate state-to-state interests regardless of societal consequences and longer-run effects. Whether the peoples of East Europe should be made to bear a permanent burden for the sake of European stability is a moral, as well as a political, question. Furthermore, the costs of this stability to West Europeans are becoming more evident. There is an emerging European sense that treating the Soviet military threat as more formidable than it is has serious, perhaps disastrous, consequences for all Europeans. The risk of catastrophic war is accentuated by the European realization that their 'selection' as a possible nuclear battlefield in 'a theatre war' is being shaped by non-European strategists. In effect, the superpowers were treating Europe as expendable, if necessary; as the ultimate firebreak to all-out war. And further, that European sovereign rights were deeply abridged by locating control over diplomacy, especially strategic military policy, in the capitals of the two superpowers.

Undoubtedly, part of this reappraisal of the European arrangements achieved at Yalta is the altered state of European political consciousness. At this stage, Europe has, of course, fully recovered from its wartime traumas. Also, the benefits of the post-1945 trade-offs are less evident. Western Europe might do better economically if its alliance relationship to the United States were loosened and its hostile stance towards the Soviet Union reduced. The Soviet Union, initially the beneficiary of an exploitative relationship to Europe, has found itself subject to growing economic responsibilities, some quite burdensome. It might be quite receptive to a rearrangement of its relations with East European countries if the results included a lessening of its burdens as well as an improvement of its image.

On balance, then, it might now be feasible for the main parties to agree that postwar arrangements have outlived their historic function and need to be superseded in some positive direction. It is so difficult to face these questions openly because the postwar arrangements were and remain 'illegitimate' from the viewpoint of political ideology prevailing on all sides. One could hardly expect Western European leaders in the midst of domestic struggles against strong Communist Parties to admit that they welcomed a German solution that kept almost half of the country in Soviet hands and under stern Communist control. Nor could the Soviets admit that they were glad to have American troops in Germany to keep a lid upon possible eruptions of new forms of German militarism built around the mission of reunification. After all, if the humiliation of Versailles helped produce Hitler, was it so unlikely that the division of Germany against the will of its people might lead to the emergence of radical forms of revisionist thinking in West Germany? Nor could the Americans admit that they were tired of intervening in Europe to help save liberal economic and political institutions, and that they had concluded in the aftermath of Yalta to remain on the continent to exert leadership and influence as the best assurance that World War III would not take place and that the liberal democracies would remain in the Western camp. It is possible, also, to conceive of Soviet occupation of Eastern Europe as an analogous departure from a tradition of territorial defence of the Russian heartland. For different reasons, then, the superpowers both seemed to demand for themselves after 1945 an active and paternalistic presence in Europe. As well, both justified their extraterritorial projection of military power on to the European region by reference to the threat posed by their rival.

These geopolitical sub-texts are still operative, although rarely acknowledged and often vigorously denied. They explain part of the reluctance to explore alternative lines of policy in a forthright manner; this refusal to be explicit has lent a rhetorical and propagandistic tone to the public debate. To find a new approach to European security, acceptable to both superpowers, requires a willingness to consider what might be gained and lost by altering the highly militarized and politically rigid system of security that has brought a 'hard' peace, but nevertheless, a peace, since 1945.

There is yet another element present. Political events surrounding the fortieth anniversary of the end of the European phase of World War II disclosed how intense feelings remain about the recent past. President Reagan's controversial visit to the German cemetery at Bitberg with its SS graves underscored sensitivities about any action that might be understood to condone the Nazi past. More significantly, the political backlash caused by such a provocative display of insensitivity to the feelings of the victims of Hitler's policy on the part of the Reagan administration demonstrated that the struggle against Fascism is not quite finished.[3] In this regard, the continuing and active search for the last surviving notorious Nazi war criminal, Josef Mengele, in Paraguay and elsewhere, was a symbolic quest, as well as a specific example of the demand for retributive justice. The *reverse* sensitivities of a powerful character were revealed when Kurt Waldheim was elected President of Austria despite the revelations of his connections with Nazi policies and practices. There appears to be a tendency for those who mobilize their energies around an anti-Communist crusade to overlook anti-Fascism or to regard it as a lesser or past evil. In its extreme form, it looks back on World War II as a struggle in which the forces of the West triumphed over Germany without any significant help from the Soviet Union. This kind of radical rightist revisionism seeks to downplay both the success of the allied *joint* struggle and to withhold expressions of sympathy (for losses) or admiration (for contribution) for the Soviet role in the war effort.

In contrast, to encourage a more cooperative set of future options it seems important to accent and affirm the realities of this shared past, especially given the heavy Soviet losses in the war. It seems evident, also, that such acknowledgement would be deeply appreciated by both Soviet leaders and people. The Soviet approach on these matters has been generally more constructive. Mr Gorbachev, for instance, while overstating the Soviet role in victory in World War II during anniversary events, has at least expressed gratitude for the losses suffered and the contributions made by the other allied powers.

One of the further impediments to moving beyond the presently rigid set of circumstances in Europe arises from the inability of political leaders to admit mistakes, especially in relation to their rivals. The Soviet Union with its ideological pretension that its government is an unconditionally positive historical force has, as a consequence, no capacity to engage in public self-criticism, or even to allow its citizenry a legitimate domain for criticism, controversy and pluralistic interpretation. Any change in public direction must come from the elite responsible for an unsatisfactory status quo, and somehow be disguised as a shift or acknowledgement of error or failure. It is not clear that the Vietnam War would have ended when it did without the role of a domestic opposition in the United States. During the Reagan presidency, the American political orientation has become self-righteously ideological, promoting a tendency to claim a comparable infallibility for all positions of foreign policy. One consequence is to make rivals grow defensive, assuring that even a mutually unsatisfactory geopolitical circumstance will be kept in a frozen condition. If this assessment is correct, then the largest cost of President Reagan's foreign policy may be virtually invisible. It may consist of a failure to seize this historic opportunity to inaugurate a new phase of European history based upon a greater measure of continental integration and stability than has ever been possible in the past, as well as a political consciousness in Europe that is fatigued by *all* types of tension and militarization.

III

There is a fairly wide spectrum of agreement then that the postwar arrangements for Europe could now be replaced by something better. But what? The main disagreements are whether the new arrangements should affect West–West relations as well as East–East and whether there should be a reduced reliance on military alliances and readiness as a basis for European security. Underneath these disagreements are matters of agenda: is the call for revising Yalta a matter only of bringing human rights and political democracy East of the Elbe, or is it, as well, the attainment of peace, independence and economic well-being for the continent as a whole? My emphasis on the broader agenda of regional self-determination contrasts with the Reagan administration's partisan call for pushing the Russians out of Eastern Europe. There are some important intermediate positions, as well.

One of these is set forth by Zbigniew Brzezinski in his widely discussed *Foreign Affairs* article that seeks to find a new mix of techniques (sticks and carrots) to pressure Moscow to let go of Eastern Europe.[4] The essence of Brzezinski's position is contained in the following sentence, italicized in his version to assure that readers will appreciate its importance: "*The historic balance of Europe will be changed gradually in the West's favor only if Russia comes to be faced west of Elbe rather less by America and rather more by Europe*.'[5] The reasoning set forth to support this adjustment to the end of the postwar world is based on the leading notion that "the division of Europe is not only the unnatural consequence of the destruction of Europe in the course of two world wars;' additionally, 'in the long run it is also an inherently unstable and potentially dangerous situation'. The prescriptive remedy of a restored and unified Europe cannot, however, be achieved, according to Brzezinski by 'an American victory over Russia' nor 'by an explicit Russian acceptance, through a negotiated agreement, of Eastern Europe's emancipation from Russian vassalage',[6] Rather, Brzezinski's quest for '[a] wider Europe' rests on what he calls 'a deliberate but subtly induced process of change, by historical stealth so to speak, which can neither be quickly detected nor easily resisted'.[7] There is, of course, something archly American about former President Carter's National Security Adviser, presumably with still unsated ambitions, proposing on the pages of *Foreign Affairs*, a journal immediately translated for the benefit of Moscow specialists, to alter the shape of Europe by historical stealth!

Brzezinski has throughout his career displayed remarkable timing in putting forth ideas for foreign policy initiatives. Here, unlike any other mainstream analyst, he is responding to the current fluidity of the European situation with a proposal for a major adjustment. What is more, Brzezinski is correct in considering the prospect for reform to depend on moves towards greater European autonomy, both because this is what Europeans increasingly demand and because Europeans in the West are much more likely than the United States to negotiate successfully a Soviet withdrawal from Eastern Europe, especially if it appears as if both superpowers are simultaneously loosening their grip on the continent.

Brzezinski urges a partial substitution of European military assertiveness for that of the United States (although without decoupling), a programme to reverse the postwar experience of Eastern Europe by the application of a variety of indirect pressures, and the establishment of a sense of Europe as a natural whole, yet leaning westward, by facilitating participation by East Europeans in all-European bodies. This notion that a somewhat reduced American military presence on the ground (regional deterrence based on American nuclear capabilities would persist) offset by 'increased Franco–German military cooperation and eventual integration' is little more than a reshuffle of the Cold War deck of geopolitical cards with insufficient incentives for a constructive Soviet response. The Soviet pretext in Eastern Europe is associated with a threat from the West, especially from Germany and France. After the 1985 Bonn Summit, such a conception of the future of Europe seems remote indeed. The most striking development at Bonn was the sign of severe strains within the NATO framework, especially in Franco–German relations. France seeks to promote regional autonomy and a more independent relationship to the United States, refusing President Reagan's offer to participate in the research and development efforts of the Strategic Defense Initiative, opposing the American attempt to overthrow the Sandinistas in Nicaragua, and generally anchoring its security on its independent nuclear deterrent which it refuses to extend to Germany. Germany, denied nuclear weapons, feels dependent on the traditional NATO framework for security, including deference to American diplomacy and a general willingness to tie its technological future to a subordinate role in relation to the United States. The Soviet Union still seems genuinely alarmed by any current indication that German military capabilities could be further revived and then used in a threatening international manner; Moscow's intense reaction to recent reports that Bonn was acquiring its own ballistic missile capabilities supports this interpretation.

To suppose that intensified European militarization carried out in an atmosphere of greater ideological agitation designed to democratize political life in Eastern Europe can encourage a Soviet loosening is highly unrealistic. It would likely present the Soviet Union with more menacing prospects than existed during the bipolar phase of Yalta, more menacing because the fear of German aggressiveness is greater than that of American aggressiveness, and because, indeed, Germany possesses potentially revisionist foreign policy goals that might tempt it under certain circumstances to take high risks of war for the sake of reunification. There is a lack of political imagination and understanding evident in Brzezinski's approach. Since he believes that the Soviet Union would exploit any lessening of military resolve in the West, and still harbors expansionist ambitions on the continent of the sort he attributes to Molotov in the closing months of World War II, there is not much room for flexibility. It is probably true that Soviet leaders would welcome a partial withdrawal of the American military presence in Europe, but not at the expense of a heightening of East–West tensions and the augmented militarization of Western Europe countries. The end-point of Brzezinski's 'restored Europe' seems assuredly anti-Soviet and pro-American, or at least pro-Western. Indeed, Brzezinski's objectives are expressed in the geopolitical language of shifting the European balance in the West's favour rather than in value terms, or even in terms of a bargain based on mutual interests. In short, Brzezinski offers carrots that are short, untempting stubs, while his sticks are heavy, clumsy bludgeons.

IV

There exist far more constructive opportunities at this stage for European adjustment. A new approach to European security which regards the pursuit of peace, economic viability, human rights and democracy as mutually reinforcing has recently been expressed by, among others, the Hungarian novelist George Konrad.[8] To summon a senior military officer to grasp the reins of power in Poland can be interpreted as an admission of failure by Moscow of its overall effort to build state socialism in the countries of Eastern Europe. It is a failure in the primary sense of being unable to obtain the allegiance, or even the acquiescence, of the peoples in the bloc countries, except by overt military rule. As such, Poland represents both a damaging stigma and an unpredictable powder keg. It complicates economic relations and diplomatic normalcy beyond the bloc, as well as providing a principal rationale for provocative forms of militarization in Western Europe. A new generation of leaders in Moscow, even if initially inhibited by the old guard in foreign affairs for a few years, may grow receptive to an alternative calculus of Soviet state interests in Europe, provided it is presented in a non-confrontational form, in contrast to that adopted uncritically by Stalin at the end of World War II. Reports of contacts between East European intellectuals and policy-makers and the middle level of the Soviet bureaucracy (from which, according to Arkady Shevchenko, the Soviet Foreign Ministry official who defected in 1978, and others, Gorbachev represents the first to ascend to the pinnacle of state power) confirm the existence of policy explorations within the bloc along these lines that include participants from Moscow.[9]

The political climate may be right, as well, in Eastern Europe. Anti-regime elements in these countries realize that their efforts to tear themselves away from the Soviet orbit play into the hands of Kremlin, party bureaucrats and domestic hardliners, and cannot succeed. Tanks and secret police can prevail over a hostile citizenry in the developed countries of the West, even if the population is substantially mobilized around heroic leaders, in a way which is impossible in Afghanistan or Vietnam. The experience of Hungary in 1956, Czechoslovakia in 1968 and Poland over the last few years is being widely interpreted in this way. Is there, then, a middle path between resistance and resignation? Konrad's formulation in *Antipolitics* is suggestive: 'I ask the authorities not to feel threatened by the independent intelligentsia. I ask the intelligentsia not to alarm the authorities.'[10] This posture rests on Konrad's belief that allowing a reform process to flourish depends on replacing the politics of confrontation with the 'antipolitics' of mutual reassurance. Three further aspects of Konrad's approach are important to mention. First, it is a mistake to threaten the official leadership by attacking the legitimacy of the basic relationship between state, party and civil society. Secondly, it is possible to persuade the official leadership, if not confronted, to adopt some reformist ideas ('It doesn't say much for the reputation of our wares if we are unable to sell any of our ideas at all to those in power.')[11] Thirdly, it seems evident that East European governments, if they do not feel threatened from below, themselves seek greater autonomy in relation to the Soviet Union, and increasingly appreciate the role of demilitarization at home and abroad in the pursuit of such a goal.

Konrad's view of how to undo Yalta is quite different, despite a superficial resemblance, to Brzezinski's counsel of 'historical stealth'. Konrad is talking about what could happen if the threats from within and without could be transformed into reformist quests for new positions of mutual advantage, while Brzezinski is talking about regionalizing the Cold War. Whether Konrad's prescriptions are too optimistic with regard to the potential responsiveness of Communist elites to moderate opposition forces is a serious concern, as yet untested. Perhaps the relatively favourable post-1956 evolution of Hungary makes Konrad unduly hopeful of what can be achieved without struggle. Although Konrad himself might not agree with this assessment, it is probably true to say that of all the Eastern bloc countries, only Hungary seems to have a reasonably popular leader in Janos Kadar – who it is said by close observers of the Hungarian scene might even win a free election – together with a relatively successful economy that has worked reasonably well for at least some sectors of society. One advantage of Konrad's view is that it favours demilitarization for Europe as a whole. One disadvantage is that it could split oppositional groups over tactics or produce a new wave of disillusionment.

The path of demilitarization seems far more promising than any attempt to take geopolitical advantage of the new European fluidity in the manner of Brzezinski. Several linked elements are contained in the idea of demilitarization: as used here, it refers to a process that seeks to make security *within* and *among* states depend less on military threats and capabilities and more on political, economic and cultural conditions of consent, participation and mutual advantage. It emphasizes trial and error, as well as shared gains arising from reduced risks of war in international and internal atmospheres of less hostility and more reassurance. As applied to Europe, demilitarization seeks to take advantage of the special situation of growing dissatisfaction on the part of most Europeans with the status quo, especially those aspects associated with internal and regional militarization, as well as with superpower hegemony.

At the same time, this condition of receptivity should not be overstated. Any superpower 'withdrawal' or downward adjustment of presence will be attacked at home as evidence of 'decline', if not 'defeat'. Military bureaucracies are entrenched in the policy-making nexus of all state structures, and can be counted on to oppose any reductions in their current roles. Present political leadership in the main Western countries continues to subscribe to the Cold War view that Soviet policy is responsive only to the political language of force. At the same time, it is probable that part of the Soviet leadership may perceive demilitarization as little more than a Western strategem to unravel a system of regional security that has upheld Soviet vital interests.

One of the least noticed, most hopeful developments of the past few years is the rising emphasis upon democracy and human rights issues by peace activists in Western Europe and the discovery of armaments and peace issues by dissidents in Eastern Europe (with the partial exception of Poland, where much of the leadership of Solidarity welcomed Reagan's conception of East–West relations, but the new 'Freedom and Peace' group is thinking on different lines). The political dynamic here of challenging leaders from below has an uncertain set of impacts. It undoubtedly stiffens resistance by essentially anti-democratic state structures. Yet these structures also seek to weaken these movements by cooption and accommodation. The outcome of this interplay will depend on whether both sides reinforce constructive tendencies on the governmental level, as governments alone can take the needed demilitarizing initiatives at this stage. Much depends, also, on whether the main political actors reward or punish demilitarizing initiatives (e.g. budget cuts, votes against particular weapons systems, improvement in human rights) by their adversary, and convey the same message to their publics.

The breakdown of detente in the United States was encouraged by a carefully orchestrated campaign (Committee on the Present Danger) designed to alarm Americans about the consequences of alleged 'weakness' in the military sphere relative to the Soviet Union and about detente being a one-way street in Moscow's favour. Undoubtedly, more restrained Soviet behaviour would have strengthened Western support for detente – no Cuban troops in Africa, no invasion of Afghanistan, shifts of budget allocations to the civilian sector, and more forthcoming approaches to the defence of human rights and democracy. Demilitarization can succeed only if the political will emerges in both superpowers, as well as an intelligent appreciation of the anxieties, social forces and interests that work against such moderations of conflict.

The European peace movement, most notably END (European Nuclear Disarmament), offers an attractive set of proposals designed to overcome unpopular military/political circumstances existing in both halves of Europe. Instead of repudiating NATO altogether, the new emphasis in END is to make a common front around the symbolism of 'dealignment', seeking to get rid of, or diminish the role of the military blocs, and not just to undermine the Soviet pretext for staying in Europe. Such a perspective does represent an attempt to act upon an all-European interest in dissolving the blocs, a regional interest that cuts against the grain of alliance affiliations, and admits to dissatisfaction with the behaviour of both superpowers. END is beginning to draw a new distinction between overcoming the hierarchical distortions of the bloc system and disrupting the contractual character of the postwar alliances. Making this distinction represents an attempt to balance the European search for autonomy and peace against the interests, commitments and dignity of the superpowers as alliance leaders still harbouring bad memories of what happens when Europe is left to its own geopolitical devices. This type of political and normative adjustment seeks to preserve some elements of the Yalta framework while overcoming its development as a core justification for a diplomacy of spheres of influence in Europe.

Dealignment is also significant as a means to recover European autonomy and sovereign rights, as well as to exert greater European control over the continent's own economic and military security. In these fundamental senses, democracy and human rights are at stake in the West as well as the East. Dealignment, then, presents an attractive and untested opportunity for East and West Europe, as well as for Moscow, yet its prospects depend upon the resolution of critical tactical questions – pressure versus reassurance; legitimizing the framework of geopolitics versus transforming the framework.

But what about Washington? At present, there is little understanding, and no support, for demilitarizing adjustments of this type in Europe. True, a part of the most militarist sector in American policy-making circles seemingly arrives at a comparable position to that of END by way of disgust over European behaviour. The disgust arises in alleged reaction to the queasiness and supposed pacifism of West Europeans (what Brzezinski berates as 'Europe's cultural hedonism and political complacence'[12] and 'the inevitable appeal of escapist notions regarding disarmament, nuclear freezes, and the like'). These Reaganites interpret such tendencies from a less engaged and imaginative perspective than Brzezinski, preferring in the end to let go of Europe, and shift even more attention to the Pacific Basin rather than enmesh the United States in a humiliating role of defending at great cost those who do not fully share anti-Soviet values or an American world view, and refuse to bear their fair share of defence burdens.

It should be understood that this 'renounce Europe' position appeals only to a fringe, at present, even among the neo-conservatives. It has been put forward as an option by Irving Kristol and others, partly, I think, to remind West European elites that they should not take United States support for granted. The dominant position among Reaganites remains one of militarily reinforcing the geopolitical frontiers of the postwar world, of which the partition of Europe remains the most dramatic and significant. In a sense, Reagan's approach is to push back the geopolitical frontiers of the postwar world by means of an intensified militarization, the very reverse of what is being advocated here. This outlook accounts for the effort to cast missile deployment and the call for increased outlays of funds for European defence as part of a necessary effort to redress a regional military imbalance that liberals and arms control advocates from the Democratic Party had allegedly allowed to swing in the Soviet favour. In this regard, the Reaganite approach, unlike that of the Democratic Party hawks, fails even to acknowledge the growing strain on postwar arrangements arising from a variety of military, economic and political sources. Indeed, the more assertive voices in the Reagan administration invert the pressure for adjustment by insisting upon a shift from the stance of 'containment' to that of 'roll-back', a shift that undoubtedly raises some eyebrows among their Soviet counterparts.

The most constructive role for both superpowers would be to encourage a regional dynamic of demilitarization by stages, reinforced by arms control, especially of a denuclearizing character. The possibility of establishing a nuclear-free zone in Central Europe seems negotiable and could be a significant confidence-building step, especially if coupled with unilateral gestures on both sides to refrain from provocative military manoeuvres that are perceived by political rivals as rehearsals for war. An abrupt renunciation of the superpower presences in Europe could be harmful even if it occurred in concert. It could lead to a nervous set of reactions in both parts of Europe, prompting an embrace of militarism in West Germany and the worst kind of domestic repression in Poland and, possibly, Czechoslovakia and East Germany, thereby raising tension levels and causing either a reversal of superpower withdrawal, or heightened dangers of intra-European warfare. A positive form of adjustment to the end of the postwar world requires patience as well as vision, and it depends on an awareness that the path of demilitarization must be cleared by stages and by trial and error.

Any of these orientations could become dangerous to the extent that they link American policy goals in Europe to militarization and reject the possibility of a more favourable East–West arrangement. If a withdrawal from the United States' postwar role is undertaken to shock Europeans into realizing their own vulnerability and dependence, it could prompt NATO governments to make a stronger defence effort. It might also raise the spectre of German militarization prompting offsetting Soviet steps. For similar reasons, Brzezinski's mixed political/military strategy of regionalizing the geopolitical game also risks breakdowns of order within and beyond the region.

The European peace movement's perspective strongly rests its case for superpower withdrawal on reassuring Moscow about the future of Germany; a minority endorse a permanently neutralized, unified and loosely confederated, German state, but the majority regard a divided and, possibly, demilitarized, Germany as a necessary dimension of reassurance. In this regard, East and West Europe would 'compensate' for the end of superpower hegemony and bloc politics by a kind of complex, double-edged embrace of Finlandization, possibly leaning slightly more in geopolitical stance towards Moscow than Washington, but basically seeking to be independent in outlook of both. Such an extended Finlandization might eventually mean the dissolution of both European alliances, a cautious non-aligned diplomacy and a refusal to become directly involved with developments in Eastern Europe or the Soviet Union. Such a shift in orientation would be reinforced strongly by economic factors, giving Europe a more promising position in the overall competitive struggle for shares of the world market, with special and preferred access to the Euro-Soviet market; if possible, such arrangements would be sustained by informal deference by the United States and Japan.

Naturally, the establishment of peace in Europe cannot be achieved by a single grand gesture. A new course must be charted, with receptivity on all sides. Given the history of the past forty years, there are no grounds for easy optimism. At the same time, there is an emerging consensus among otherwise divergent positions that it is time to explore alternatives to the bloc system, and seek practical ways either to undo the variously interpreted 'dirty legacy' of Yalta or to move beyond the Yalta phase of postwar adjustment in Europe. Conflictual strategies to reach such goals have consistently failed in the past, generally producing a hardening of opposed positions, the reverse of proclaimed goals. The moment seems right to try something new, not merely a shift in the pattern of militarization, but a political shift that facilitates overcoming a mutually destructive and very expensive pattern of militarization. The solid appeal of this shift is not only a matter of geopolitical sanity, obviously not a strong element shaping the politics of the superpowers, but it offers the prospect of real economic gains, as well as an enhancement of regional and strategic security, and the possible strengthening of sovereign rights for countries in both halves of a divided Europe. With the present Kremlin leadership being relatively forthcoming, this might be the time to test the possibility for making the fifth decade of Yalta the last one that has to look back to 1945 to explain the unhappy predicament of a Europe functioning as storm centre for geopolitics in the nuclear age. Unfortunately, there is no current disposition in Washington to undertake such a test. In the next few years more demilitarizing perspectives might gain dominant influence through electoral politics in several European countries, including West Germany and England. This could confront the United States with a virtual *fait accompli*, especially if Moscow shrewdly refrains from encouraging these developments too openly. Such a prospect converts what could be a positive development for Europe, as measured both by security and human rights, into the semblance of a defeat for the United States. A more imaginative American foreign policy would itself participate actively in this process of adjustment, welcoming the occasion for an orderly withdrawal of its overlong European military presence.

V

The presence of the superpowers in Europe can in no fundamental way be regarded as equivalent. The Soviet presence possesses a seemingly unconditional character, was resented by the peoples of the countries concerned from the outset and has been sustained by intimidation and coercion. It is revealing that where Communism triumphed in Europe without the intervention of the Red Army, as in Albania and Yugoslavia, the local leadership broke decisively with the Soviet Union and went along an independent path that was overtly hostile to Moscow. It is hardly surprising that the men in the Kremlin assume that loosening their military grip on Eastern Europe would lead in time to an abrupt repudiation of a Soviet-orientated foreign policy, no matter what reassurances were given, and might even occur in such a way as to destabilize political life in the Soviet heartland.

By comparison, the American extension of influence in Western Europe has been generally consensual, leading to prosperous economies and democratic political orders, relying on only occasional and indirect interventionary manipulations, usually of a covert and virtually invisible character, as well as the side-effects of economic and cultural hegemony. In the daily lives of the peoples of Europe these differences in postwar destiny are critical and, for those in the West, worth fighting to preserve, at least if it does not result in nuclear incineration. In many ways these differences are expressed by the differing concerns at the frontier. In the East the frontiers are heavily guarded to keep people from leaving, whereas in the West monitoring activities concentrate on keeping unwanted people from entering.

At the same time, even in the West the postwar arrangements are growing less satisfactory. American objections to East–West trade work against European efforts to achieve economic and political stability in the environment of the 1980s. Perhaps even more importantly, longer term prospects for the economic well-being of all Europeans seem increasingly to hinge on East–West normalization, permitting secure and expanding trade relations on a regional basis, as well as extending to Soviet markets. Also, a growing proportion of the population of West European countries finds the postwar pattern of subordination to American leadership threatening and unacceptable. West European sovereign rights on ultimate issues of survival and defence are increasingly perceived as seriously eroded by command structures and the hierarchy of relationships that exist within the NATO alliance. Western Europe has come to realize that it has delegated crisis decision-making to Washington. Such delegation undermines sovereignty and political democracy in the most crucial domain of national policy, as well as passively committing the countries of Western Europe to a potentially suicidal course of action, based on reliance upon nuclear weapons in a manner irreconcilable with widely held religious beliefs, ethical standards and international legal obligations.

In the immediate postwar world of devastation and vulnerability, the acceptance of American leadership seemed a natural price to pay for reassurance that Soviet pressures would be contained, especially when combined with the promise of economic reconstruction contained in the Marshall Plan. This situation was also shaped by a certain anxiety that Moscow-orientated Communist Parties might assume power in such key West European countries as France and Italy. By now, the calculus of benefits and burdens has altered considerably. Except for conservatives, there is a general disposition to discount the Soviet military threat and to regard the possibility of Finlandization as quite remote and relatively benign, especially if compared to either a war-prone NATO orientation or second-class and diminishing participation in the world economy.

The experience of reassessment in Eastern Europe has proceeded along a different main line. For Eastern Europe the main challenge all along has been to regain political independence and human rights by mounting a struggle for national self-determination that repudiates, or at least dilutes

Soviet control. The boundaries of acceptable autonomy are rather rigid, and if crossed, generate direct Soviet intervention, as occurred in Hungary (1956) and Czechoslovakia (1968). On both occasions reorientations of the official Communist leadership directly challenged Soviet hegemony, and gave vent to strong popular democratizing and anti-Soviet sentiments. As a consequence, Soviet leaders undoubtedly were alarmed by the bloc consequences of these national challenges, and possibly by fears that what was permitted in one country would have to be granted to the others. While ruthlessly suppressing direct challenges, less threatening postures by East European governments have been tolerated. Rumania's independence on foreign policy issues and Hungary's relative openness with respect to domestic economic and social innovation suggest tactical opportunities for East European governments to promote national interests in a manner more imaginative than is suggested by satellite status and its assumed implication of bland submission to Moscow. Of course, events in Poland over the past several years illustrate the thin line between initiatives at the societal level and a suppressive intervention at the regional level. It seems evident that Soviet leaders greatly prefer farming out their repressive missions to national leaders than intervening directly, as their approach to the Solidarity movement illustrates. Their interventionary threat remains credible as a result of their past practice, as well as by the sustained military campaign to destroy a powerful popular movement of resistance in Afghanistan.

All sides have learned from the experience of resistance and repression in Eastern Europe, and none of the main political actors can take much satisfaction from the current situation. Soviet hegemony is secure in a sense, but manifestly illegitimate and costly in a variety of ways to maintain. Social movements in Eastern bloc countries have come to understand that they can expect no outside help from the West and that there is no way to batter down Soviet dominance over the political life of their homeland through direct encounter. It has been assumed, correctly I believe, that any Western military challenge directed at undoing Soviet hegemony within its European bloc is too risky. The Soviet Union has fostered the impression that Western intervention in bloc affairs would ignite World War III. This impression has been accepted as credible in Washington regardless of who is in office. What has distinguished President Reagan's diplomacy from that of his predecessors is his refusal to provide Soviet leaders with reassurance as to the permanence of the geopolitical status quo as part of a post-World War II 'settlement'. In that respect, calling the current division of Europe unacceptable and temporary can be taken, at the very least, as a signal of encouragement to anti-Soviet oppositional activity.

Most conjectural is the reaction to this course of events by the new Soviet leadership. Soviet leaders, quite predictably, are extremely defensive about these direct attacks on Yalta mounted during the Reagan years, attacks which seem correctly associated with the militant revival of a Cold War atmosphere. These attacks have been accompanied by the apparent unwillingness of the Reaganites to accept either the Nixon/Brezhnev 1972 Declaration of Principles for relations between the two superpowers or those portions of the Helsinki Accords that provided reassurance about the stability of existing European boundaries. Soviet leaders associate these stands with the renewal of Cold War pressures, including an effort to isolate and encircle the Soviet Union, and react with the adoption of militarist rhetoric of their own. Despite these rigidifying elements, Soviet experiences in Afghanistan and Eastern Europe may well have produced some sombre second thoughts about the costs of achieving border security by imposing their will upon neighbouring countries, with force as necessary.

Of course, the Soviet leadership never admits to second thoughts in public. There is no tradition of overt self-criticism, no role for a legitimate opposition that debates policy. Yet Soviet foreign policy exhibits a kind of trial-and-error prudence. Mistakes once made are not generally repeated, whether it be a matter of seeking to place missiles in the Western hemisphere, challenging Western access to Berlin, or becoming heavily committed militarily to anti-Communist nationalist leaders such as Egypt's Sadat. And in Eastern Europe, too, there is evidence for a Soviet search for less heavy-handed methods than were used to dislodge by brute force the Nagy and Dubcek leaderships in Hungary and Czechoslovakia. In the post-intervention period, especially in Hungary, a definite Soviet effort was made to moderate the style of rule, stimulate economic and social progress, and to minimize to the extent possible the visibility of the Soviet military presence and the imposition of Moscow's political will. Soviet forbearance in relation to Polish developments during the past several years is as impressive as is Soviet pressure upon the party machinery in Poland to follow a hard line towards Solidarity. Of course, so long as Moscow-orientated bureaucrats retain control over the Polish state it is often possible to exert influence indirectly.

In truth, we do not know the shape of the internal debate among the Soviet elite on 'intervention' in the tumultuous post-Brezhnev period. So far, Mr Gorbachev has not unambiguously revealed any new disposition to reverse the course of the Afghan war, and perhaps his position is not strong enough to do so even if he believed such an initiative would be desirable for the sake of overall Soviet interests. As the American experience in Vietnam showed, it is exceedingly difficult for a major state to admit to the failure of a major foreign policy undertaking once its military prestige is engaged, even in the face of large-scale and intense domestic opposition. As Soviet policy is carried on without such an opposition, the bureaucratic momentum in support of intervention may be virtually impossible to reverse.

A direct consequence of the militarization of Europe has been to bring once again the threat of devastating warfare east of the Urals, this time in the shockingly ultimate form of nuclear missiles. Even without the European blocs, strategic nuclear weapons in silos, aircraft and submarines pose a constant threat to the Soviet heartland. This declining relevance of geography to security should encourage a political approach to Europe. There are obvious benefits for Moscow that could flow from a dissolution of the bloc system. A softening of relations to the West could assure the Soviet Union reliable access to a much wider range of modern technology. These considerations may gain weight as the newer leaders begin to appreciate that 'security' cannot be achieved in the nuclear age by buffer zones and territorial defence. More than ever before the Maginot Syndrome, both looking back to the last great war for guidance and regarding the geographical defence of territory as the essence of security, endangers and deprives governments of opportunities for better overall adjustments by way of improving the political climate through mutually reassuring (or non-provocative) postures of deterrence and defence.

Washington is also entrapped in a pre-nuclear time warp, seeking to make adjustments to the changing scene by extremely expensive technological innovations in weapons systems and strategic doctrine that have the overall effect of making the Soviets strain to catch up or to discourage any sense of exploitable advantage. This interaction has the terrible consequence of encouraging preemptive strategies in crisis situations; going first rather than risking being 'disarmed'. It also means reducing the decision time for responding in a crisis, entrusting a larger role to preprogrammed reactions and relying upon automated procedures. These tendencies seem insensitive to the great risks of provocative weapons systems and the vagaries of an unpredictable arms race. United States policy-makers refuse to admit that, on balance, striving to stay ahead is much more dangerous than falling behind, whatever that could mean at current force levels. Of course, better than any kind of resolve to win an arms race, would be a serious effort to find strategic and diplomatic formulae for stabilizing the strategic military environment. Such a focus is somewhat different than the call for 'a freeze'. Here, the main goal is defensive defence – to configure forces and verification methods, including espionage by satellite and otherwise, to assure both sides of defensive and retaliatory intentions and capacity. That is, the United States needs, in its own interest, to convince the Soviet Union that it has no intention or capacity to attack and that it could under all circumstances retaliate effectively after a Soviet attack. Similarly, the Russians should seek to convey the same message to Washington.

We must not lose sight of the positive side to Yalta, while seeking to do away with its dark side. Yalta successfully established some geopolitical boundaries, or spheres of influence, that clarified in advance the occasions on which intervention would produce World War III. The West abided by these inhibitions in relation to the dramatic moments of Soviet brutality on Eastern Europe. However great Western sympathies for the struggles of the Poles, Czechs, Hungarians and East Germans, there was little disposition to challenge Soviet intervention. Similarly, if Communist Parties in France or Italy had gained the upper hand, even by constitutional means, it seems virtually certain that the Soviet Union would have stood meekly by in the event that the United States made moves to dismantle such a regime, as seemed likely from the Sonnenfeldt Doctrine and other expressions of intention. Yalta was one of several attempts to set forth some agreed rules of the game.

The dark side of Yalta remains, of course, its implications for human rights and self-determination, as well as its tendency to make the postwar European atmosphere one of continental division amounting to a prewar fix. The challenge remains to create conditions for lasting peace. As it has turned out these postwar arrangements have mainly meant a loss for the peoples occupied by the Red Army, but not entirely. It has meant the permanent militarization of the continent as a whole under the auspices of the two superpowers with negative effects on the sovereign rights and political culture of Western Europe of a sort discussed earlier. It has also implied an outer limit on West European political freedom, although one never fully tested. We do know that the United States, through the CIA, funded conservative labour and student organizations, cultural activities, and rightist political parties, especially in Italy, with a primary goal of containing the influence of the Communist Party. Yet, by and large, postwar Western Europe has prospered, at least up to now, by its participation in bloc politics.

Eastern Europe has not. It has been economically and politically stifled by a much heavier hand of outside dominance. Yalta, then, is perceived from this angle as a betrayal of these peoples, consigning them to the untender mercies of unchallenged Soviet hegemony. The convergent circumstances that may make something new happen consist of these elements: in the West, a desire to reach eastwards to overcome economic stagnancy and partially circumvent American/Japanese dominance of the world trading system and a concern that unless the military environment established to uphold the status quo is reformed there could be either a breakdown leading to the devastation of the continent or a further expansion in popular discontent to a level where radicalism posed a real threat to established interests. Further, even the superpowers realize that a new era might be advantageous. The Soviets are burdened economically by their role in Eastern Europe and they have no prospect of being accepted as legitimate guardians of an acceptable order; their attempt to make Yalta acceptable to the peoples under their hegemony has definitively failed. With the trade deficit so high, American leaders could be persuaded that it might be better to let Europe work out its own destiny at this stage. Such persuasion must encompass the sub-text of Germany, that is, whether a divided and occupied Germany is still a vital condition for the stability of Europe; if it is perceived to be, then East–West tensions are needed to provide 'a cover story'.

The difficulty of framing an alternative policy here is compounded by matters of delicacy. Opening up the German dimension would involve, first of all, a real conviction that Fascism and Prussianism are more or less dead as serious forces in the country, or that a post-occupation framework can be devised to keep German militarism in check for the indefinite future. The view is often expressed that the removal of the American military presence would leave Germany vulnerable and exposed, and might provoke a second Versailles mood, possibly opening the way for a new surge of German militarism. It is these scenarios that help undergird the status quo long after its natural life. The various interpretations of the all-European commitment to the promotion of human rights and political democracy in the Helsinki Accords are quite revealing. As with Yalta, there is a considerable difference between the Left, Right and Centre in the West with regard to the human rights provisions (so-called Basket III) of Helsinki. The non-Communist and anti-state Left regards this opening as a vital way to push for detente from below, insisting that peace and demilitarization cannot be achieved without prior progress in the area of human rights and democracy. For the liberal/realist Centre, these Basket III provisions are mainly occasions for hostile propaganda useful to instruct societies in the West about the dreadful character of life in the East. For the Right, these provisions are a Trojan horse by which to mount their roll-back campaign against Yalta, that is, against the Soviet sphere of influence in Eastern Europe, or at the least, they are a tool by which to wrest Soviet geopolitical concessions outside of Europe in exchange for some kind of grudging toleration of the Soviet role within Eastern Europe.

NOTES

1 See Paul Johnson, 'The Ghosts of Yalta Haunt Us Still', *Wall Street Journal*, 7 February 1985, p. 30.
2 John Gittings, 'How Concord Turned to Mistrust', *Manchester Guardian Weekly*, 17 February 1985.
3 Cf. M. Kalb's account of his visit to Bitberg in the aftermath of the Reagan stopover, *New York Times*, 14 May 1985.
4 Zbigniew Brzezinski, 'The Future of Yalta', *Foreign Affairs*, 63 (Winter 1984/5), pp. 279–302.
5 Ibid., p. 294.
6 Ibid., p. 295.
7 Ibid.
8 'The Post-Yalta Debate', Interview with George Konrad, *World Policy Journal* (Summer 1985).
9 Arkady N. Shevchenko, 'How Soon Will Gorbachev have Real Clout?', *New York Times*, 21 March 1985, p. 27.
10 George Konrad, *Antipolitics* (London: Quartet 1984), p. 120.
11 Ibid.
12 Brzezinski, 'The Future of Yalta', p. 299.

3

The Nature of Bipolarity: An Argument Against the Status Quo

GIAN GIACOMO MIGONE

We are accustomed to thinking that the world is first and foremost divided by a conflict between East and West. The present administration in Washington is a strong proponent of such a view which, of course, is both expedient and, to a considerable degree, self-fulfilling. Traditionally, this view leaves as little margin as possible for anybody who would like to take a non-aligned position. Within the alliances, a bipolar interpretation of the world is the best justification for strong leadership and strict discipline on the part of lesser allies. At the same time, it is the theoretical premise on which the arms race rests. For its part, Moscow has acted eagerly to sustain it with the invasion of Afghanistan, normalization of Poland, the deployment of new nuclear weapons and great readiness to establish control over all those countries of the Third World which do not readily enter the American fold.

There is a growing concern in Europe today that the present tension between East and West hides a deeper conflict, rooted less in ideology than in facts, facts that oppose those who are committed to the status quo to those whose interest lies in trying to modify it to their advantage. Though the Reagan administration may not accept Moscow on equal terms, both are committed to a hierarchy of nations which keeps everybody else in their place. Though this deeper conflict is by no means confined to Europe, it is rooted in the division of Europe. The limited sovereignty of Eastern European countries is self-evident. But even the different issues which have poisoned relations between the United States and Western Europe – the deployment of INF missiles (Intermediate Nuclear Forces), East–West trade, high interest rates, even American unilateral intervention in the Mediterranean – stem from the post-World

War II settlement. Some historical perspective will help clarify the issue.[1]

HEGEMONY, DOMINATION AND THE POSTWAR SYSTEM

The partition of Europe after World War II did not take place at Yalta. As Stalin pointed out in one of his conversations with Milovan Djilas, it was the military presence of the wartime allies which ultimately settled the geopolitical map of Europe. Though superpower control cannot be reduced to military factors, the presence of American and Soviet troops, which became permanent under the alliance system, should not be underestimated. In the case of Eastern European countries, it is probably the essential condition for the survival of the present internal regimes and of the Warsaw Pact. In the West it is necessary to distinguish between different countries. There is hardly any doubt that as far as the Mediterranean members of NATO are concerned – what has been referred to in the past as the 'soft underbelly of the alliance' – internal events in every single country (with the exception of France) have been deeply affected by the American military presence and, above all, by the special bilateral relationships established by the armed services which are an essential feature of the NATO framework. Naturally, the machinations of the secret services are very much included in this pattern. In the case of Greece and Turkey, such a relationship has been an important component of successful *coups d'état*. In the case of Italy, sectors of the American national security establishment have given encouragement to abortive coups. But the pathological aspects of these bilateral ties within the alliance framework are not the most important. Sometimes a weapon is most effective for its intimidatory value rather than its actual use. De Gaulle's break with the treaty organization but not with the alliance did not have a purely ideological significance. It was a very practical decision to re-establish direct national control over every aspect of French national security as well as military policy.

Naturally, the direct presence of troops and the structure of the military alliances are not in themselves sufficient to ensure the hegemony of the superpowers over their respective spheres of influence. What distinguishes hegemony from sheer domination is the capacity to exercise power in such a way as to satisfy real needs, thus ensuring some degree of consensus on the part of the dependent nations. One could also add that the surrogate for hegemony is domination, and that the most obvious means of domination is force. The Soviet capacity for hegemony was from the beginning very limited. To varying degrees Soviet troops supplemented the Communist cause in the various Eastern European countries. Furthermore, Soviet ideology itself was such as to offer no flexibility or pluralism, and limited reliance on consensus. But lack of economic resources weakened the Soviet quest for hegemony more than any other single factor. The Soviet Union not only had little to offer, and much to demand in this respect, but, to fend off American influence, had to force its satellites to refuse what was actually offered them through participation in the Marshall Plan. Since the late 1940s Soviet capacity for hegemony has certainly not increased. Whatever appeal Soviet Communism had has been weakened by the formation of power-hungry and sometimes corrupt national bureaucracies which rely on the threat of external intervention in order to survive. When, in spite of this threat, significant changes have taken place within single countries and single Communist parties, the Soviet Union has been forced to intervene. Only the capacity to use military power in those instances has preserved Soviet control over its satellites. When control is principally ensured by military power, such power obviously cannot be dispensed with. Where it has not been applied, as in Yugoslavia and, to some extent, in Rumania, the Soviet Union has lost control. Even the long-term effect, from the Soviet point of view, of the Polish military coup is open to doubt. It is the first time that Moscow has achieved normalization without paying the price of direct military intervention. But forces of opposition are far from destroyed and the fact that the solution to the crisis was carried out by the Polish military themselves may turn out to be significant in the long run.

It is not clear what the Gorbachev era may have to offer lesser members of the Warsaw Pact. While it is reasonably certain that the new leadership in the Kremlin is prepared to make considerable concessions to slow down the arms race in order to gain breathing space for internal reform, it has given no signal that it will lessen its hold over Eastern Europe. It should not be forgotten that Krushchev invaded Hungary immediately after the XXth Congress of the CPSU.

American capacity for hegemony over its European sphere of influence has been greater, though it is today declining. The early period of the Truman administration has rightly been considered the high-point of American leadership. More important than the military superiority of the United States relative to the Soviet Union, which had not yet acquired full nuclear capabilities, were the United States' comparatively unlimited economic resources and ideological vitality. The Marshall Plan became a formidable Cold War weapon precisely because it was primarily conceived to meet other ends. As after World War I, reconstruction and pacification of Europe fulfilled a need of the American economy, which had been expanded by war production. Monetary stabilization and productivity – the two cornerstones of American aid – served the purpose of European reconstruction, in a free market context, with the capitalist and managerial establishment firmly in the saddle. Even then, harsher means were sometimes used. Greece was stabilized by the allies through military intervention which led to a dictatorship. In Portugal and Spain, already-existing dictatorships could rely upon American support. Though the Italian postwar crisis did not end in military intervention and dictatorship, it was certainly no picnic. In France, Belgium and Germany (as well as in Italy) the working class movement was split and the neutralist left excluded from any form of government power.

All this notwithstanding, it was not direct intervention or manipulation of the political process which established American hegemony over Western Europe as a whole. American policy was successful in consolidating in power a pro-American, essentially conservative, establishment precisely because it satisfied some popular needs which went far beyond those who benefited politically. American economic aid primarily corresponded to enlightened American self-interest, and had little to do with the humanitarian verbiage in which it was clothed; but it nevertheless fed empty stomachs. While the Marshall Plan offered prospects for economic growth, if not social change, the Western democratic model offered genuine appeal to large sectors of the working class with a Christian or social democratic tradition, especially if contrasted with what was taking place in Eastern Europe. The simple fact that the Soviet Union had to resort to military force in order to establish control over Eastern Europe strengthened American hegemony in the West. Even the quality of the conservative leadership which established itself in Western Europe in those years was a tribute to American strength and leadership. The comparison between the Adenauers, the Schumanns, the De Gasperis and latterday pro-American, European leadership is in itself significant. It is no coincidence that the United States in the late forties and early fifties could even exercise leadership in the direction of European unification. It was the tenacity of European national habits and interests, not lack of American self-confidence, which acted against such efforts at the time.

THE ROLE OF DETENTE

The Korean War, the continuous tension over Berlin, the invasion of Hungary and the military build-up in the climate of Dullesian rhetoric served to harden existing divisions in Europe in the course of the fifties. But it was the beginning of detente at Camp David, preceded by the XXth Congress of the CPSU, which gave new stimuli to the role of the superpowers. There is no more powerful force of legitimization of superpower leadership than those leaderships' capacity to negotiate with each other in peaceful terms, especially after periods of tension. European leaders and the public opinion they represent were, and probably still are, dangerously inclined to consider a summit meeting in itself beneficial, regardless of practical results. In such cases there is a readiness to delegate enormous power to the United States and the Soviet Union, which supposedly represent the interests of the rest of the world. This happened at Camp David in 1959 and happened again in the Nixon–Kissinger era.

The aftermath of the 1985 Geneva meeting between President Reagan and Mr Gorbachev, as conducted by Washington, is a perfect example of the manipulative use of summit diplomacy. At the meeting nothing took place, because the Reagan administration was not ready to grant the new Soviet leader the breathing space in the arms race which he so obviously needed. Nevertheless, the two leaders joined each other in pleasant generalities which world opinion – too scared by preceding tension – did not have the heart to brush off with cynicism. Perhaps the very failure of the subsequent Rekyavik summit can be explained by its improvised nature. Both leaders needed an agreement for different reasons which created a genuine opportunity for disarmament in everybody's interest, beyond the traditional manipulation of summit diplomacy. Gorbachev's far-reaching proposals forced Reagan to take refuge behind a rigid defence of SDI. In the aftermath of Irangate it is not clear whether added tension or a less ambitious agreement will follow. In either case the main purpose of summit diplomacy will have been achieved: to legitimize its protagonists. It is the alternate use of tension and detente which strengthens the privileged position of the dominant powers.

From the European point of view, the most serious event of the 1960s was the invasion of Czechoslovakia, but even the fall of Salvador Allende in Chile had a direct and long-term impact on thinking in Europe. Chile was only distant geographically, since its strong democratic traditions and fairly developed economy put it in the same category as some European countries. In both cases, the superpowers re-established their domination in a ruthless manner. The United States was successful in supporting a bloody military coup by stifling the Chilean economy and orchestrating covert operations. The Soviet Union once again had to resort to direct military intervention. In both cases the superpower not directly concerned limited even verbal protests to a minimum and withheld any form of practical support. These parallel episodes brought home the lesson, particularly relevant to the European situation, that the two superpowers interpreted their self-interest in such a way as to preclude any meeting point between democracy and socialist policies within their respective spheres of interest. Allende attempted a socialist transformation of society while respecting individual rights and democratic principles. Dubcek wanted to reinstate democratic pluralism and individual liberties within a reformed socialist economic system. A major cause of their failure was the unspoken agreement of the superpowers that parliamentary democracy should remain inextricably wedded to the capitalist system and that any attempt to separate socialism from the Soviet autocratic model should be thwarted. It became quite evident that both Moscow and Washington considered the meeting of the two fundamental popular aspirations of this age – liberty and equality – as a threat to their respective positions. With Kissingerian gusto for conceptual clarity, the so-called Sonnenfeldt Doctrine proclaimed that Eurocommunism – which signalled precisely that double aspiration – was a danger because it represented a potential rallying point for democratic aspirations in Eastern Europe. If Eurocommunism was permitted to weaken Soviet domination, it would automatically threaten United States leadership in the West. The Nixon administration, as well as its colleagues in the Kremlin, subscribed to the well-known principle according to which heresy is more threatening to the mother church than a clearly defined opposing religion (or indeed atheism).[2]

These limitations to European sovereignty tend to consolidate existing social systems, making any kind of radical reform very dangerous in Eastern Europe and more difficult in the West. But it is naturally in the field of foreign and military policy that superpower controls and pressure make themselves most felt. In order to justify the military alliances, the arms race and their dominating role, each superpower needs to be able to point to the threat represented by the other. This is particularly true in the case of the United States because its government has to take public opinion, both American and foreign, into greater account. Traditionally the Soviet Union represents an ideological threat of world revolution: radical change in any Western society has been linked to Soviet expansion. This axiom has been weakened by the obviously conservative nature of Soviet-orientated Communist regimes and by the increasingly democratic and pluralistic orientation not only of social democratic parties but also of the Italian PCI, the only Communist party which, because of its size, has the possibility of presiding over a government in a Western country. None the less, the myth is far from dead, since even the Swedish conservatives frequently accused Olof Palme of wanting to Sovietize the country. But NATO doctrines rest on the premise that a Soviet military threat against Western Europe not only exists but could take the form of outright invasion. Now, while the Soviet Union has shown great readiness in repressing independent aspirations in Eastern Europe and also in taking advantage of struggles for independence in the Third World, it is hard to think of it as seriously contemplating territorial expansion at the expense of Western Europe. As E. P. Thompson has pointed out, in an interview, its problems are rather of a digestive nature.

This ideologically unattractive and basically conservative Soviet Union has created serious problems from the point of view of American and NATO policy, which badly need to be sustained by the aggressiveness, cohesion and ideological credibility of its major opponent. Gorbachev's peace offensives have not made things easier. The emphasis which the Reagan administration from the very beginning placed on 'international terrorism' functions as a surrogate to prop up the customary Soviet threat. In point of fact terrorism has grown dramatically during these past years, but both its forms and its protagonists are so varied as to defy any effort to consider it as a consistent whole. Such efforts can lead to momentous mistakes, similar to those which ensued from the American habit of the fifties and sixties of directing foreign policy against 'international Communism'. Yesterday as today, the reason for such a preoccupation is the persisting need of Washington to indicate to its domestic opinion a unified and threatening enemy which justifies the sacrifices which are called for. But such all too obvious simplification also has the purpose of building up a unified international front, led by the United States. International Communism was led by Moscow (even after the Sino–Soviet rift). International terrorism is a convenient concept because it permits the identification of actors which are, from time to time, the most expedient targets of unilateral strikes. At the same time, these manipulators have friendly ties with Moscow and thus strengthen a bipolar foreign policy.

In order to understand the political consequences of military conflicts, a theoretical distinction can be helpful.

THEORETICAL AND ACTUAL CONFLICTS

Two kinds of international conflict exist in the world today: one could be called the theoretical type of conflict and the other, the actual type. A theoretical conflict is that embodied in the opposition between the United States and the Soviet Union, between East and West. This is expressed in the desire of the superpowers to make the rest of the world choose sides through military alliances, thus reciprocally justifying the arms race. This type of conflict is theoretical in the sense that its logical consequence, nuclear war, has not yet happened, in spite of the fact that the superpowers tend to reduce every actual conflict to terms fitting this polarity.

Actual conflicts, by contrast, arise when nations or peoples oppose the hierarchy based on the bipolarity of the superpowers, by pursuing autonomous policies even within the alliance system.

Obviously, it is the threat posed by the theoretical conflict which permits the dominant powers to control the actual conflicts. It strengthens the military blocs; it forces the arms race to escalate; it coerces Third World nations to sacrifice autonomy for the sake of avoiding nuclear conflagration. Thus theoretical conflict is in itself a weapon to reinforce nuclear monopoly, limit the actual conflicts and maintain current power relationships. Although the actual conflicts are by no means confined to Europe, they are rooted in the division of Europe.

The peace movement has up until now been only partially successful in challenging this scheme. The movement is no longer that of the 1950s, made up of people who could be called fellow-travellers of the Soviet Union since they were trying to equalize the balance of power which favoured the United States in that period. In the 1980s the movement has acquired the awareness that the threat to peace does not come from one side only. Neither does it come from imbalance. It stems from the increasing spiral of armaments beyond the control of the peoples, and of most governments, of the world. From this awareness follows the criticism of bipolarity, albeit an insufficient criticism, which characterizes today's movement.

Its weakness, however, consists in the lack of attention given to actual conflicts, which are a major cause of the arms race and the threat to peace. Let me give an example. In Italy the focus of the movement has been the missile site at Comiso, in so far as the installation of cruise and Pershing II would further expose the nation to danger in the case of war. Such a struggle is just and necessary, but it neglects the immediate political and economic effects not only of the missile site, but also of the general military presence of the United States in Italy and of NATO's role in internal politics: the *de facto* violation of sovereignty that this entails. It focuses on the theoretical conflict and its possible future consequences rather than on the immediate effects of the actual conflict.

Several supporters of INF have made no bones about the fact that the deployment of these weapons has very little, if any, military relevance. Both the United States and, since the advent of Gorbachev, the Soviet Union have offered a zero option: i.e., the elimination of all medium range nuclear missiles on both sides. Yet, as of today, no such agreement has been reached. The point is that these weapons are primarily important not for their effect on the nuclear balance (which is not based on any form of bean counting) but for the added control they establish on the part of the dominant, nuclear powers over the countries where the missiles are located.

To sum up, the INF weapons increase the danger of a theoretical conflict, in that they add to the momentum of the arms race, but they are presently being used in the actual conflict in which they weaken the sovereignty of nations where they are located – these nations are, paradoxically, excluded from the disarmament negotiations which directly concern them.

In other words, any increase in the American military and nuclear presence in any Western European nation augments the dangers of war for those peoples and, in immediate terms, underscores the subordination of that country to decision-makers outside its borders. This daily increases the alienation of peoples, parliaments and governments from what should be their natural prerogatives. At the same time it strengthens the Soviet hold over Eastern Europe.

The pro-American critics of the peace movement insist that the desire for a neutral Europe means a Finlandization policy which would see national autonomy controlled by Moscow. Such critics neglect the fact that Europe is already in a much worse position, even with regard to the most elementary principles of liberal democracy. Western Europe has already been Finlandized – by the United States. The extent varies from nation to nation, increasing as one proceeds from the North Sea towards the Mediterranean. The United States limits the rights of European peoples to choose their own governments, to control their own economies, to acquire raw materials independently.

In Eastern Europe the situation is even worse. It is in a state of partial military occupation in which every attempt to claim individual or collective liberty is met with force or repression. As K. S. Karol has pointed out, Finlandization could be an excellent goal for Eastern Europe, while Western Europe should strive for independence.

In spite of appearances, both superpowers not only want to maintain control over their respective alliances but also have a vested interest in the cohesion of the other camp. It was not only Henry Kissinger who firmly believed that any act of destabilization within one of the blocs would also weaken the other bloc, because it would threaten its legitimacy. After all, the cohesion of an alliance depends on the menace, and therefore the cohesion, of the other alliance.

Even President Reagan, in fact, does not dare to play Dulles's game of roll-back (which was a game of words in any case). This became extremely clear during the climax of the Polish crisis (the spring of 1981) when the White House not only did not seriously attempt to prevent a Soviet invasion, but in fact encouraged it by holding back help to Kania from American banks, sending General Haig to China to orchestrate military cooperation and daring the Kremlin to intervene by stating that the Soviet

Union was no longer a first-rate power because it was not able to keep order within its own empire. Nor is it any coincidence that, after the military coup had taken place, from the many proposed sanctions the only significant step the administration seriously attempted to enforce was in fact directed against Western Europe. Had the building of the pipeline to supply Western Europe with Soviet gas been stopped, Soviet economic interests would no doubt have been hurt, but the main consequence would have been Western Europe's continued and almost exclusive dependency on fuel directly or indirectly controlled by the United States. Thus, while the superpowers seem to be on opposing sides of the theoretical conflict, they are really allies in the strategy of the actual conflict.

Yet, in spite of all this, the Soviet–American condominium over Europe remains precarious. As far as the United States is concerned, the continuous use of unilateral pressure is in itself evidence that the traditional hegemonic relationship, based on consensus, no longer holds. This is particularly visible in the economic field, where high American interest rates have weakened European economies but have also indicated the incapacity of the dollar to face all its responsibilities within the international monetary system as a whole.

Superficially we receive the impression that the superpowers' control over Europe has been reasserted. A few years of exasperated bipolarism have produced some results. The Polish experiment has been arrested (though not totally destroyed). As of today the governments of Britain, Germany, Italy, Belgium and The Netherlands have accepted the cruise and Pershing II missiles. The peacekeeping operation in the Lebanon, while not achieving much else, has successfully eliminated any European role in the Middle Eastern question, at least for the time being. European attempts to formulate a policy in crisis situations in the Third World, while significant for their novelty, have not yet produced any results: this is true in situations as different as Nicaragua and South Africa. The Strategic Defense Initiative has served the purpose of dividing European governments and establishing links between the United States and individual Western European industries.

At the same time, even the deployment of the new missiles cannot hide the fact that the malaise within NATO is so significant that it cannot be eliminated by more consultation or some adaptation of the institutional framework.[3] On the basis of the record of at least the last two American administrations, more consultation is not likely to take place and a NATO directorate would, in all likelihood, create more problems than it would solve. Even a European NATO supreme commander (SACEUR) would hardly resolve the issues at stake. No 'grand design' is at hand. The time is past when western public opinion and parliaments were prepared to delegate the debate on NATO and national security to those who used to be called the 'theologians' during the Kennedy administration. Likewise, it is hard to imagine that American hegemony can somehow transform itself into domination of Western Europe, with a more direct use of force.

It is, to say the least, doubtful whether the Reagan administration has effectively eliminated the Vietnam syndrome, even in the most vulnerable parts of the Third World. Grenada and Libya prove that American intervention can take place successfully only where its price, in terms of money and American lives, is very low. The basic problem of American foreign policy – the disproportion between its aims and the human and economic resources Congress and the voters are prepared to allocate – remains, regardless of geography. At the same time the increasing lawlessness of American foreign policy is in itself an indication of crisis. The strictures imposed by Congress and American public opinion have encouraged the tendency towards short term unilateral military actions that do not involve direct use of American troops, as well as different forms of covert action (perhaps even using the excuse of international terrorism which can be convenient for everybody concerned). As Gibbon pointed out a long time ago, any empire that cannot respect the rules it has laid down for itself and others has entered a phase of decline.

The Soviet Union has never been able to establish a hegemony based on consensus in Eastern Europe. Over the years controls based on force have not been transformed into consensus hegemony. On the contrary, the economic crisis and persistent conflicts of national identity have become more difficult to manage militarily, and more and more expensive.

While not weakening his hold over Eastern Europe, Mr Gorbachev's diplomacy seems interested in addressing Western Europe as an independent entity. An important step in this direction has been the acceptance of the French *force de frappe*. It remains to be seen how Soviet diplomacy would respond to a European initiative which set forth requests concerning greater autonomy for territories under Soviet control – the only way to prevent present Soviet policy having the sole effect of dividing the Western alliance without any reciprocal concessions.

In conclusion, we might say that the United States is not able completely to transform its crisis-ridden hegemony into domination; neither can the Soviet Union transform its crisis-ridden domination into hegemony.

BEYOND BIPOLARITY

What is it, then, that continues to maintain the division of Europe and the superpower status of the United States and the Soviet Union?

In the first place, the internal divisions of Western Europe are the result as well as the cause of America's role. Certain decisive sectors of the ruling classes remain historically linked to American power, even if conflicts of interest with the United States and pressure of public opinion force them into positions of even greater autonomy.

Secondly, though the superpowers are losing the ability to control effectively their respective spheres of interest, they are able to use their *mutual* dependence effectively. In this manner, the use of what I have referred to as the theoretical type of conflict stands as a formidable weapon in the hands of both superpowers for the purpose of keeping discipline in the ranks. This is true in moments of high tension when the threat of global war seems imminent: the leadership role of the two dominant nations has to be respected in order to avoid the outbreak of armed conflict. In times of dialogue and negotiation, they posture as responsible and paternal proponents of the fragile prospects of peace. But what ensures their control over the rest of the world is their capacity to alternate the situations of crisis and negotiation. The risk exists that the possibility of war causes nations not to try to control the power wielded by the increasingly irresponsible superpowers, but to delegate even more power to them as they negotiate, ceding power from a sense of relief, an illusion of having escaped from danger.

On the other hand, the need of the superpowers to use rearmament and threats of war in order to control increasingly reluctant lesser allies is at the root of the present danger. By now it is clear that peace and its proponents cannot rely exclusively on the fear of war. The fear of war does, at first, produce mobilization, but, if it is not followed by a widespread understanding of the causes of the danger, it is easily transformed into the more or less uncontrolled ceding of power to those who are armed, once they declare themselves ready to negotiate.

But this still does not get to the heart of the problem. The peace movement must take on as a priority a role in what I have termed actual conflicts. If peace is menaced by power struggles based on the roles of the dominant powers, then peace must be defended by changing this, by freeing the peoples and individual leaders involved from the extra-national conditioning that limits their independence.

If peace is based on freedom, then the struggles for freedom must become the first concern of the peace movement if there is to be any escape from the web of nuclear blackmail spun by the superpowers. In other words, the theoretical conflict can be avoided only by winning each actual conflict. The peace movement will only survive and grow if it extends its campaign against armaments into the support and encouragement of every expression of independence from the two dominant powers, whether these may be struggles for liberty in Poland or the fight of a Central American nation for freedom from American intervention without embracing Soviet leadership. In order to become successful as a peace movement, the movement also has to become a liberation movement.

Before the nuclear age, the liquidation of empires was brought about by wars or catastrophes of similar dimensions. It is possible that the danger of absolute destruction – which is distinctive of the nuclear age – brings with it an opportunity for radical change of the world balance of power, without war. In other words, our survival depends on the possibility that some other way can be found to modify a status quo that, in the end, will lead to war.

NOTES

1 A related treatment of these questions can also be found in G. G. Migone, 'Le Relazioni Stati Uniti–Europa e il declino delle superpotenze', in Pier Paolo D'Attorre (ed.), *La governabilita degli Stati Uniti. Mutamenti e continuita nell 'America contemporanea* (Milan: Franco Angeli, 1983). For a much earlier version of the same kind of thinking, see: G. G. Migone, 'La Realtà Internazionale tra federalismo e Neonazionalismo', *Relazioni Sociali*, 7 (April 1967).

2 For a similar argument, see R. Falk, *The End of World Order* (New York: London, Holmes & Meier, 1983).

3 Typical of this way of thinking is K. Kaiser, W. Lord, Th. de Montbrial and D. Watt, *Western Security: What has Changed? What Should be Done?* (New York and London: Council on Foreign Relations, 1981).

4

American Domestic Politics and the Atlantic Alliance: Crisis and Controversy

ALAN WOLFE

I

In the aftermath of World War II, the United States became intimately involved in the affairs of Europe, both economically through the Marshall Plan and militarily through the North Atlantic Treaty Organization. From the viewpoint of the 1980s, this statement is unremarkable, for some kind of Atlantic alliance has been in place for a generation and has taken on the appearance of being 'natural'. But from the standpoint of American history, the Atlantic alliance was the exception, not the rule. Long isolationist in general, and suspicious of Europe in particular, Americans needed to be convinced of the need to play a role in European affairs. As Senator Vandenberg pointed out to President Truman, it was necessary to 'scare the hell out of the American people' before his constituents in Michigan would allow him to support the emerging Atlantic alliance.

Why did the United States take the unprecedented step of tying its fortunes to Europe, thereby repudiating the spirit of George Washington's Farewell Address ('no entangling alliances') and reversing its proclivity to ignore the rest of the world? American policy-makers have little doubt about the answer. The position of Soviet troops on the European continent, they have argued, left them with little choice. When Harry Truman asked Clark Clifford in 1946 to prepare a memorandum on Soviet intentions, Clifford was told by the US State Department that Soviet ambitions in Eastern Europe could only be 'contained' by 'armed resistance on the part of other major powers in areas where they feel their vital interests to be endangered'.[1] By 1948–9, there was no longer any doubt or dissent within the US foreign policy establishment about the necessity of a permanent American presence in Western Europe to counter what was seen as Soviet aggression in Eastern Europe.

Time – and the inevitable publication of documents that comes with time – has led a number of scholars to question the adequacy of the Soviet threat as an explanation for American involvement in European affairs. There was, of course, no nuclear threat from the Soviet Union in 1946, making overall American superiority obvious to all. And even in the conventional arms field, as recent research by Matthew Evangelista has demonstrated, no 'overwhelming' Soviet advantage existed.[2] (Visions of the Red Army sweeping through Belgium generally did not acknowledge both the casualties suffered by the Soviet Union in World War II and the limited, and conservative, strategic Soviet objectives.) Both superpowers, in other words, were jockeying for position in Europe with whatever resources they could muster from the residue of World War II. If there was a 'threat' to the autonomy of Europe, it came from both superpowers, each viewing the intentions of the other as an excuse to maintain its control over predetermined spheres of influence.

If the Soviet threat does not hold as a sufficient explanation for the unusual American willingness to participate in an Atlantic alliance, something else must. A number of scholars, especially those of a Marxist bent, have been arguing that the explanation lies in the realm of economics. The most sophisticated of these theories, in my view, is that of Fred Block, who – along with European writers like Mary Kaldor – views the creation of a free trade, liberal and global order as the highest priority of American policy-makers in the postwar period.[3] Given strong protectionist traditions in the United States, plus substantial popular resistance to foreign 'give-aways', the only hope for American approval of the Bretton Woods Agreement, the British Loan and, finally, the Marshall Plan lay in the cultivation of a military threat to America's trading partners. The Cold War mood of the late 1940s and early 1950s legitimated a sharp turn in American foreign economic policy. A military alliance, solidified by American efforts to rearm the continent, would protect the entire economic structure that liberal free traders had brought into being:

> Military aid to Europe after the Marshall Plan would eliminate any pressure for Europe to cut itself off, because there would be a continuing source of dollar aid. This would also make it possible to finance the exports of certain industries that would still be dependent on foreign markets even after rearmament. Finally, European rearmament under American leadership would make Europe dependent on American military hardware. This dependence could then be used to prevent Europe from drifting away from the United States.[4]

There is a good deal of truth in such 'economic' explanations of the birth of the Atlantic alliance, and my purpose is not to argue with them.

Instead, I wish rather to propose that economic explanations do not go far enough. A substantial part of the explanation for the origins of the Atlantic alliance, I will argue, lies in some of the peculiar features of the domestic political scene in America. The nature of these features must be taken into account in any effort to understand the current relationship between attempts at European autonomy from the United States and American domestic politics.

The Atlantic alliance was forged by politicians and policy-makers who viewed themselves as 'liberals' in American political terminology, the inheritors of the New Deal and the legacy of Franklin Delano Roosevelt. The strongest possible opposition to an assertion of American particip-ation in European hands came from the right-wing of the political spectrum – especially from those who possessed an 'Asia-first' view of the world. To understand the origins of the Atlantic alliance, one must recognize that the liberal coalition that had governed since 1932 was in serious political danger. Just as Churchill was to be replaced – right in the middle of the Potsdam Conference – by Attlee, it was assumed by almost all political commentators that in 1948 Harry Truman and the Democrats would go down to defeat at the hands of Thomas E. Dewey and the Republicans.

By the late 1940s, public support for such Democratic innovations as expensive social welfare programmes had run its course. There was an enormous demand for tax reduction and a return to the simpler world of small government and localism. Although the rest of the advanced capitalist world was prepared for a turn to the Left in the form of social democracy, America was clearly headed in the opposite direction. Without a strategy for responding to this mood, the Democrats would become the opposition party and New Deal liberalism a relic of the past. To stay in power, the Democrats needed a theme that would simultaneously give them a conservative tinge and thereby protect them from the Right, while also enabling them to rationalize domestic spending and retain the loyalty of the electoral groups on the Left. It seemed an impossible task; yet the Cold War satisfied both needs. By shifting to the right of the Republican Party on the dimension of anti-Communism, liberals could both prove their loyalty and bring into being a form of Keynesianism based on military, rather than social, expenditure.

To summarize a complicated history, the adoption of a Cold War posture to supplement New Deal liberalism contained a number of irreplaceable advantages for American liberals:

(1) Cold War themes could unify a contentious elite. Without the personal magnetism of Franklin Roosevelt, the Democratic Party threat-

ened to unravel into petty factions in the postwar period. To take the most obvious example, the Southern wing of the party was prepared to walk out of the party if too great a commitment was made to civil rights and labour legislation, a walk-out symbolized by the 'Dixiecrat' nomination of South Carolina's Strom Thurmond in 1948. At the same time, the urban liberals from the North-East – who saw themselves as the true heirs of the New Deal – also were tempted to leave the party and to support the candidacy of former Vice President Henry Wallace in 1948. In other words, if the Democrats were not to be destroyed by the Republicans, they seemed sure to destroy themselves. That this did not happen is in large measure traceable to the unifying appeals of Cold War liberals. Hubert Humphrey, for example, made the civil rights speech that prompted the Dixiecrat walk-out in 1948, yet his anti-Communism kept him safely within the party and against the Wallace effort. At the same time, the promise to locate military bases in the South, combined with a strong tradition of Southern support for the military, was extremely persuasive to both Senate and House Committee chairmen, who quietly discouraged the Thurmond effort in order to retain their patronage rights. Only a combination of Cold War militancy and liberalism was capable of keeping the Humphreys and the Ellenders and Russells safely within an increasingly contentious and disunified majority party.

(2) The Cold War and the Atlantic alliance required enormous expenditure – a tripling of the military budget in the view of the authors of NSC–68, the top secret overview of American strategic interests in the postwar period. While it might seem as if substantial new taxes would be needed to pay for this effort, thereby making the Democrats politically vulnerable, this need not be the case, as the authors of NSC–68 noted. Military expenditure could contribute to economic growth, raising the overall level of demand, encouraging investment and thereby financing itself. Indeed, as I have argued at length elsewhere, growth, not liberalism, became the catch-word of the Democratic Party, and military Keynesianism was essential to growth.[5]

(3) The Cold War solved the problem of excessive partisanship and substituted in its place a pattern of bipartisan cooperation that lasted for an entire generation. The Congressional elections of 1946 revealed an extremely bitter degree of partisan rancour, as Republicans charged Democrats with treason and various other heinous crimes. Bipartisanship curbed the excesses of Republican extravagance and enabled moderate and liberal Republicans to isolate the extremists in their own ranks. At the same time, it gave some space to the Democrats for their programmes, permitting them to prove their respectability to conservative public opinion. While it is often claimed that bipartisanship was a brilliant

manoeuvre by which the Democrats won Republican support for globalism, it can also be interpreted as a significant victory for the Republicans, who forced the Democrats to argue on the grounds of anti-Communism, thereby driving the Democratic Party ever further away from the New Deal and closer to Republican themes.[6] Without the Cold War, no centrist position existed that could have succeeded in bringing the moderate factions within each of the parties closer to each other and removing the more ideological groupings in both parties further from political power.

(4) Finally, Cold War emergencies provided a political rhetoric and vocabulary that would give substance to a liberalism that was being atrophied. Roosevelt had made the essence of the New Deal *social* security; postwar Democrats would shape their programme around *national* security. There was an obvious link. As William E. Leuchtenberg has noted, even Roosevelt was fond of using the language of war in order to argue for domestic programmes.[7] The Cold War and the New Deal existed within the same language of discourse: both demanded action by government; both required planning. Intellectuals needed to come to Washington to organize both crusades. Both were responses to dire emergency – economic chaos in the one, international chaos in the other. From Harry Truman to John F. Kennedy to Jimmy Carter, postwar Democrats found the metaphor of war and security indispensable to their world view. No longer liberals, they ran the risk of standing for nothing. The Cold War gave them something to 'be about', and, remarkably, they could 'be about' it without arousing the fierce opposition that domestic programmes inevitably engender.

All these points can be summarized in the following manner. As observers from James Madison in the eighteenth century to Samuel P. Huntington in the twentieth are fond of pointing out, America has a feudal political system, one based on small baronies of privilege and power, unable to concentrate its energies for the sake of national plans as a whole. Yet in the postwar period, something more than traditional politics was demanded if America was going to play the ambitious global role its leaders envisioned. Since it is impossible to lodge a twentieth-century empire inside an eighteenth-century polity, it was the political system that would have to yield. In the past, 'activist' presidents like Lincoln, Teddy Roosevelt and Woodrow Wilson had discovered in war a sufficient state of emergency to make governance possible.[8] For all postwar presidents who aspired to activism, a permanent state of war – which is, domestically, what the Cold War promised – was perhaps the only way to justify an agenda emphasizing policy coordination and planning in a political system organized for brokerage and patronage.

Europe played an obvious role in this process, for not only was the continent the most similar to America in background, but American troops had just returned from participating in a war for its future. Cold War rhetoric emphasizing the threat to Europe would be far more effective in terms of the domestic functions described above than alleged Communist takeovers, in, say, the Philippines or Iran. (Even Greece and Turkey, part of Europe, were insufficient really to arouse American fears; it was only when Northern Europe was seen as threatened that the Cold War reached its take-off point, giving the postwar world the anomaly of a *North* Atlantic Treaty that included Italy, Greece and Turkey. For all of these reasons, an American presence in Western Europe was foreordained given the directions taken by US domestic politics. It is, in fact, difficult to imagine how the postwar American political system would have functioned at all in the absence of a Cold War threat to Europe. In short, to put the matter in the bluntest possible way, *Western Europe was held hostage to American domestic politics. Europe would have to give up its autonomy in order to make the American political system work.*

Since the late 1940s, Atlantic relations have been governed by an unexpressed but none the less acknowledged form of social contract. European elites would accept American aid and all of its benefits in return for allowing American politicians to score domestic political points off the European situation. John F. Kennedy would be allowed to march in Berlin, 'grandstanding' back home in ways that most Europeans understood to be pure theatre, unrelated to the actual military and political realities on the continent, in return for America assuming a large share of the burden of European defence. The only problem with the arrangement was that it put European leaders in a potential conflict of interest between their own people and American politicians; when such situations arose, European policy-makers were expected to put their Atlanticist affiliations ahead of their own domestic realities, even if there were political costs attached to so doing.

This system could work – but only so long as the benefits from cooperation with the United States far outweighed the political costs to European elites of subsuming their domestic needs to American political realities. Now that the benefits have been declining, the whole structure is falling apart, with significant consequences both for Europe and for American political realities.

II

There were undoubted benefits for European elites in the patchwork system that was called the Atlantic alliance. The three most important were military protection, economic assistance and the contagiousness of a culture of consumption that compared extremely favourably with the Eastern model.

American military protection was an offer too good to refuse. For societies devastated economically from world war, the idea of being allowed to devote government and industry to economic reconstruction without prohibitive defence costs came with what seemed to be a low price – diplomatic subservience to American interests. (Only de Gaulle found the price too high.) European economies, given room to expand, did expand, helped along by a second source of benefit – direct economic assistance from the United States. And along with economic aid came an American way of life which, however distasteful to aristocratically inclined European elites, served as an important source of legitimating symbols for ordinary people. No head of state wishes to circumscribe his or her room for action, but under these conditions, a willingness to play a secondary role to American interests seemed perhaps justified when so much was offered in return.

Yet the effects on American domestic politics of such an asymmetrical alliance system were serious. To understand those effects, one must begin with a recognition of the unique character of the imperial order created after World War II. The United States' efforts were by no means the first attempt to create a world-wide system of political hegemony. Yet unlike the Roman or British empires, America seemed determined to be simultaneously the major world power and also to retain its parochial innocence towards global affairs. Americans wanted a form of *isolationist imperialism*, all of the benefits of global hegemony without any of the costs. And thus Americans supported extremely hawkish politicians, but rebelled against them when their policies spilled American blood. They voted consistently for a huge military establishment but rejected paying the taxes to finance it. They sought to extend their influence everywhere but did not care to learn the names of the countries to which they sought to extend their influence. They wanted, in a word, to influence the world but not be influenced by it. If the world did not correspond to American stereotypes about how it was supposed to work, then it was the world that would be forced to change, not the stereotypes. Rarely in history has any country sacrificed so many lives in order to protect images and perceptions, not real strategic or economic interests.

The effect of European subservience to American domestic needs in the early postwar period was to reinforce and strengthen the parochial nature of American foreign relations. Thus, NATO and the Marshall Plan were viewed by most Americans as a unilateral extension of American generosity, not as an attempt to shore up a Pax Americana. What to many

Europeans constituted, over time, a form of interference, was seen by Americans as a gift. The latent anti-Europeanism in American culture, in other words, was extended in the postwar period even as Europe became part of the American imperium. The Europeans, Americans were told, were too divided and confused to meet the challenge posed by Communism, so the United States would meet it for them. They were still too decadent and socialist to know how to run a capitalist economy, so the United States would help them. They were likely to divide into regional and linguistic groupings, so they would be encouraged to integrate into the Common Market. They did not know who their own best leaders would be, so the United States would pick their leaders for them. Americans assumed that they had a right to give Europeans moral lectures on Communism or economic growth simply because, without American help, most Americans believed, there would not be any Europe.

Over time, a combination of anti-European images combined with active US involvement in European affairs created a set of myths in America about the nature of postwar Europe. The most important can be called the myth of the selfish and spoiled child. Any attempt made by Europeans to recognize a degree of autonomy from America's immediate interests was viewed as the efforts of a spoiled brat to turn against the generous hand that was feeding it. This myth helps account for the *hurt* tone in American opinion when considering European efforts to find their own way in the world. 'After all we did for them,' one hears repeatedly, 'how could they . . .', and there then follows a complaint about trading with the Russians, or opposing the neutron bomb or demonstrating against Pershing missiles.

The Atlantic alliance, Theodore Draper has insisted, was never an alliance at all, since America pledged to come to the defence of Europe, but Europe could not come to the defence of America.[9] A unilateral power relationship expressed as a bilateral commitment could only cause trouble, Draper continues, and those troubles are now upon us. In a similar way, one can describe the imagery of the Atlantic alliance – an imagery that assumes a good deal of importance under the conditions of modern democratic politics – as similarly skewed. In theory, America and Europe would merge their fates. But in reality, America expected Europe to blend into America – to adopt its strategic outlook, to share its commitment to liberal capitalism, to watch its television programmes, to speak its language, and, most crucially, to accept the first premise of American opinion toward Europe, that it remain divided along the Cold War axis. It would have been far better, in a world that does not exist, if NATO had been deliberately described, not as an alliance, but as a one-way American guarantee. Similarly, it would have been far healthier for the American public to have been told that the dividing line down the middle of Europe was created by the way World War II ended and would therefore have to be temporary instead of viewing that line as the boundary between freedom and slavery, or, as Dwight D. Eisenhower once put it, between the forces of light and the forces of darkness.

As European political leaders, in return for American benefits, allowed American politicians to reinforce a set of images about Europe based more on American romantic fantasies about how the world works than on actual geostrategic realities, a gap between American and European perceptions was allowed to widen – to the point where it may never again be possible to bridge. Any relationship between the Europe that Americans read about in their press, even (or should I say, especially) in the *New York Times*, and the actual Europe that exists is purely coincidental. There are, in short, two Europes: real Europe and the Europe of American imagination. The former is an economic giant capable of deciding on its own what kind of attitude it wants toward the Soviet Union. The latter, as one reads the dispatches of John Vinocur and James Markham, is a place where tried and true friends of the United States find themselves under attack by the forces of anti-Americanism, pacifism, neutralism and fascism. (The peace movement in Germany is consistently portrayed in the *New York Times* as the heir to Nazi desires for *lebensraum*.)

In the postwar period, then, the United States became the major power in Europe without ever acknowledging the real reasons for its actions. Unable to see itself for what it was – a superpower engaged in the dangerous business of extending its power wherever possible – it chose to spin itself into an ideological web. Few American politicians were capable of asserting that the United States should provide economic aid to Europe because it was good for capital. Even fewer could summon up the courage to say that an American military presence was needed on the continent because superpowers throw their weight around by showing the fleet. Instead, it was said that the United States gave Europe money and troops to protect democracy and to insure that the European countries would retain their autonomy. It is no wonder, then, that a state of shock is generated in the United States when European governments, acting democratically and autonomously, decide that the American embrace is a bit suffocating.

In the late 1940s, when the Cold War began, members of the US foreign policy elite like Dean Acheson were quite capable of recognizing that there was a gap between what they told the American people about Europe and what American foreign policy actually was. (Acheson informed readers of his autobiography of the need of US officials to speak a language 'clearer than truth' – e.g., a lie.)[10] Policy-makers found it advantageous to make a distinction between appearance and reality, for their dealings with European governments were based on straightforward questions of interest, while their attempts to justify the American imperium at home were based on ideology. *The single greatest factor affecting the relationship between American domestic politics and events in Western Europe is the collapse of the American ability to divorce ideology from interest.* In the Reagan administration we witness a group of policy-makers who have confused what was said in public with what was done in private; they listened so long and so intently to the ideology that was being put forward for gullible public consumption that they forgot it was ideology and took it for the real world. Unlike during the period when the Cold War began, American policy-makers are today confronting Europe with the same rhetoric and imagery that they present to their own people. European leaders, who were willing to permit American politicians to use that kind of world view in Nebraska, now find *themselves* lectured to in the same language. Such was the ultimate legacy of an Atlantic alliance that proceeded on the assumption that a myth of a helpless Europe would be allowed to become a vital factor in the organization of American domestic politics.

III

The differences that have emerged between the United States and Europe in the 1980s are fundamentally differences over the meaning of World War II. For many Europeans, the war was a victory over fascism and a defeat for Germany. The former demanded a postwar order that, through social democracy and liberalism, would never again allow the extreme right to manipulate domestic fears of insecurity. The latter insisted on a geostrategic settlement that would in future not permit any one European nation state to become so powerful that it would threaten all the others. Each of these two premises led to an eventual accommodation with the Soviet Union, for shrill domestic anti-Communism was incompatible with reformist politics and detente would relax the need for the remilitarization of any of the European states. From this perspective, what is remarkable about Soviet–European detente in the 1980s is not that it is happening, but that it took so long. The exception was the American presence in Europe, while the rule, which has reasserted itself, was for Europe to deal with its own problems.

America interpreted World War II in an exactly opposite way, ideologically in opposition to Communism and geostrategically against the Soviet Union. For most Americans, Nazi Germany was a surrogate enemy, an accident of history, a temporary distraction from what one American ex-president has called 'the real war'. These assumptions give rise to an entirely different set of priorities for organizing the postwar world: a permanently divided Europe; conservative domestic governments; fever-pitch anti-Communism. For Americans, a US presence in Europe came to be taken for granted, while motions towards European neutralism were equated with Soviet-style Communism.

The United States and Europe are more seriously divided than at any point since World War II. There are substantial economic and strategic reasons for these divisions, ones that have been written about at great length. But there are also important political and symbolic differences, literally distinct world views through which Americans and Europeans interpret what goes on around them. The crisis in the Atlantic alliance is so serious, in my opinion, because its two sides literally think differently. It is only a matter of time before those differences in interpretation spill over into anger and mutual hostility, the inevitable result of a widening gap between the basic assumptions of each side.

Already one can see a significantly higher level of public disgust with Europe within the United States. The old Republican right, with its Asia-first inclination and distrust of old world pretensions, still makes itself heard periodically in Congress. In 1982, for example, under the leadership of conservatives like Ted Stevens (Alaska) and Jake Garn (Utah), the US Senate made a serious effort to cut military strength in Europe 23,000 troops below the Pentagon request. A bill introduced by a conservative Congressman from Michigan would demand a 50 per cent cut in American troops to any NATO country that did not increase its military spending by 3 per cent (in real terms) each year.[11] One of the most interesting aspects of this anti-European sentiment is that it has been linked to 'Mansfieldism' efforts by liberals in Congress to cut US troop commitments in Europe. From both ends of the political spectrum, opposition to Atlanticism is being expressed.

The political lines with respect to the Atlantic alliance are drawn differently in the 1980s than they were in the 1940s. Then it was the Right which opposed Atlanticism while the Left supported it. Now there are two kinds of Atlanticist persuasions within the establishment and two kinds of Atlanticist opposition at the fringes. American domestic opinion toward Europe is highly fractured and inconsistent, as to a lesser degree are elite attitudes, but, none the less, it is possible to detect various kinds of approach.

During the Carter administration it appeared as if a new Atlanticism was to be reborn under the leadership of the Trilateral Commission, formed by a private initiative of David Rockerfeller in 1973 to bring together elites in North America, Western Europe and Japan to build a consensus around international economic policy. Recognizing the limits of

American economic and political hegemony, the Trilateralists seemed to advocate more of a shared leadership among Western elites – Atlanticism with a more refined division of labour. This tendency still exists in strong measure, even though it remains in opposition during the Reagan years. It has organized itself around the following themes:

1 Endorsement of a no-first-use pledge or similar attempt to reassure European domestic opinion that the United States is not a war-mongering society.[12]
2 Substantial build-up of conventional arms, such as the programme proposed by the European Security Study.[13]
3 Alliance with a successor generation of European leadership pledged to a more assertive role within a revised NATO structure for the European countries, such as the kind of proposals made by Hedley Bull.[14]
4 Greater reliance on economic integration, including free trade commitments, than the more 'Prussian' combination of autarchy and military strength advocated by the Reagan administration.

In short, the first tendency that can be identified within the American elite is *revised Atlanticism*, an effort to remake the Alliance of the 1940s under the changed economic and political realities of the 1980s. Should the Reagan agenda prove increasingly unpopular – a real possibility if enormous deficits lead to inflation – there will be waiting in the wings a fairly complete liberal alternative, basing itself on lower military spending, fewer nuclear weapons, more balanced budgets and promises of something left over for domestic programmes. In the particular economic circumstance of declining American capitalism, this agenda makes a great deal of realistic sense, and it is quite possible that revised Atlanticism will be the dominant elite sentiment of the latter part of the decade. But even though its economic aspects are realistic, it faces a deep, and potentially devastating, political weakness. Unlike original Atlanticism, the revised version cannot exaggerate the Soviet threat, for to do so would undermine its claim to fiscal sanity. Yet without the Soviet threat, there is no reason for popular opinion to support any kind of Atlanticist programme at all, since Americans can be convinced to join their fate to Europe only on the basis of anti-Communism. This was exactly the fate of Trilateralism in the Carter years; it began as an effort to reorganize American priorities but found itself unable to win mass appeal in an atmosphere of militarist hysteria. Revised Atlanticism, in a word, is economically salient but politically weak.

Exactly the opposite situation holds for the second elite alternative to the Atlantic alliance – *brinksmanship revisited*. Unlike the isolationist right of the late 1940s, the Reagan administration does not seek to cut off ties to Europe and redirect American energy towards the Pacific. All things considered, it feels a strong need to affirm its links to Europe – but only on American terms. Brinksmanship revisited is based on the following principles:

1 Europe is still so militarily dependent on the United States that it has little choice but to follow the American lead, even if it does not agree.
2 America should therefore play 'hard-ball', acting unilaterally (as in Grenada and Libya) and afterwards seeking European support for its actions, pulling out all stops to get that support.
3 While such actions will inevitably disrupt the Atlantic alliance by alienating European domestic opinion and by placing Atlanticist politicians like Chancellor Kohl in untenable positions, there are real advantages: (a) the weakness of Europe is constantly reaffirmed; (b) American domestic opinion is satisfied; and (c) the effect is to enhance Soviet secrecy and unilateralism, thereby confirming all along what Washington claims to be Moscow's nature.
4 A strong foreign policy based on military strength will contribute to Europe's economic weakness by forcing European countries to increase their defence spending, thereby helping out American companies with respect to overseas competition.

Reaganism, in other words, is premised on two propositions: it insists on a geostrategic contest against the Russians which demands European cooperation, and it insists on an economic contest against Europe which, ironically, demands Soviet cooperation. (If the Russians refuse to play the role that American aggressiveness assigns to them, European governments cannot be induced to raise their military spending.) Brinksmanship, as its name implies, is entirely a short-run strategy, an effort to gain the maximum leverage out of the current imbalance in US–European relations. Precisely because of its short-term character, it is politically popular; one does not lose points in American electoral politics by lecturing European politicians on the evils of trade with the Russians, even while one sells the same Russians wheat. Yet brinksmanship revisited is economic dynamite, exacerbating tensions with America's 'natural' trading partners and maximizing long-term hostility as the balance of economic power shifts away from the United States.

The seriousness of the emerging split between the United States and Europe is indicated by the differences between one alternative that makes economic sense but has little political support and another with major political support that reinforces economic difficulties. For the foreseeable future, American policy towards Europe, in my opinion, is likely to swing back and forth from one pole to the other. I see no way that these two positions can merge into a compromise in the way that happened in the late 1940s because the conditions of US hegemony no longer exist.

One way of expressing this same point is to say that American politics with respect to Europe will increasingly depend on what happens in Europe. There, I would argue, the option of reconstituting the Atlantic alliance of old is, simply, no longer an option. There are only two possibilities: the emergence of a revised Atlanticism on the European side that seeks an accommodation with similarly inclined elites on the American side or a popular movement in Europe for withdrawal from the Atlantic alliance that seeks to make links with similar American sentiment to let Europe go its own way. If the latter kind of sentiment continues to grow in Europe, it will find that there are two kinds of sympathetic sentiment, from the Right and from the Left, that may find it impossible to agree on anything else.

A resurgence of extremely conservative American isolationism in the aftermath of European dealignment from the United States can easily be envisaged. As I argued above, American military and economic aid to Europe in the postwar period was not accompanied by an especially positive image of Europe in the eyes of mass popular opinion; Europeans, while praised as staunch allies, were also treated in a condescending manner, as if without American assistance they would be lost souls. Isolationism, in short, never disappeared, even when interventionism was at its highest. The heartland of American conservatism, the West and South-West, looks elsewhere than to Europe for both economic and cultural ties, especially to Asia and Mexico. Only the Atlantic Coast retains its European heritage, yet as demographic changes shift within the United States, America becomes more of a Pacific and less of an Atlantic power. (Indeed, the very term 'Atlantic alliance' no longer describes the American reality, even though Europeans are still Atlantic-bound.) Finally in this context, there has been a surge of immigration in the United States from places other than Europe, and political experts predict that in the immediate future, Asian and Hispanic voters – with few ties to the Democratic Party like immigrants of old – may be the key to future electoral balances of power.

The initial, and more popular, reaction to European dealignment might be described as *vindictive anti-Europeanism*. Given a long tradition of suspiciousness towards Europe in American political culture, conservative reactions against the Atlantic alliance are likely to appeal to large numbers of people in an economic atmosphere of protectionism and a political climate of self-justificatory chauvinism. To the degree that such latent anger towards Europe is translated into Congressional action, it will take the form, most likely, of symbolic gestures and periodic demagogic actions. There are reasons to doubt that it will translate into an effective programme based on a concrete and thoughtful strategy of responding to European dealignment. Such politics of frustration are nothing new in American history; cycles of xenophobia and anger at outsiders occur with enormous regularity. In most cases, they serve the function of promoting ambitious local politicians into the national spotlight and of mobilizing symbolic anger more than they serve the interests of any particular interest group or class. Given the ties that exist between multinational corporations on the one hand and the Pentagon on the other with European elites, there will, in fact, be extremely strong pressure mobilized *against* vindictive anti-Europeanism. One will witness the spectacle of military chiefs and corporate heads taking the 'progressive' position on ties to Europe, while populistic and democratic bursts of anger from the heartland will be portrayed as 'reactionary'.

It would be a mistake, in my opinion, for Europeans seeking greater autonomy and distance from Atlanticism to count very heavily on such isolationist sentiment in the United States – even if both groups might share for a time the common objective of dealignment. Right-wing isolationism is not only chauvinist, it is also quite militaristic and would be sure to combine any move towards a reduction of forces within Europe with demands for a Fortress America based on the latest in high-technology nuclear weapons. The most distinguishing feature of American isolationism is its inconsistency, swinging rapidly back and forth from extreme pacificism to belligerent militarism. Conservative isolationism in America, in the past, tended towards anti-war sentiment when the war was against Hitler and pro-war sentiment when the enemy was the Soviet Union. One might predict, based on this, that if Europe were to move simultaneously towards both dealignment and democratic socialism, isolationist anti-Europeanism within the United States would transform itself overnight into demands for immediate intervention to reshape Europe along more conservative lines.

This leaves, as a final tendency within the United States, movements sympathetic to European autonomy from an internationalist perspective. I refer to the politics of what is increasingly being called the *other Atlantic alliance*: the links between the European peace movement and the movement for a nuclear freeze in the United States. While there has been substantial public support for the nuclear freeze in America, this has not succeeded in establishing an institutional check on the Pentagon capable of blocking funding for even the most reprehensible of weapons, such as nerve gas. The allies of the European peace movement, in other words, are politically and bureaucratically weak compared to the allies of official Atlanticism. None the less, the best strategy towards European dealignment combined with long-term support for a more autonomous Europe within the United States still lies in trying to expand the sphere in which non-militaristic internationalism can express itself.

The strongest obstacle along this course will lie in the support for conventional military spending. This became, for example, a key point in the Democratic Party's platform of 1984. In order to appeal to traditional Cold War Democrats as well as to win support in military and business circles, Mondale strongly advocated more conventional arms to protect Europe against the Soviet menace. Since everyone in the United States aspires to the Aristotelian virtues of balance and moderation, a programme of no more nuclear weapons combined with many more conventional weapons strikes many Americans as reasonable and sensible. Many Americans who oppose nuclear weapons indicate their support for conventional weapons, thereby enabling them to feel that they have satisfied their fear of both nuclear war and the Soviet Union at the same time.

The European peace movement has shown a remarkable ability to intervene in the domestic US debate and to educate Americans to European realities. The freeze movement itself was clearly inspired by the success of massive European demonstrations against Pershing and cruise missiles. This educational campaign, however, has only just begun. The next step will be to demonstrate some not especially known truths about conventional weapons: that they are as destructive as low-yield nuclear weapons; that they run the risk of actually lowering, rather than raising, the threshold against the use of nuclear weapons; that the Soviet conventional advantage is subject to threat inflation; and that the best defence of humane and democratic values in Europe lies not with weapons at all but with political solidarity.

There is an American peace movement willing to hear, and to convey, messages like these, but, when compared to all the other groupings of attitudes towards Europe, it is small, under-financed and has little access to the mainstream media. None the less, it is the only realistic ally that movements for European dealignment have in the United States. A second generation of Atlanticists seeks to loosen NATO ties only to strengthen them; Reaganism and Pentagonism have nothing in common with European neutralism; and conservative isolationism is dangerous and unpredictable. The task of building up internationalist sentiment in the United States to accept a dealigned Europe is a long and difficult job, but few would have predicted either the success of the nuclear freeze or the impact of the European peace movement in the United States ten years ago. The main advantage possessed by both the American peace movement and efforts at European dealignment is that they speak for the future, while defenders of NATO as it presently stands live only in the 1940s. The world is changing radically; it is time for American domestic politics to change with it.

NOTES

1 Quoted in Daniel Yergin, *Shattered Peace* (Boston: Houghton Mifflin, 1978), p. 243.

2 Matthew A. Evangelista, 'Stalin's Postwar Army Reappraised', *International Security*, 7 (Winter 1982–3), pp. 110–38.

3 Fred L. Block, *The Origins of International Economic Disorder* (Berkeley and Los Angeles: University of California Press, 1977) and Mary Kaldor, *The Disintegrating West* (New York: Hill and Wang, 1978).

4 Block, *Origins of International Economic Disorder*, p. 107.

5 Alan Wolfe, *America's Impasse* (New York: Pantheon, 1981).

6 Richard Falk, 'Lifting the Curse of Bipartisanship', *World Policy Journal*, 1 (Fall 1983), pp. 127–57.

7 William E. Leuchtenberg, 'The New Deal and the Analogue of War', in John Braeman et al., (eds), *Change and Continuity in Twentieth Century America* (Columbus, Ohio: Ohio State University Press, 1964), pp. 105–25.

8 Walter Karp, *The Politics of War* (New York: Harper, 1979).

9 Theodore Draper, *Present History* (New York: Random House, 1983), pp. 51–114.

10 Dean Acheson, *Present at the Creation* (New York: Norton, 1979), p. 375.

11 For background on these developments, see Laurence Radway, 'Let Europe be Europe', *World Policy Journal*, 1 (Fall 1983), pp. 23–43.

12 McGeorge Bundy, George F. Kennan, Robert S. McNamara and Gerard Smith, 'Nuclear Weapons and the Atlantic Alliance', *Foreign Affairs* (Spring 1982), pp. 753–68.

13 Report of the European Security Study, *Strengthening Conventional Defense in Europe* (New York: St Martin's Press, 1983). I have discussed this report in much greater length in 'NATO at the Crossroads', *Boston Review* (October 1983), pp. 25–7.

14 Hedley Bull, 'European Self-Reliance and the Reform of NATO', *Foreign Affairs*, 61 (Spring 1983), pp. 874–92.

5

NATO and Domestic Politics: Britain, Italy and West Germany during Cold War and Detente

BEN LOWE

This chapter is divided into two parts. The main purpose of the first section is to explain how Western European governments became caught up in NATO, and the active role played by the European Right (the social democrat and christian democrat Right). The consequence was what might be called the 'Finlandization' of Western Europe – the development of one-sided politics in the old continent with dire consequences, in particular, for the forces of the radical non-Communist Left. In the second section I shall discuss more recent developments, emphasizing above all how Atlanticists sought to suppress the radical movements that erupted with the advent of detente, and how they strove to use detente to rationalize the system that had developed during the period of Cold War. The term 'Atlanticist' will be explained later, but broadly it is used to describe the pro-NATO elements within the establishment.

The chapter's emphasis is on the role of the European establishments in NATO – in both its origins and its various phases of development. In no sense is this meant to suggest that the European role in the formation and development of the Atlantic alliance was primary. Indeed, I would be quite emphatic that NATO's formation was only possible because it served the interests of powerful factions within the US establishment and that the United States has been the dominant power in the alliance throughout its existence. However, the purpose of this chapter is to discuss the domestic effect of NATO membership and Cold War politics, and here the role of European establishments, albeit often in alliance with Washington, is extremely important. The analysis implies that any dealignment strategy necessarily involves a change in the constellation of domestic political forces through a process of democratization. By the same token, any challenge to the European establishments, on a whole range of issues not necessarily connected to the nuclear question, can only be effective in the situation where there is greater international space for manoeuvre.

By focusing above all on West Germany, Britain and Italy, I intend to highlight three different reasons for America's economic-political commitment to Europe in countries that are closely integrated into NATO, politically as well as militarily. But while illuminating the *multiple causes* of American hegemony in Western Europe, these countries' experiences reveal remarkably similar effects in terms of domestic politics. Such effects are examined for each country in turn. Similar conclusions could probably be drawn about other countries, although the experience of countries more marginal to the alliance may be somewhat different.

NATO'S ORIGINS, COLD WAR AND DOMESTIC POLITICS

West Germany

Germany lies at the centre of Europe. In 1945, it was held responsible for two wars that had all but destroyed Europe, it had twice invaded Russia and it had twice occupied France. Whether the country was now rebuilt or dismantled would have a profound and far-reaching effect on other European countries. Plainly, a policy for Germany in the late 1940s was a policy for Europe.

American policy-makers were divided over Germany throughout the 1940s. By 1945 it was evident that the main division was between the anti-Communists, who wanted Germany to act as an ally against Communism (which meant a policy favouring German industrialization), and the traders, who believed that America's superior economic and trading strength would prevail if stability could be achieved in Europe, and who saw Germany as the main threat to stability should it revive (which meant a policy of deindustrialization).

Before 1945, with the traders dominant, the policy was the same as Moscow's – deindustrialization. By 1945, there was a stalemate, which meant that the dismantling of industry was at best half-hearted in the years that followed. By 1947, the anti-Communists were being joined by economic strategists who had by now concluded that Europe's economic recovery required Western European economic coordination combined with a hefty dose of US aid. Strong commercial interests also favoured the industrialization of western Germany, as they envisaged a return to capacious prewar markets and profits, and saw these as necessary to stave off recession at home.

Already, in 1946, the British and American zones in western Germany had been combined. In 1947, following the declaration of Marshall's aid programme, the two countries moved closer towards the creation of a political system in western Germany and encouraged the area's economic recovery.

The Soviet Union now went on the offensive – with threats to West Berlin – in order to keep open the possibility of Germany's remaining united and neutral. But there was anxiety, too, in France, both on the Right and the Left. Without a guarantee against the threat a revived West German state might pose to France, Paris would stay out of the Western anti-Communist camp. The Brussels Treaty of March 1948 with Britain, Holland, Belgium and Luxembourg provided something of a guarantee against Germany. But it was only the North Atlantic Treaty that gave France the full guarantee its leaders sought.

For American policy-makers, the problems bedevilling Europe – including economic crisis, political disarray, nationalist and colonial rivalry – were problems for the United States too, given the economic need to expand overseas. Moreover, it was argued in Washington that Europe's problems could only be solved satisfactorily if western Europe as a whole was involved. So France had at all costs to become part of the Western camp, pooling its potential economic strength, its technological expertise and the resources of its colonies.

The French leaders were preoccupied with both Germany's revival as a military power, and the increasingly aggressive nature of the Soviet Union – itself a direct response to the prospect of German revival. Therefore, the establishment of a West German state much enhanced the possibility of a cohesive Western bloc, but only because the United States was strong enough to contain West Germany should aggressive nationalism once again rear its head.

Anglo–US policy for Germany resulted in the division of Europe.[1] There had often been spheres of influence in Europe in the past, with great powers exerting influence over smaller powers. This was no less the case, albeit with greater ideological input, after Yalta and Potsdam. What changed following the various events of 1947 that effectively launched the Cold War (see below on Truman and Marshall) was that spheres of influence now became closed hemispheres, with no possibility of direct influence by outside powers. Moreover, these hemispheres became mutually dependent and mutually exclusive, with the part-fabricated 'enemy without' used frequently as a blunt-edged weapon against dissident elements within.[2] Nowhere was the pain of the process more keenly felt than in Czechoslovakia. Until early 1948, Czechoslovakia's elections were as free as any in the West, and the Communists gained the highest percentage of the vote. With the onset of Cold War, and Stalin's evident willingness to play the game by rules set by Western strategists, Czechoslovakia was to be a 'Soviet bloc' country. Even US State Department planners like George Kennan said as much in policy papers.[3] So Czech democracy was sacrificed.

One consequence of these developments was the West German state, a child of Cold War, a living symbol of Cold War, and a source of continuing tension throughout the Cold War. The beneficiaries inside the new state were the industrialists, the political Right and (a little later) the military. Nazis, too, benefited. Even before the new state was born, former Nazis were reinstated in high positions in the judiciary, diplomatic service, the civil service, the education system, the police and industry. Under Reinhard Gehlen, Hitler's former intelligence chief on the eastern front, there were also Nazis engaged in preparatory work on the new German army, the Bundeswehr, from 1948.[4] Moreover, although the Christian Democrats (CDU) appeared to be very much in control of the political machinery of the new state, ex-Nazis played a pivotal role there, too.[5] One could almost talk about an informal alliance coming into being between the CDU and ex-Nazis throughout the state machinery, with anti-Communism as the binding element.

Before the Cold War developed in Germany, the political scene was extremely lively. As Nazism's grip was broken, there was a broad support for radical social programmes including widespread socialization, communal ownership and the extension of civil liberties. Even the Christian Democrats, in their early years, expressed broad support for such policies – demanding in their 1947 Ahlen Programme, for example, the abolition of the capitalist system and the establishment of a 'new social and economic order'.[6] The strongest party was the Social Democrat Party (SPD) and the Communist Party (KDP) had a sizeable vote in some areas. A few months before the first West German elections, few would have considered a Christian Democrat victory conceivable.

The right-wing Christian Democrats were able to outflank not only their own left wing but also the other parties through appealing to a trans-class anti-Communism, pro-clericalism and pro-Americanism. People were persuaded that the first would ensure that external or internal threats to the social order would be repulsed, the second would ensure the morality of the new state, while the third – because of the Marshall Plan – would ensure prosperity. The party had no real commitment to such popular concerns as civil liberties, German reunification or social programmes (although some welfare concessions were certainly made).

The Cold War context allowed this Christian Democrat formula to become ever more successful. Radical socialists, for their part, found their room for manoeuvre extremely limited. The polarization of the international political scene into stylized caricatures of capitalism and Communism left little room for democratic anti-capitalists. Vainly, the SPD tried to sell itself as an anti-Communist party committed to reunification, civil liberties, social welfare, class politics and anti-militarism. But its support rarely rose much above a third of the electorate – largely, it would appear, because in the Cold War atmosphere the SPD's anti-Americanism allowed opponents to append a 'pro-Communist' badge to the party's lapel in the popular mind.

In the early 1950s the emphasis in West Germany was less on 'freedom and democracy' than on the *defence* of these via the defence of the constitutional order. Because of the stress on defending constitutional provisions, it was possible to justify the erosion of civil liberties in the 'interests of the country as a whole'. The principle threat in the minds of West German officialdom was the Communist Party, and from 1951–52 every effort was made to legitimize its prohibition. Although British intelligence personnel tasked with discrediting the KPD found nothing they could readily use – short of fabrication[7] – the Party was eventually banned, along with various 'front' organizations. The SPD, for its part, was subject to general surveillance and harrassment, while changes in the criminal as well as civil law from 1951 allowed a witchhunt to proceed against thousands of sundry political activists, particularly within the civil and public service, with the full authority of the 'constitutional state' behind the hunters. As one liberal lawyer later wrote, political criminal law went 'beyond its classical function of defence against threats to the internal and external security of the state to become an instrument of inquisition into all heretics and dissidents'.[8]

A key element in the Christian Democrats' success through the 1950s was the informal but deep relationship between Adenauer and leading anti-Communists in the US administration. The German Chancellor always knew that he could advocate the most daring policies – German rearmament, membership of NATO, partial sovereignty – confident in the knowledge that he would have the support of leading officials in the White House, State Department and Pentagon and, further, that he could use this support to secure popular approval for such policies in both the United States and West Germany.

The American connection, combined with anti-Communism and clericalism, held together the disparate elements of the West German state behind what was, in effect, a facade of 'liberal democracy'. The first seventeen years of the West German state were marked by effective one-party rule (the small and right-wing Free Democrats sometimes acting as coalition partner); by a strict authoritarianism; by restrictions on the right to work (Berufsverbote in the public service for a number of years); by the prohibition and widespread detention of Communists; by a political atmosphere that associated all radical and anti-capitalist elements with the Kremlin; by a rigid and backward-looking education system; and by a political culture that allowed ex-Nazis – including generals from World War II, SS officers, Gestapo and high-ranking politicians – to return to prominent positions in society.

It was only in the mid-1960s, as we shall see, that this was to begin to change. In the meantime, the SPD had abandoned its anti-capitalist programme at the Bad Godenberg conference in 1959, and had consented to support NATO and implicitly to accept for the time being the division of Germany. It was now a party firmly within the 'Atlanticist consensus' – even if its policies still differed in certain important respects from those of the Christian Democrats and others.

With the shift in the SPD, just ten years after the formation of the new West German state, there was no longer any party political representation for views which, in the period immediately preceding the state's formation, had enjoyed majority support within the West German population. The fact that the sea-change in German opinion had begun before West Germany's entry into NATO is irrelevant to the general argument here. The process that led to NATO's creation and to the creation of the West German state – with all the implications this had for West German politics – was one and the same. It resulted from the new American role in Europe, from Anglo–US policies for Europe and their interaction with Soviet and French policies, from the export of America's domestic conflict over foreign policy goals to European soil and from the activities of the West German Right.

Britain

Britain was the most active European participant in the formation of NATO. Aware of Britain's inevitable imperial decline, Conservative and Labour leaders alike sought to maintain Britain's role as a great power through three forms of alliance – one with the United States, another with Europe, the other with the Commonwealth (Empire). Britain's strong position in each alliance would be guaranteed by the benefits derived from the other two. In particular, by sharing parts of the Empire with America, more of it could be retained in 'Anglo-Saxon' hands; and by tempting US troops into Europe as part of a joint commitment to the survival of both European capitalism and Europe's imperial territory, Britain could sustain a greater military presence elsewhere to defend the Empire. One extra component, and the most appropriate symbol, perhaps, of a dying empire seeking to keep up the appearance of 'greatness', was the decision in 1947 to develop nuclear weapons.

The plans of American officials – particularly in the State Department – overlapped with these British interests in a number of respects. American-based international capital (banking/industry) was generally eager to move into Europe's empires, and wanted more open access to Europe's consumer markets. By this time, the American commitment to anti-colonialism was double-edged, despite the official rhetoric. Although in the long term the perspective was to replace political–military structures of colonial rule with more indirect means of domination (multinationals and international financial institutions), the administration was willing to prop up colonial rule in many areas (Africa, Indochina, parts of the Middle East) for as long as there were no strong reasons to support independence.[9]

This coincidence of view made Anglo–US collaboration possible in the postwar period. The relative strength of Britain in Western Europe – the biggest army by far, the global financial role of the City of London, the size of the Empire – combined with long-established cultural ties between the two establishments was sufficient to create the 'special relationship'. The first test came in 1946, when Britain requested a huge loan to stave off economic collapse. Thanks to Keynes's stress on Britain's global responsibilities and Churchill's anti-Communist rhetoric at Fulton, the loan was granted. Still more significant was Britain's request for US assistance in suppressing radical forces in Greece and propping up the government in Turkey in early 1947. By taking over responsibility for this area (albeit only through Truman's thunderburst of anti-Communist bluster, designed to sway Congress), the United States gained a foothold in the eastern Mediterranean – an area vital to general control over the oil-rich Middle East.[10]

In the initial discussions over the Atlantic alliance just under a year later, Britain's Foreign Secretary, Bevin, principally conceived of an alliance of Europe's main colonial powers – those in the Brussels Pact – being backed up in some way by the United States and being linked through other mechanisms to the other European countries.[11] The idea was to bring Western countries together in a *political* union designed to combat the Communist 'enemy within'. The views of Atlanticists like Marshall and Hickerson in Washington was not dramatically different, but they saw the Rio Treaty of mid-1947 as the model for a new transatlantic alliance. This treaty contained a provision under which US forces could intervene in Latin American countries without being subject to a Soviet veto in the United Nations. It was felt that the North Atlantic Treaty ought to contain such a provision; this would facilitate the passage of the treaty in Congress, and also establish America's right to intervene in Western Europe in emergencies (see also below, on Italy).[12] Of course, unlike the Rio Treaty, the United States was not the only major power involved in the Atlantic alliance: policy-makers in Washington always expected that the other major powers would provide in large part for their own defence. Whether or not they would be *left* to fend for themselves in a war was an issue in the first discussions over NATO and has been a source of tension within the alliance ever since.

The United States was not prepared to commit itself formally to Europe's defence without some major concessions on the part of the European governments, including the opening up of domestic markets and the erosion of colonial privileges. Thus the British government, having pushed for the alliance for strong reasons of its own, found that it was being caught up in more than it had bargained for. It was forced to make concessions to the United States on 'imperial preference' and the role of sterling. And it had to accept politically the anti-Communist fireball raging across the Atlantic as the US establishment fought out its foreign policy battles.[13] Nevertheless, for reasons of *imperial defence*, the British establishment favoured the special relationship with the United States, even if it meant that Britain was the subordinate partner.

The left wing of the Labour Party held sway over much of domestic policy in the late 1940s, but the party's right wing was able to gain control of foreign policy, especially once the Cold War developed in 1946–8. The polarization of the world into two camps, which was keenly supported by the Labour right and the more fanatic Conservatives, made it impossible for the left wing to sustain an independent foreign policy. Despite the attempts by radicals to find a middle ground between pro-Americanism and pro-Sovietism, the political space for their ideas shrank as the Cold War developed – and increasingly this affected domestic policy as much as foreign policy. It was not so much that the defeat of the Left was inevitable at this time. It was more that the Right obtained considerable advantage from the polarization of politics in the northern world.

Internationally, the arms build-up took off in a big way from 1950 – allegedly because of war in Korea. Now that the United Nations was evidently not going to be an effective world policeman, the United States decided that it would need to commit vast funds itself to the protection of its global investments.[14]

Far from the Atlantic alliance relieving Britain's heavy burdens, the new boom aggravated them. Labour had to choose now between arms spending and the welfare state. The National Health Service was the loser, with the abandonment of Labour's commitment to a 'free service', and several left wingers resigned from the government. Soon afterwards, as Shonfield shows in his detailed history of Western capitalism,[15] the Conservatives came to power with a quasi-monetarist programme favouring warfare over welfare, and reinforcing the domination of financial capital over the economy. In spite of a shift to Keynesianism in the mid-1950s, high military spending persisted, as did the autonomous role of financial capital (which preferred on the whole to invest elsewhere). Britain was left with one of the lowest investment levels in the Western world through the 1950s and 1960s, and the economy declined steadily in relation to its rivals. The Labour Left, for its part, was effectively neutralized until the early 1970s, despite a brief flourish a decade earlier.

For the first 20 years of NATO's existence (except at the very beginning) there was an unquestioning allegiance on the part of the three major parties to Britain's membership of NATO and its special relationship with the United States. This remained the case despite America's humiliation of the British government over Suez (the White House opposed the invasion, having helped to provoke it), over Skybolt missiles (a British 'independent deterrent' which the United States decided not to produce at the last minute, thus forcing Britain to buy a missile from another production line) and on numerous other occasions. But this was deemed acceptable because the relationship with the United States was directly related to the survival of a certain kind of Britain.

Britain had the military clout and the financial capital of a major power, but increasingly it had the economy of a secondary power. As the military and the financiers were given their head (as we have seen again with Thatcherism), so the economy declined still further, starved like never before of the necessary kinds of investment. The tie with the United States has served above all to keep in power those elements of the establishment most committed to this topsy-turvy set-up.

Nevertheless, it was also the case that Britain did not experience the same level of domestic political repression during periods of Cold War as in West Germany, Italy or even the United States. In some ways, all the main elements of repression were present in Britain: from early 1948 there was political vetting of permanent civil servants, which led to 135 people losing their jobs or being removed to 'safe' areas over a seven-year period. The vetting was much extended, under US pressure, from 1952. The 'political police', notably the Special Branch, were certainly active, with officers infiltrating trade unions and carrying out extensive surveillance of Communists and radical trade unionists. The Labour government actively encouraged an anti-Communist offensive in the trade unions, which resulted in the removal of several officials and the prohibition of Communist officials in several unions. Peace groups were banned in the Labour Party on the grounds that they were 'Soviet Fronts'; and there was plenty more.[16]

Despite these efforts, the effects were negligible compared to elsewhere, and the question is 'Why?'. It was partly because Labour politicians themselves were behind the anti-Communist offensive. Moreover, the Communist Party was an insignificant force in the labour and trade union movement in relation to the Labour Party (it was no accident that the period of the Communist Party's offensive in the trade unions coincided with a general decline in trade union militancy, while their earlier period of quiescence coincided with widespread strike activity).

The Tories, for their part, were not interested in launching a McCarthy-style campaign against Labour establishment figures. They never recovered fully from the size of the Labour Party's victory in 1945, which indicated mass support for an end to such hallmarks of earlier Tory administrations as mass unemployment and widespread poverty. And they no doubt never forgot that Churchill's attempt to identify Labour Party socialism with Nazism in 1945 backfired on the Tories in no uncertain terms.

It was not something specific to Britain or 'the British' that held off more serious levels of Cold War repression, then, but rather more specific factors related to the domestic circumstances at the time. All told, Cold War at the macro level did the trick, and the Labour right wing helped it on its way. No more was needed. No more was sought.

Italy

For much of the 1945–7 period, Socialists (openly Marxist) and Communists held power in Italy, along with the weaker Christian Democrats. By late 1946, the US State Department was resolved to undermine the strength of the left-wing forces by any means necessary. In particular, there would be a 'judicious mixture' of psychological operations (subversion) and moral encouragement of pro-American elements combined with heavy economic aid that was 'so damned pro-Italian that even the dumbest wop would sense the draft'.[17] The United States was concerned that a left-wing victory in Italy could remove Europe's fourth largest economy from the US sphere and, worse still, could prove infectious in France and elsewhere. Moreover, should pro-Communist elements come to dominate Italy, the Soviet Union would be able to prevent the United States from gaining general control, along with Britain, of the Mediterranean.

In May 1947, shortly before the announcement of the Marshall Plan, General Marshall made it clear to Italy's Premier, de Gasperi, through a diplomatic note,[18] that Italy could receive large doses of aid if the Communists and Socialists were removed from power. Within days de Gasperi dissolved the government, and he was only to reconstitute it when he had found sufficient support on the far Right to create a centre-Right government. The Communists (PCI) have never entered power since.

By the time of the Pentagon discussions in March 1948, when the American delegation stressed the need for Italy to be in NATO if the Communists were to be defeated,[19] there was a concerted operation under way in Italy. The newly created CIA was providing funds to various bodies, there was media propaganda, aid was pumped in at the times best suited to propaganda purposes, members of the Vatican were financed to loosen their tongues for pro-American speeches, etc.[20] Despite all polls and predictions to the contrary, the Christian Democrats won the elections, which took place in April. (Years later, there was another CIA-run operation for the 1958 elections, when the Communists again seemed possible victors.)

The American interest in opposing any radical threat to the status quo was particularly strong in Italy, France, Greece, Belgium and Iceland. These were all countries that were considered strategically and economically important and where Communist and other forces were in a position to take power through the electoral process. It was President Truman, in his speech proclaiming the Truman Doctrine in March 1947, who first publicly declared America's determination to defeat these political forces in Western Europe, although he confined his request for military aid, at this juncture, to Greece and Turkey. With the Marshall Plan, announced three months later, US strategists sought to undermine Communism by removing its material basis. It was believed that the strength of Communist and Socialist parties derived from the severity of Western Europe's economic crisis, and that the programme of aid and other economic mechanisms designed to relieve that crisis could sap the strength of the radical forces.

NATO proved an extra guarantee against a Communist (or, in Italy, also Socialist) electoral victory for the following reasons:

1 Article 4 of the North Atlantic Treaty allowed for intervention when the 'political independence' or 'security' of any member is threatened. The original draft of this, from March 1948, talked in terms of 'indirect aggression', defined as an internal *coup d'état* or 'internal change favourable to an aggressor', e.g. a Communist/Socialist electoral victory. Indeed, as of 9 March 1948 – i.e. even before NATO – the United States had contingency plans for a military mobilization and possible intervention in the event of a Communist or Socialist electoral

victory. And from the founding of NATO up until at least 1961 it was the position of the State Department and the CIA that the US should undertake a full intervention. Only in 1961, under Kennedy, did officials in Washington press for the Socialists to be allowed to come to power – this after the Socialist Party had decided to accept Italian membership of NATO. But the PCI was still seen as a real threat.[21]

2 NATO provided a military–political adjunct to the Marshall Plan. American investors and financiers needed a long-term guarantee of political stability, otherwise they would fail to provide the high levels of investment required for economic stability. The North Atlantic Treaty provided the guarantee. The integration of the Italian armed forces into the NATO military structure was also seen as a direct political bulwark against the PCI. The kind of domestic military coup that later occurred in Greece and Turkey was always an implicit possibility in postwar Italy.

The Italian Right, along with its friends in the Vatican, actively sought US political intervention, especially for the 1948 elections. It also played an active role in stimulating anti-Communist sentiment, so it cannot be said that Cold War politics came only from the outside. The alliance with the United States, and the rise of Cold War tension with predictable consequences for the polarization of Italian politics, had the following effects:

1 The strengthening of the Christian Democratic Right against the Left in its own party as well as against other left-wing forces.
2 The survival of the Communist Party, by virtue of its widespread support within the Italian working class and its consequent ability to benefit from the polarization of international politics along capitalist–Communist lines.
3 The sowing of divisions within a declining Socialist Party so that the Socialists became increasingly marginalized as the political situation polarized. As elsewhere, it was the more independent-minded, radical Socialists who were the main losers in Cold War.

NATO and the Cold War enabled the Christian Democrats to maintain a grip on power for over twenty years – although their hostility to radical/progressive change and their association with countless political scandals allowed the PCI to gain control of an increasing number of city administrations. By 1976 there were two parties in power, one at the national level, one at the local level. Moreover, the PCI was again in the position where it might win national elections.

It was this situation that prompted the United States, along with certain NATO allies, to intervene politically to prevent the PCI from taking power. US Secretary of State Kissinger led the offensive, arguing that 'it is inconceivable that the United States could maintain ground forces in Europe if there is a major communist participation in western governments', and asserting that it was not possible to have a 'Titoist Italy' (i.e. modelled on Yugoslavia) in NATO without far-reaching changes in alliance structures.[22] West German Chancellor Schmidt, for his part, admitted to reporters that the United States, West Germany and Britain had agreed privately at a meeting in Puerto Rico that no future loans would be granted to an Italian government containing Communists at cabinet level. In addition, there were threats of investments being withdrawn, of economic chaos, of international isolation, of detente breaking down and of tensions in the EEC. Finally, it was made clear that there could be no Italian participation in NATO's Nuclear Planning Group with Communists in government. All this was something of an over-reaction, it might be said, given that the PCI now accepted NATO and had long since declared its effective independence from the Soviet Union. However, the PCI failed to win the election.

DETENTE AND DEMOCRACY

During the 1950s, right-wing conservatism held sway throughout Western Europe – a remarkable mirror image, albeit in a more flexible system, of the rigid Stalinism imposed on the eastern bloc. Observing their electoral support declining, and losing confidence in their ability to return to power, socialist and social democratic parties in countries like Britain, West Germany and Italy took a right turn. For party ideologues, the shift was a necessary response to rising working class incomes and apparent confirmation of capitalism's ability as a system to 'deliver the goods'. The shift appears to have been successful in electoral terms – with all three parties entering government by the early 1970s. Nevertheless, the thawing of the Cold War and the subsequent shake-up of the European political scene by new radical movements showed the extent to which a substantial constituency for a more radical politics had survived the era of mass consumerism. Given the significance of these changes during the 1960s, it is worth briefly examining their roots.

The success of Western capitalism in the 1950s and 1960s was contingent on a number of factors, among which was the opening of new markets to the rapidly expanding and increasingly internationalized companies of the United States, Britain etc. They were able to grow initially because the mass of workers became consumers for a broad range of products developed earlier in the century.[23]

The Cold War from 1947 to 1964–5 provided the context in which the new markets in Western Europe could be exploited to the full, and in which rival European nationalisms could be quelled in the face of what was perceived to be the greater *external* threat. It further created an environment in which Western access to the more important raw materials in the Third World could be maintained either through well-armed 'puppet' rulers, through economic pressure or through direct military intervention.

But the Cold War could not continue indefinitely. In the United States there was the painful realization during the Cuban missile crisis that overwhelming military/nuclear superiority did not necessarily mean a nuclear war could be fought against the Soviet Union.[24] This prompted moves towards a Test Ban Treaty and other East–West talks. In West Germany the erection of the Berlin Wall in 1961 acted as a spur to certain social democrats to push for recognition of the physical–geographical nature of the East–West divide. To people like the Mayor of Berlin, Willi Brandt, it seemed that, if the presence of the 'external threat' could be neutralized through a negotiated deal between East and West Germany, the political consequences in West Germany, in particular the opening up of the German polity to more critical and radical forces, could only benefit the SPD.

De Gaulle was a factor, too. The General's experience of Anglo–US domination of NATO, which kept France excluded from a number of 'inner secrets' and policy decisions, helped him see through the delusion of Atlanticism (above all the image of the 'Soviet threat') earlier than most. The gradual loosening of the French relationship with America under de Gaulle's leadership, in particular from 1962, was an inspiration to many.

In West Germany the SPD gained ground steadily in the mid-1960s, and by 1966 it was able to gain a modicum of power when it entered the Grand Coalition government with the Christian Democrats. The more power it gained, moreover, the more it advanced towards recognizing East Germany and establishing cultural and trading links. But all the time detente was about *stabilizing* the East–West system, not undermining it. This was to prove important later on.

The beginnings of detente in the mid-1960s coincided with an awakening of a new kind of political movement. Largely student-based, predominantly middle-class, motivated in large part by the Vietnam War, this movement represented the first sign of open hostility to the more negative ideological and cultural effects of the Cold War system. The ossification of the political system was clearly a major target, but so too were the education system, the aridity of cultural life, the new consumer society, and the vast corporations that now affected so many aspects of life in Western society. Later, racial and sexual discrimination were to become central concerns, and there was to be a growing awareness of the importance of class politics. But the important point, for our purposes, is that this movement was a *second offspring of detente*, accompanying the rebirth of a much sanitized social democracy, and in many ways filling the gap left by the shift that had occurred in social democracy.

It was not until the mid-1970s that these developments came to a head. Social democracy was now on the ascendant in many European countries. At the same time, the radical movements of the 1960s had grown in maturity, complexity and confidence. They in no way posed an electoral threat to the social democrats, but they were a constant thorn in their side and a constant reminder of their more radical past.

It was during this period that Pax Americana was suffering its worst crisis since NATO was founded. The main dimensions of the crisis were as follows: the United States had suffered a heavy military defeat in Indochina, and there was now strong domestic opposition to any further interventions in the event of a challenge to the United States' imperial rule; the decline of the dollar brought about, in 1971, the end of the gold–dollar convertibility that had contributed so much to postwar economic stability, while it was also a clear indication of the relative decline in US economic strength; OPEC had recently challenged the right of the West to obtain its oil on the cheap, and had helped turn a creeping recession into the worst economic crisis in decades; and the end of military rule in strategically important countries in southern Europe had contributed to a frailty and discord in the Western alliance, as had rarely been seen hitherto. In the context of the crisis, the new radical movements were viewed as a source of unwanted pressure and instability.

In Britain the dominance achieved by right-wing social democrats within the Labour Party in 1947–8 had been eroded by changes in the labour movement and the emergence of a new alternative movement within and outside the party. For the German SPD, the problem was different, in that the labour movement in Germany had not been infected by a new radicalism, as in Britain. But the problem was in some ways more acute, in that the alternative movement that had emerged from the earlier student movement was more broad-based, more militant and more damaging to the legitimacy of SPD rule. Likewise in Italy, where the social democrats, Christian Democrats and even many leading Communists were united in seeing the extra-parliamentary opposition as a threat to the very fabric of society.

Within the Trilateral Commission, which had been established to bring together elites of the advanced capitalist world in 1973, European social democrats, as well as many conservatives with a similar perspective, found allies within the US establishment. There was no conspiracy here, rather a coming together of like-minded politicians, business people and others who shared similar concerns about the state of the world and about the crisis facing parliamentary democracy.

In 1975 various members of the Commission produced a report on the 'crisis of democracy' for discussion at Commission meetings. The section by one author, Samuel P. Huntington – an academic and an official in the governments of Nixon and Ford – is particularly interesting in that it can be seen as one of the first attempts to define the *politics of Atlanticism* in face of the first major challenge confronting it. Huntington comes to the conclusion that 'Some of the problems of governance in the United States today stem from an *excess of democracy*. . . . The effective operation of a democratic political system usually requires some measure of apathy and non-involvement.' He talks about the time when American democracy was unproblematic, the time when 'it was governed by the President acting with the support and co-operation of key individuals and groups in the Executive Office, the Federal bureaucracy, Congress and the more important businesses, banks, law firms, foundations, and media, which constitute the private establishment'.[25]

This system, which remained stable throughout the period of Cold War, came under threat because of what Huntington defines as a 'democratic surge'; this manifested itself in 'citizen participation in the form of marches, demonstrations, protest movements and "cause" organizations . . . markedly higher levels of self-consciousness on the part of blacks, Indians, chicanos, white ethnic groups, students and women . . . previously passive or unorganized groups in the population now embarked on concerted efforts to establish their claims to opportunities, positions, rewards and privileges which they had not considered themselves entitled to before.'

For Huntington, this 'democratic surge' for rights previously denied is a 'distemper' or disease. He argues that a government must have the right to govern, the manager the right to manage. Above all, foreign policy and defence must remain in the right hands, protected as far as possible from the 'adversary' media and the 'critical' intelligentsia. Otherwise, a government may lose its ability to 'impose on its people the sacrifices necessary to deal with foreign policy and defense'.[26]

The Trilateral Report, though read widely among government and business leaders in Japan and the West, did not necessarily shape a new consensus – not least because establishment liberals found its prognosis hard to stomach. Nevertheless, it helped rationalize an Atlanticist reaction to the 'backside' of detente – the side that was not part of the grand plan of the detente strategists, and which threatened to undermine the stabilization process in northern Europe.

From 1974 to 1978 all the leading Western European countries introduced legislation specifically aimed at curtailing or containing extra-parliamentary political activity. The Reale Law introduced in Italy in 1975, purportedly against terrorism, eroded basic civil liberties in such a way as to limit the scope for street-based political activity and radical political theorizing ('developing a rationale for the overthrow of the state').

West Germany, which had already banned radicals from public service with the 1972 Berufsverbote, toughened this ban in 1975 to include all those 'closely associated' with radicals. It created new elite police squads, toughened judicial powers and gave the police new powers for personal and household searches. Police powers were extended to a remarkable degree throughout Western Europe, especially from 1974–75. Riot squads became a regular sight on TV screens throughout Europe, often with no riotous affray to justify their intervention. The arrest of people on demonstrations or other forms of protest, if only to remove them from the scene or to intimidate others, became more frequent. Finally, political censorship became more common, following enabling legislation, in West Germany and Italy, and many newspapers and books were banned.

In most cases the new laws and police powers were introduced immediately after a terrorist offence. But the laws and powers had been prepared well in advance of the offence in question, and their main target was less the offending terrorists than the movements of utopian revolutionaries, black or ethnic minority activists, feminists and other radicals who formed part of Huntington's 'democratic surge'.[27]

In West Germany the radical movement changed shape in the wake of the offensive and regrouped largely in and around the Greens and the left wing of the SPD. In Italy the movement suffered more than elsewhere in terms of demobilization, but the peace movement has emerged as a vehicle through which a number of lamed or disappeared civil liberties can be given new life. In Britain the government had less to contend with and the measures appeared to be more modest.[28] Nevertheless, a Prevention of Terrorism Act was introduced in 1974, setting the precedent for the subtle but steady erosion of long-established civil liberties. And the state has armed the police with new powers and riot weapons in preparation for an offensive against the main thorn in the side of the ruling establishment – trade union power. After a series of skirmishes, this moved into top gear during the miners' strike of 1984.

The key points that emerge from the above are as follows:

(1) In the late 1940s, European christian democrats aligned with the US government to launch an offensive against their domestic opponents, thereby creating the Atlanticist consensus. In the mid-1970s it was largely European social democrats, who, having now adopted Atlanticism as an article of faith, found their American allies useful in articulating a response to the first real challenge to the Atlanticist consensus. (Only in Britain were the main protagonists on the Atlanticist side social democrats on both occasions.) In each case, it was the commitment to Atlanticism – in its political, ideological and cultural dimensions – that determined the response, not the party affiliations.

(2) There was a remarkable multi-party consensus behind Atlanticism in the Europe of the 1960s and early 1970s, at the same time as party and intra-party differences. In Britain, there were varying attitudes both within and between the Tory and Labour Parties over whether to shift from a 'special relationship' with the United States to a close relationship with Europe, and equally there were different approaches to radical trade unionisms and to the social movements (feminism, anti-racism, etc.). Overall, though, the approach of the two parties was unmistakably Atlanticist. On defence, energy, foreign and nuclear (civil and military) matters, policies were consistently developed by a tiny political elite in the interests of a scarcely larger political–military–industrial elite (the latter with an American accent often creeping in). On the cultural–ideological front, Labour was perhaps more receptive to change, but persisted with an explicitly racist policy on immigration and did little to improve the position of ethnic minorities, women or other people whose rights had so long been denied.

The picture was similar in West Germany, where the social democrats were responsible for most of the repressive measures of the 1970s. In Italy, the main opposition party, the PCI, never gained power at a national level. At a local level it was certainly more committed to welfare policies than its main rivals, and its close relationship with the majority of Italian trade unionists clearly made for a different approach to working class political activity. However, the new policy of 'historical compromise' from the mid-1970s represented an accommodation to some key aspects of Atlanticism in foreign and military policies. The PCI would henceforth accept Italian membership of NATO, and was to agree in the early 1980s not to oppose the deployment of cruise missiles in Sicily.[29]

(3) The question of detente, democracy and civil liberties is not only pertinent to Eastern Europe, as many claim. Detente potentially creates new openings for democratic change in Western Europe, but only if fundamental civil liberties can be won and retained. The need for civil liberties to be retained in Western Europe as detente weakens the hold of elitism and conservatism should not be ignored. The lesson of the period from 1974 is that one of the main weapons that the Atlanticist elites will use against movements challenging the cultures, ideologies, policies and programmes of Atlanticism is to restrict their freedom of movement, association and expression. In the pre-New Cold War days of the 1970s, Britain suffered less in these respects. But the right-wing Conservative government that came to power in 1979 has shown that, once the first inroads into civil liberties have been made, others can soon follow with a minimum of protest. Moreover, it is striking how the same measures of surveillance, infiltration, random arrest, stop and search and restriction of movement used against the peace movement have also been used, in varying ways, against a workers' movement such as the miners.[30] It is a mark of how the Atlanticist consensus can shift when the level of East–West conflict intensifies, that few of the recent repressive measures would have been considered acceptable in Britain ten or fifteen years ago.

Detente may come again in the next years, and with it another social explosion. The principal concerns this time may be different, reflecting rising unemployment, the technological revolution, and a somewhat greater preoccupation with peace issues than a decade before. But the need for wider civil liberties in order for this explosion to exploit its full potential is no less urgent than in the previous manifestation.

(4) The question of detente and democratic change goes beyond the issue of civil liberties. With hindsight, it is possible to see that, from the establishment's point of view, detente was fundamentally about stabilizing the Cold War system. By removing some of the latter's absurdities and irrationalities, it was hoped to extend its life while also allowing marginally more freedom of choice over who could enter power. But there were distinct limits to this rationalization. When the Labour government of the mid-1970s in Britain sought to introduce a wide range of radical measures in 1974–6, pressure mounted from both international institutions and the British Treasury. Atlanticists within the Labour Party, including most importantly Denis Healey, supported a move against the Labour left, and a deal was worked out with the International Monetary Fund for a massive loan combined with an austerity programme.[31] In Italy, as we have already seen, numerous international initiatives were undertaken from 1976 to 1978 to keep the Communist Party out of government. In 1978 this may have even involved cooperation

between American and Italian intelligence services, together with the top reaches of the Italian police, military and judiciary.[32]

In the above cases, NATO itself was not under threat. Nevertheless, the position of many of the Atlanticist elites in Western Europe was undoubtedly threatened. Some might argue that this was more imagined than real in the case of Italy, where the fanatical anti-Communists in the P2 masonic lodge are now known to have played a significant role. On the other hand, one may wonder whether the postwar Italian establishment could have survived a PCI government without major ructions and whether it was the very perception of this that led leading Socialists and Christian Democrats to involve themselves with P2 (see n. 32).

New Cold War

One of the main ingredients of the New Cold War has been the deployment of cruise and Pershing II missiles in Western Europe. The decision to deploy these missiles was not necessarily a Cold War decision, and it could have been implemented without the return to ideological East–West confrontation witnessed from 1979. However, as a decision that presupposed the survival for many years of several aspects of the Cold War *system*, it left itself open to reinterpretation within the new political and ideological environment. This was the in-built contradiction in both the right-wing social democrat position and the experiment in Trilateralism.

British, Italian and West German social democrats played a not insignificant role in the 1979 two-track decision. Britain's Fred Mulley, James Callaghan and Denis Healey recommended cruise missiles for the European theatre (but on ships rather than on land) as early as August 1977. Germany's Helmut Schmidt made his famous intervention in October 1977 – not because the United States was not already planning to introduce new theatre weapons, but instead because the weapons being considered within the Washington establishment had too short a range to strike the Soviet Union and therefore turn a hypothetical European war into a global war[33] (see also below). The role of the Italian Socialist Party leaders came somewhat later, but was no less significant. With Italian acquiescence in cruise deployment vital to the success of the whole NATO enterprise, the party's leader, Craxi, simply ordered the party to comply. Many Socialists were appalled, but seven leading members who complained that Craxi had abolished inner-party democracy were summarily expelled and the revolt was temporarily quelled. With Italian support for cruise deployment secured, NATO was able to proceed with an otherwise kamikaze decision, and greater pressure could be brought to bear on the recalcitrant Dutch and Belgians.[34]

Why did these political leaders play such a role? For the Atlanticist social democrats, a stable detente meant a strong defence, and that meant strengthening all nuclear forces, including those in the European 'theatre'. The possibility of public opposition in Europe was recognized (the first signs were evident with the opposition to the neutron bomb), but the British and West German governments did not take into account the possibility of a return to the Cold War, nor that the Americans might use the apparent European request for theatre nuclear weapons as a means to impose weapons and a new doctrine for their use which would reawaken mass anxiety about the prospect of nuclear war.

The catch in the European social democrats' position reflected an ambiguity in the general perspective and outlook of the body most responsible for maintaining cohesion in Atlanticist thinking in the mid-1970s, namely the Trilateral Commission. Although the Commission considered that responsibility for western power in the world should be shared more equally in future between North America, Japan and Western Europe, this was contingent on the strategy working in the United States' long-term interests. In part this meant that US banks and multinationals must not see their interests threatened by revolutionary developments in the Third World, and in part it meant that the Europeans and Japanese must be seen to take a meaningful share of responsibility.

Neither the American nor the European establishments were fully united behind Trilateralism, even if members of all the major parties from countries in the three areas attended its meetings. In the United States a small hawkish faction was determined to reverse America's defeat in Vietnam and its setbacks in Angola, Mozambique and elsewhere in the mid-1970s. A number of them formed the Committee on the Present Danger in 1976 in order to campaign vigorously for a more interventionist stance in the Third World, a new arms build-up and a more strident anti-Communism. In Europe, the German government in particular was unimpressed by President Carter's administration, staffed as it may have been by numerous Trilateralists, and it demanded a greater leadership role on the part of the United States.

It was within a small group discussing general strategic matters that the two critical groups came together. The Euro-American Workshop brought together such hawkish American thinkers as Albert Wohlstetter with Helmut Schmidt's top defence advisers and military strategists from Britain and Norway. The Europeans were kept well informed on developments in the United States, and were persuaded to initiate a campaign for a more long-range version of cruise missiles in Europe. Wohlstetter and other US hawks sought to use cruise to undermine President Carter's initiative at the SALT II negotiations (this being thought too dove-ish).

In 1979, when developments in the Third World and above all in Iran caused serious setbacks for American interests world wide, the Committee on the Present Danger and related groups saw the constituency for their views transformed almost overnight. Suddenly, cruise missiles were no longer simply being used in intra-establishment politicking, their role now was to be that of a symbol of the West's new approach to the Soviet Union and the Third World. The New Cold War ship was launched, with cruise at the top of the masthead.

As the New Cold War has developed, the pressures and counter-pressures within Washington have intensified, but in the meantime, Europe has taken its fair share of the new ideological and political offensive. It is indicative that, this time around, the Europeans have generally avoided yielding to the American demands for greater military spending, and popular resistance in Denmark and Holland has prevented the governments of these countries falling in with the Euromissiles decision in the way expected of them. Further, on crucial foreign policy issues such as the Soviet invasion of Afghanistan, Martial Law in Poland and the revolution in Nicaragua, most European governments refused to yield to American pressure to respond aggressively. In the energy field, too, there was European resistance, with Europeans persisting with their arrangements with Moscow for gas from Siberia, despite Washington's opposition. For all these reasons, NATO went through one of its shakiest periods to date from 1981 to 1983.

As a bare-faced attempt to restore American hegemony in Europe following the torrid period of the 1970s, the New Cold War had not been a great success for the United States. European Atlanticists do continue to demand US leadership in the alliance, but they also insist on recognition by Washington that Europeans have valid interests of their own. Since the end of 1983, NATO has to some extent begun to adjust the balance between the United States and Europe, even while reaffirming America's dominant position. The barrage of abuse from Washington directed at the relatively low levels of military spending in continental Europe and the allies' 'softness' towards the Soviet bloc has become barely a whimper. The High Level Group within the Nuclear Planning Group (established in 1977) has given European strategists the chance to influence nuclear policy up to a point, and they did this at Montebello in 1983, with the decision to remove 1,400 nuclear weapons from Europe (the decision has since been partially mothballed, however, as many in Washington objected; some of the old ways continue . . .).

The Independent European Group – a 1976 creation which first really came to life during 1984 – has allowed European arms producers to collaborate more effectively with each other in the face of American competition (although again there is a twist, as there is now greater transatlantic as well as intra-European collaboration, so the United States is still in a powerful position).

NATO officials would like to believe that these developments will ease the Alliance out of its multi-faceted crisis. They are likely to be disappointed. Popular opposition to NATO's military policies continues, despite the neatly constructed illusion of a shift away from early and primary reliance on nuclear weapons; Greece and Denmark remain unreliable allies; France and Spain remain outside the military wing of NATO and seem unlikely to change their position; and there are major difficulties brewing on the issues of military production and soldier recruitment.[35]

But if NATO appears less than healthy, the politics and ideology of *Atlanticism* remain remarkably resilient in the mid-1980s, and nowhere is this more evident than in France and Spain. In France, a socialist government elected in 1981 tried vainly to protect its domestic policies from international pressure through a pro-Atlanticist foreign policy (pro-NATO, pro-cruise and Pershing II). None the less, international pressure mounted not least through extraordinarily high real interest rates in the United States and France found itself increasingly trapped every way it turned. In time, both foreign and domestic policies had fallen broadly within an Atlanticist framework, and *The Times* was able to proclaim, with evident satisfaction, 'C'est magnifique, mais . . . ce n'est pas le socialisme'.[36]

In Spain, the socialist government that came to power in 1982 has done everything it could to keep the country within the Atlanticist fold, while being forced to make certain concessions on NATO membership in order to hold domestic opposition at bay. Thus Spain hopes to play a full role in the EEC, in the 'civilian' wing of NATO (as well as certain military aspects, such as exercises and arms procurement), in international financial institutions etc. Moreover, Spanish opposition to American policies in Central America has given way to a much more conciliatory stance close to the State Department's. Meanwhile, European and US Atlanticists did all they could to help the socialists turn round the substantial Spanish majority in favour of leaving NATO (52:19 at the end of 1984; swung round to 39:51 in the referendum on NATO in March 1986). In this process, Britain made concessions on Gibraltar – a key issue with Spanish nationalists, and the EEC managed, despite internal differences, to facilitate Spain's entry into the Common Market shortly before the national referendum on NATO membership. The timing helped the government capitalize on popular support for the EEC and identify the EEC with the Western alliance in the popular mind. The final swing in opinion on NATO was then achieved through dire threats by the

Prime Minister that an anti-NATO vote would lead to Spain's economic ruin as the US and other NATO members would react by disinvesting *en masse* and causing a collapse of the Spanish economy.

CONCLUSION

It is evident that as long as the Cold War system exists – i.e. the military blocs, US hegemony in Western Europe complementing Soviet domination in Eastern Europe, Atlanticist ideologies surviving as an expression of US hegemony – the United States will continue to exert a powerful influence on political, economic and military developments in Western Europe. This may be because of direct economic, diplomatic or military intervention; it may be because of pressure through the international institutions of the broad Western alliance (NATO, IMF, World Bank etc.); it may be because conflicts within the United States over global strategy unleash an ideological tornado that has the effect of destroying some political forces while ossifying the political system as a whole in Europe; it may be because Europe becomes caught up in a macabre plan to 'roll back' Communism through military force or blackmail; or it may be ensured through a more subtle and direct means of pressure, as follows: Western European supporters of NATO can use the implied threat of US economic intervention (as in Spain in early 1986) to strengthen public support for their Atlanticist policies; they may use NATO institutions as allies in a domestic political conflict – as, for example, during the Euromissiles crisis; or they may take advantage of an ideological climate fostered by more hawkish Americans to marginalize critical or dissident political forces – as we have seen in Britain under Mrs Thatcher. In each case, either the ideology, the structures or the mechanisms of US hegemony proved useful to Atlanticist Europeans.

More attention ought to be paid to the role of Atlanticist forces in Western Europe in reinforcing American hegemony. It is not enough to rail against US intervention, US pressure and US bluff and bluster. Most of the time, it is not Americans who are reinforcing and stabilizing the Cold War system in Western Europe, it is those Europeans who support that system.

Yet even though it is evident that the Cold War system has negative ramifications for Europe, it is also plain to see that the task of escaping from that system is very hard. The system operates through political, economic and military mechanisms, and through established norms and codes. It militates against democracy to be sure, but that does not make it any easier to find a political route out of it. It militates against an economic system that might bring social justice, but what economic programme do we have to offer as an alternative? It is militarily extremely dangerous, carrying with it the daily risk of total annihilation. Yet, military policy is intimately tied up with political and economic policies, so we come back to the fundamental question as how to resolve these.

The central problem is how to deal with European Atlanticists – whatever colour political coat they wear – *at the same time as* the Americans. We have seen all too clearly how an Atlanticist detente, stabilizing and rationalizing the Cold War system, only provided a short breathing space for the flourishing of half-open democracy. We have seen how the pro-detente Atlanticists limited that new democracy, and sought a return to pluralist elitism, shorn of mass participation. And we have seen how, when the hawks regained the advantage in the United States, the structures were all in place for a new Cold War.

Given that the right questions are asked, grounds for optimism lie in the fact that this New Cold War (or 'Hot Peace') has shown not only the necessity but also the possibility for a renewed *challenge from below* to European Atlanticism. Elsewhere in this volume (especially chapters 6 and 7) there is discussion of the growing fissures that have opened up between Western Europe and the United States during the recent period of East–West detente. It is evident, too, that Atlanticist Europeans have been sharply divided over a number of key issues, not least the Strategic Defense Initiative (Star Wars), the attack on Libya and the deployment of the Euromissiles.

On the one hand, we see Europeans whose principal motivation is undivided loyalty to the American Right. Led by Mrs Thatcher and Chancellor Kohl, these lend their full support to the Euromissiles, and give their backing to Star Wars in so far as it is not seen to undermine either deterrence or the ABM (Anti-Ballistic Missile) Treaty.

Lined up against these loyalists are the more independent-minded Atlanticists who hold that public support for NATO in Europe can only be sustained henceforth via the removal of some or all of the Euromissiles and through the rapid demise of the Star Wars programme. This position, advocated most clearly by Britain's Denis Healey, enjoys the support of many European members of the Socialist International. An additional component, supported by the whole of the Socialist International in Europe and by many liberal conservatives, is support for a stronger 'European pillar' in NATO and closer European cooperation in military matters.

It would appear that the latter Atlanticists, acutely aware of the threat to the alliance posed by the conflicts and tensions of recent years, are seeking to redefine the US–European relationship on a more equal or consensual basis in order to maintain the overall structure of the Cold–War system. For those concerned with peace and democracy, this attempted redefinition offers new opportunities that it would be dangerous to ignore.

Thus, in the present context of lessening European dependence on the United States, we must push also for growing independence, within Europe, from Atlanticism. This may mean opting for a more participatory, localized democracy; it may mean a challenge to elitism and traditional hierarchies; it may mean more urgent efforts in the direction of sexual and racial equality; it may mean a renewed challenge to the power of the multinationals and the international banks and the development of an alternative economic strategy that prioritizes social needs and qualitatively improved jobs *as well as* leisure time in a context where technological change opens up possibilities for longstanding working class demands to be fulfilled; it may mean a different approach to overseas aid and to liberation movements, with development on the Third World's terms being the priority within a general context of self-determination; it may mean a radical new approach to military policy, with the notion of 'defence' re-defined, nuclear weapons abolished and alternative employment provided; it may mean new educational and health policies. Above all, the need is there for an explosion of new creative energy in Europe, developing on the advances already made in the peace movement, and allowing us to take maximum advantage of the gradual loosening of the Western alliance and the likely openings spawned by the thawing of Cold War in order to set Europe finally on the path to peace and liberation.

NOTES

1 The West's responsibility for the division of Germany is not accepted by all historians. However, the more documentary evidence becomes available, the more it points to Western rather than Soviet complicity. See, for example, J. and G. Kolko, *The Limits of Power* (New York: Harper & Row, 1972), chs 6, 12, 18; Richard Barnet, *The Alliance* (New York: Simon & Schuster, 1983), pp. 38–46; 'United States Assistance to other Countries from the Standpoint of National Security'. Report by the Joint Strategic Survey Committee, Foreign Relations of the United States, vol. 1 (1947), pp. 73–8. For more orthodox accounts, but ones which nevertheless point to Western complicity in many respects, see Hardley Arkes, *Bureaucracy, the Marshall Plan and the National Interest* (Princeton, NJ: Princeton University Press, 1972) and James L. Richardson, *Germany and the Atlantic Alliance* (Cambridge, Mass: Harvard University Press, 1966).

2 As Michael Cox so persuasively puts its, 'Outwardly, a great conflict of two

social systems and between two superpowers was occurring. In reality, the great contest was more apparent than real, conducted between forces of totally unequal economic and military capability. Real though the antagonism was in the broad historical sense, after 1947 the two poles within the world system effectively existed in an interdependent and functional relationship in which the mutual opposition between the two facilitated the stability and reproduction of both.' 'Western Capitalism and the Cold War System,' in Martin Shaw (ed.), *War State and Society* (London: Macmillan, 1984), p. 154.

3 See 'Resume of World Situation', PPS 13 (Policy Planning Staff), Foreign Relations of the United States, vol. 1, (1947), pp. 772–7.

4 See Barnet, *The Alliance*, pp. 38–9; William Graf, 'Anti-Communism in the Federal Republic of Germany', in R. Miliband, J. Saville and M. Liebman (eds), *Socialist Register 1984* (London: Merlin, 1984), pp. 167, 172; Reinhard Gehlen, *The Service*, (New York: World Publishers, 1972).

5 One-third of Adenauer's first cabinet were ex-Nazis, and his early cabinets included such ex-Nazis as Gerhard Schroeder, Minister of the Interior; Hans-Christolph Seebohm, Minister of Transportation; and Theodor Oberlander, Minister for Refugees. Ex-Nazis also occupied leading positions in the FDP, and it is striking that one finds a level of anti-Communist hysteria in the rhetoric of these two parties in the Cold War era not found anywhere else in Western Europe at the time.

6 See Graf, 'Anti-Communism', p. 170. Despite this Ahlen programme, the 1946–7 period saw the right wing of the CDU taking over the party in most parts of the Western occupied zones. See also Reinhard Kuhnl, 'Die Auseinandersetzung mit dem Faschismus in BRD und DDR', in G. Hess (ed.), *BRD–DDR, Vergleich der Gesellschaftssysteme* (Koln: Pahl-Rugenstein, 1971), pp. 248–71.

7 The fabrication included the use of homosexuals who faced conviction on the grounds of their sexual predilections and who were posed with cameras outside Western airbases so that they could appear in the papers as 'Communist spy caught red-handed at air base'. There were also carefully fabricated spy cases. British intelligence personnel who failed to brand Communists as subversives were moved elsewhere, and were replaced by more 'cooperative' people. (Evidence from member of British Intelligence in the Allied Control Commission in Germany 1947–55, interviewed by the author.)

8 Werner Maihofer, quoted in Sebastian Cobler, *Law, Order and Politics in West Germany* (Harmondsworth: Penguin, 1977), p. 7.

9 The US administration effectively abandoned its traditional anti-colonial position in early 1944. This was explained by President Roosevelt's personal envoy, Isiah Bowman, to officials in London. He informed them, in April 1944, that the US administration had now 'definitely discarded all idea of approaching (the colonial) problem from the aspect of independence. . . the goal of actual independence was too remote'. Public Record Office, PRO F.O. 371/35311. On long-term imperial planning by America's postwar planners in the 1942–5 period, see L. H. Shoup and W. Minter, *Imperial Brain Trust* (New

York: Monthly Review Press, 1977).

10 See, for example, Martin Eve, 'Anti-Communism and American Intervention in Greece', in Miliband et al. (eds), *Socialist Register*, p. 103.

11 Bevin put forward a number of different proposals in private meetings between November 1947 and February 1948, but this appears to have been his first choice. Addressing the House of Commons in January 1948, he talked of the overseas territories held by Britain, France, Belgium, Portugal and Holland which have 'raw materials, food and resources which can be turned to very great common advantage'. He felt that the exploitation of these territories was indispensable if 'Western Europe is to achieve its balance of payments and to get a world equilibrium', but that the scheme would only work 'if the power and resources of the United States' could be harnessed to it. For this reason, he proposed an Atlantic Pact – an alliance of the United States and the European empires.

12 Senator Vandenberg is most explicit on this. See Arthur M. Vandenberg, *The Private Papers of Senator Vandenberg* (London: Lowe and Brydine, 1952), p. 419. See also the report prepared by the Policy Planning Staff 'Concerning Western Union and Related Problems' (PPS 27), Foreign Relations of the United States, vol. III (1948), pp. 63–4.

13 None of Washington's policies was supported by the whole establishment in the United States in the late 1940s. Isolationists were opposed to any form of overseas commitment. Others wanted overseas commitments confined to the Western hemisphere or wanted Asia prioritized over Western Europe. It was in large part the political battles fought over these questions that generated such a high level of anti-Communist hysteria in the 1947–53 period – anti-Communism being invoked in particular by the Atlanticists and the pro-Asianists as a means to defeat their domestic rivals. See also Alan Wolfe's chapter in this volume (chapter 4).

14 The most important document rationalizing an arms build-up – the first version of which was completed and approved at the highest level before the outbreak of the Korean War – was the National Security Council memorandum known as NSC-68, which can be found in Department of State, Foreign Relations of the United States, vol. 1 (1950), pp. 235–92. See also the useful commentary in Jerry W. Sanders, *Peddlers of Crisis* (London: Pluto Press, 1983), pp. 23–46.

15 A. Shonfield, *Modern Capitalism* (London: Oxford University Press, 1969), pp. 99ff. The policies of the Conservatives post-1951 were markedly different from Thatcherist monetarism in that the earlier commitment to full employment was upheld. The Tories at that time were not anti-welfare as such, but were inclined to see the welfare state largely as a 'safety-net', and in this respect they share much with Thatcherism. Otherwise, there is no doubt about the similarity, as Shonfield shows: 'The outstanding feature of the period was a kind of vigorous spiritual back-pedalling, the expression of a nostalgia for some bygone age when market forces produced the important economic decisions, while governments merely registered them . . . there was a systematic attempt to cut down the role of the public sector and to introduce

in its place some natural or fabricated play for competing private interests' (pp. 99–100).

16 See Tony Bunyan, *The Political Police in Britain* (London: Quartet Books, 1977), pp. 124–5, and Reg Whitaker, 'Fighting the Cold War on the Home Front: America, Britain, Australia and Canada', in Miliband et al. (eds), *Socialist Register*, pp. 34–41.

17 Dowling to Matthews, Washington, 21 November 1946, 865.00/11–2146, General Records of the Department of State (RG59), NA. I am indebted to James E. Miller for unearthing this quote.

18 Ambassador Dunn, the US envoy in Rome, acted as the intermediary, and helped persuade Marshall of the nature of the danger to American interests in Italy. See Alan A. Platt and Robert Leonardi, 'American Foreign Policy and the Post War Italian Left', *Political Science Quarterly* (Summer 1978), pp. 198–9; James E. Miller, 'Chaos or Christian Democracy: The ERP as a factor in Italy's 1948 election', University of Padua, mimeo.

19 The Pentagon discussions were held secretly from 22 to 27 March with high-level representatives from Canada, the United States and Britain. They designed the North Atlantic Treaty down to small details, and little was changed in later negotiations. The Soviet spy Donald Maclean was present as a member of the British delegation. See report prepared by the Policy Planning Staff (PPS 27), Foreign Relations of the United States, vol. III (1948), pp. 63–4.

20 For a detailed account by two of the CIA operatives involved, see Robert T. Molt and Robert W. van de Velde, *Strategic Psychological Operations and American Foreign Policy* (Chicago: University of Chicago Press, 1960), esp. pp. 164–74.

21 See Platt and Leonardi, 'American Foreign Policy', pp. 201–8.

22 Quoted in the *New York Times*, 7 April 1976.

23 For a full analysis, see e.g. W. M. Scammell, *The International Economy since 1945* (London: Macmillan, 1980) and David P. Calleo and Benjamin M. Rowland, *America and the World Political Economy* (Indiana University Press and London, 1973).

24 The US administration had seen the limitations of nuclear weapons on previous occasions, notably during the Soviet invasion of Hungary in 1956. For the much greater impact on official thinking of the Cuba crisis, see the interview with Robert McNamara in Robert Scheer, *With Enough Shovels: Reagan, Bush and Nuclear War* (New York: Random House, 1982).

25 *The Crisis of Democracy*, Report on the Governability of Democracies for the Trilateral Commission (New York University Press, 1975).

26 Ibid., p. 105.

27 Information on these developments has been compiled by the author from numerous newspaper and magazine reports from the period. It is perhaps significant that NATO intelligence bodies also have a role in intelligence collection on radical groups. It emerged in 1984 that, at least since 1968, weekly police reports have been passed to the NATO liaison office in Kiel as well as British, American and Canadian intelligence bodies on political activities in West Germany. In Britain, similar police reports have for decades

been given to the British Special Branch and probably MI5. It would be surprising if the CIA did not also have access to such reports. See the *New York Guardian*, 11 July 1984, and Tony Bunyan, *The Political Police*, pp. 141–2.

28 In part, the apparent moderation in the British response can be put down to the fact that the Labour government of 1974–9 was successful in demobilizing and/or demoralizing the radical workers' and extra-parliamentary movements through a mix of partial reforms, radical rhetoric and an alliance between the Labour Right and the IMF (on this, see below in text). However, a number of plans had already been laid in the 1970–4 period for more drastic action by the state, including the use of troops to break strikes or suppress civil unrest. These plans are still being up-dated. See Bunyan, *The Political Police*, pp. 267–85 and 293–7.

29 A slightly ironic twist to this new face of the PCI was that it was thwarted in its attempt to sign a joint statement from European socialists condemning the Soviet invasion of Afghanistan. The Italian Socialists and the German SPD insisted that the PCI's name be taken off the list of signatories.

30 On civil liberties and CND, see for example *Sanity*, August 1984, pp. 16–30; articles by Nick Davies and Ian Black in the *Guardian*, 19 and 20 April 1984; and the *Sunday Telegraph*, 9 December 1984, p. 1. On the miners and civil liberties, see especially Jim Coulter, Susan Miller and Martin Walker, *State of Siege* (London: Canary Press, 1984). The testing grounds for these attacks on civil liberties were above all Northern Ireland and selected black communities in London and elsewhere.

31 The most detailed history of this episode is Joel Barnett, *Inside the Treasury* (London: Andre Deutsch, 1982).

32 The P2 Masonic lodge is now known to have involved leading figures from all these branches of the establishment. P2 was dedicated to keeping the Communists out of government in Italy, and Moro, the Christian Democratic leader, was the man most likely to upset their scheme. The Red Brigades were undoubtedly responsible for kidnapping and eventually murdering Moro, but the ease with which they carried out the kidnapping and the incompetence of the police and the security services during the week he was held leave one to wonder whether there was not a coordinating plan to 'create space' for the Red Brigades to do their damnedest. As much was suggested at the trial of the Red Brigades, with Moro's wife among those who were suspicious. On the P2 sect, see for example the *New Statesman*, 21 September 1984. The best source is probably Barberi et al., *L'Italia della P2*. (Milan: Oscar Mondadori, 1983).

33 Many commentators have read into Schmidt's speech at the IISS in London only a concern to maintain detente, and argued that this speech did not advocate theatre nuclear weapons deployment. However, it has emerged that Schmidt's advisers made it known to American officials at the time of the speech that Schmidt was making pointed remarks about Carter's SALT initiative, and that cruise's short range was one of the reasons. See, for example, R. Garthoff, 'The NATO INF Decision', *Political Science Quarterly* (Autumn 1983), pp. 198–201; Fred Kaplan, 'Warring over New Missiles for NATO', *New York Times Magazine*, 9 December 1979; and various pieces in

Richard K. Betts (ed.), *Cruise Missiles, Technology, Strategy, Politics* (Washington, DC: Brookings Institution, 1982).

34 On this episode, see Diana Johnstone, *The Politics of Euromissiles* (London: Verso, 1984), pp. 139–42.

35 Difficulties because of rapidly rising costs and the end of the 'baby boom'.

36 *The Times*, 14 December 1984.

6

Transatlantic Crisis – A Framework for an Alternative West European Peace Policy?

HANNE-MARGRET BIRCKENBACH, CHRISTIANE RIX, ALBERT STATZ AND CHRISTIAN WELLMANN

THE CRISIS IN TRANSATLANTIC RELATIONS AS A CRISIS OF CONSENSUS

The NATO decision of December 1979, to deploy cruise and Pershing missiles and negotiate simultaneously with the Soviet Union about them, triggered a debate in West Germany about current security policy and NATO strategy. A fundamental critique of military and especially nuclear concepts of security was formulated by the peace movement; but the European establishment has also become critical of the Reagan administration's current policies and this has led to a crisis of transatlantic relations. The confrontational elements of President Reagan's policies *vis-à-vis* both the East–West conflict and transatlantic differences have intensified diverging interests within the NATO alliance. Establishment critics argue that the fundamental transatlantic consensus is being jeopardized by this confrontational approach and this is why alternatives are required.

Our aim in this chapter is to illustrate the contradictions and tensions in transatlantic relations, and to consider the extent to which the USA, as the hegemonic power in the Western alliance, is able to impose its own interests on the European allies. This chapter looks at the economic and military dimensions of transatlantic relations. It is not enough to assert American dominance in the alliance to justify decoupling. What is needed is an examination of the catchword 'crisis of transatlantic relations'. The crisis provides an opportunity to press for an alternative peace policy.

The use of the term 'crisis' should not obscure the concurrence of economic and political interests and ideological common ground within the alliance. There exists a fundamental consensus on the need to promote and protect the interests of the industrialized capitalist countries *vis-à-vis* the socialist countries as well as the Third World; furthermore, there is large agreement on the need to find a common economic and political strategy for strengthening capital in the current world economic crisis, for regulating international competition and for securing political control in the face of growing opposition.

This interest (initially a very abstract one) in preserving and stabilizing the system internally and externally requires a process of compromise in concrete situations where interests diverge. Agreement on the need to iron out conflicts of interest gives rise to a framework in which the content of the general interest can be more precisely defined, and which determines the formal structures in which compromises can be achieved. The compromise formulae do not simply conceal opposing interests; they also signal real agreement (which can be translated into policy) on where unity exists and where it does not. Accordingly, the process of compromise aims to overcome differences where possible, and to agree to disagree where this is not possible. Herein lies the consensus in transatlantic relations.

Such an integrative management of differences tries to take into account the fact that the process of compromise takes place among unequals. It is understood and accepted that some interests cannot be renounced and that different nations have different capacities for carrying out policy. This is a strategy based on agreement. In contrast, a strategy which is one-sidedly confrontational jeopardizes the underlying structure for balancing interests and brings about resistance from those who consider that the current mode of reaching compromises is itself an interest that cannot be renounced.

Thus, the United States' confrontational strategy for regaining hegemony is now giving rise to a crisis within the Atlantic alliance, because the consensus about the process of compromise is called into question. The United States is trying more and more to interpret its interests in the field of economics and military strategy as those of the entire alliance. So, when talking about the crisis in transatlantic relations, one is really talking about a crisis of consensus.

The current crisis refers therefore to the structure of transatlantic relations, and thus to the international political order which developed after World War II. It is to be seen as an extensive crisis of the economic, political and military structure of international relations. But it should not simply be considered as a 'collapse' of the system. The crisis has its own internal dynamic. Crisis can be defined as decision (this decision has to be determined).

The character of the crisis as a crisis about mechanisms for reaching compromises is evident in the conflicts both about economic policy and about NATO nuclear strategy. The agreement about the need for an international economic structure linking advanced industrial countries is being undermined by the use of austerity policies to pursue national economic interests, in order to improve the ability to compete in international markets. Likewise, the strategy of flexible response was a way of glossing over divergent security interests and, at the same time, making possible a common concrete military strategy. But the increasing US insistence on its own confrontational interpretation of flexible response has called into question this form of compromise.

American policy has given rise to criticism, and this has affected the political structures of NATO, which serve as the institutional framework for reaching compromises. This has led to serious consideration of such issues as greater political and military independence within NATO, European control over the use of nuclear weapons and the redefinition of West European security in the context of an all-European peace order. There is a connection here between the establishment critique of NATO and the more fundamental alternatives discussed by the peace movement.

The United States' concern is to work out strategies through which it can impose its position on the West Europeans: the United States is making use of its still central position in the international economic system as well as its greater opportunities for influence in the military field within NATO. The West Europeans can attempt to preserve their margin of manoeuvre by reacting in various ways: giving in to American pressure and adjusting to it, so as to ensure that a minimum of independent interests can be preserved and promoted; or developing counter-strategies, which could nullify the previous consensus, and force the United States to a more integrative policy. Offensively, they might carry out a joint foreign economic policy in the EEC – however improbable it presently seems – and this might well represent a lever in a new definition of West European security. Because President Reagan's confrontational strategy could undermine the concrete consensus between Western Europe and the United States, and also put in question the fundamental basis for transatlantic relations, it is coming up against resistance within the United States itself.

In the following discussion, we will attempt to demonstrate the connection between the economic and the security–political crisis. We consider that the economic margin of manoeuvre is fundamental in determining the future course of developments in European security policy. Because the economic crisis narrows the economic margin of manoeuvre, so the space for compromise is correspondingly reduced. Just as the economic margin for manoeuvre restricts possible political strategies, so political and military strategies can be used to improve economic positions.

GROWING MILITARIZATION AS COMPENSATION FOR THE UNITED STATES' ECONOMIC DECLINE?

The United States has faced a steady relative decline of its economic hegemony since 1945. This became obvious in the 1970s when serious crises in the world economy emerged. At the same time, the United States has retained its military dominance within NATO. Of particular significance is the security guarantee it provides with its nuclear weapons. However, tendencies towards detente diminish the importance of the security guarantee. More recently, since Ronald Reagan took office, a new global strategy of confrontation has been taking shape, which is often interpreted in the following manner: the United States, by using military force and strategies once again as an instrument of politics, is attempting to 'compensate' for its economic weakness. This is to be achieved by making war 'fightable' at all levels, to make deterrence and military blackmail 'credible' again or really to fight a war.

The East–West conflict is primarily defined in military terms while the consensus in transatlantic relations has been expressed in the form of the US security guarantee. Hence a confrontational American strategy means a return to the politics of the 'Cold War' in order to rebuild America's hegemonic position.

According to the compensation thesis, this strategy of strengthening the common front of NATO members *vis-à-vis* the Warsaw Treaty Organization and of interpreting any regional conflict in terms of the East–West conflict serves American interests in different ways. The redistribution of the costs of the arms build-up within NATO is supposed to weaken the West European economies and thus strengthen the American economy. The margin of manoeuvre for Western Europe which was gained in the course of detente is also restricted. The decline of the American economy's competitive edge *vis-à-vis* the countries of the Third World is counterbalanced by the emphasis on military means to safeguard spheres of influence. In effect, the growing transatlantic conflict of interests is being pressed into a common mould apropos the East–West conflict whose specific meaning and importance is defined by the United States in terms of its own interests. The interests of the West European allies as they themselves determine them are only then taken into account when they do not run counter to the 'necessities' brought about by the East–West conflict as interpreted by the United States. By means of its security guarantee, America is attempting to impose a consensus on the West Europeans and in this way to 'blackmail' them.

Since World War II, when the economic and political–military hegemony of the United States coincided and when the United States used both forms of hegemony to bind Western Europe to the capitalist world, the security guarantee, as a mechanism for imposing American interests, has been a fundamental element of US foreign policy towards Western Europe. As regards the concrete economic significance of the 'compensation thesis' and the concrete political mechanisms whereby the American concepts of foreign and national security policy as a 'consensus' are formulated and imposed, two basic questions must be posed.

First: to what extent and in which areas has the United States lost its economically hegemonic position? What economic strategies are available to 'compensate' for this economic loss of position and to help it to regain its hegemony? If such economic policies seem unlikely to succeed, then the use of military means to 'compensate' for economic decline becomes more probable. Even if current austerity policies succeed and open up new economic, non-military policies, the question still remains whether the US security guarantee for Western Europe and the military potential of the United States are also required to support the politics of confrontation and whether, in order to manage the consequences of growing economic confrontation, the austerity policy itself will be militarized.

Secondly: Is there still sufficient common ground in security relations to make unnecessary the imposition of President Reagan's policies *against* diverging European security interests? Indeed, is the unilateral imposition of a confrontatiional global strategy possible in the face of West European resistance, given common transatlantic interests and mutual dependence? How has the transatlantic process of consensus-building evolved, in the context of the militarization of American foreign policy?

THE DECLINE OF AMERICAN ECONOMIC DOMINANCE IN THE WORLD ECONOMY

The current economic crisis could be characterized as a deep structural rupture occurring at the end of a 'long wave' of capitalist development, which began with the world economic crisis at the end of the 1920s. The technical, social, economic and political structures underlying the international division of labour could be said to have conformed to the American 'model'. The United States was not only superior in market competition, it also determined the framework in which competition took place. US hegemony meant that the United States possessed a large degree of 'autonomous' control over the entire reproductive process at the international level. The United States secured its dominance through the monetary system established under the Bretton Woods Agreement, and gradually brought about conditions of free trade, i.e. the mobility of goods and capital. Only under conditions of international economic liberalism was it possible for the United States to exploit its hegemonic position.

The consequence of this development was a growing international integration in the sphere of goods, productive capital (multinational corporations) and monetary and credit relations. The mutual dependence which thereby arose constricts considerably the space for unilateral protectionist moves: tariffs and other trade restrictions, the introduction of controls on the movement of capital or national monetary and currency policy.

The hegemonic position of the United States was weakened by the spread of the American model – not least because of the export of American capital and technology – and by the catching up of competitors. The growth rates of productivity in the United States can be considered as the key structural determinant. These fell more and more behind those of the West European countries and of Japan so that the competitive advantage of the United States disappeared; the American share of international trade declined continuously. Despite the relative shifts in competitive positions, however, it remains the case that the United States still decisively determines the development of the world economy as a result of the magnitude of its internal market, its imports and exports.

The intensification of international competition in the world economic crisis jeopardizes the political–economic postwar consensus. The possibilities for concrete compromises are increasingly restricted and the balancing of interests becomes a zero-sum game. Contrary to the logic of interdependence, there is an increasing danger of a resort to national solutions to the crisis. In managing the consequences of unilateral protectionist moves, different countries possess different margins of manoeuvre. The prospects for the United States are much better than for the West European countries, unless they develop a joint economic policy *vis-à-vis* the United States. Thus, America dominates the world economic situation (to a considerable degree) by the sheer size of its economy.

While the competitiveness of the American economy, i.e. American produced goods, has declined, the global strength of American capital has increased. American multinational corporations still have their profit and decision-making centres in the United States and offer at the same time various possibilities for promoting the United States' interests and for influencing the decision-making processes in foreign countries. It is true that the interests of American multinationals are by no means identical with the policy of the American government, but the 'transnational connection' furthers the influence of US government strategy: for example, Third World intervention; the attempt to extend American laws to the US multinational corporations in foreign countries, as was the case during the boycott of the West European gas pipeline settlement with the Soviet Union; or the American attempt to influence the renegotiation of the terms of Poland's debt by private creditors.

American hegemony is even more evident in the area of currency and credit relations: in spite of the collapse of the Bretton Woods system, the dollar continues to be the most important reserve currency; international transactions occur widely in dollars, especially in the oil business as a result of the dominance of American multinational corporations in this area. Also, up to 5 per cent of transactions in the international credit markets, such as the Euro-money market, take place on a dollar basis.

While the internal prerequisites for an absolute American hegemony are being eroded, American dominance in international capital and credit relations is increasing. But this means that the United States is increasingly dependent on foreign economic expansion, and therefore the American economy is much more vulnerable to the global economic crisis. The size of its internal market enables the United States to restructure its domestic productive capacities via international economic strategies. This, in turn, restricts the possible strategies available to other countries to solve their economic problems. In other words, the United States still has the power to organize the framework of international business and to change the international division of labour.

At the end of the long-term boom on the world market, economic conflicts are about the extent to which different national strategies can influence the future structure of the world market: which branches will become growth branches; what significance will the arms industry have; to what extent can the liberal conditions of international markets be safeguarded in this crisis; what new forms of world market penetration and/or insulation can be envisaged; and what social and political model will be imposed during the crisis, which can shape development thereafter?

AUSTERITY POLICY AS A NATIONAL AND INTERNATIONAL ANTI-CRISIS STRATEGY

A West European economic strategy of decoupling both from the United States in the politico-military sphere and *vis-à-vis* American global strategy takes place within the framework of the austerity policy which was adopted after the failure of the Keynesian policy. This resulted in the agreement that the crisis situation poses much the same problem for all countries affected. International interdependence has become a structural condition for managing the crisis so that the reorganization of the conditions of production and new forms of the international division of labour within the 'free international market' are being sought. International competition necessitates a rigorous anti-inflationary policy via the 'imperative of the balance of payments'. This is because any loss of position in the world market as a result of inflation leads to crises in the balance of payments and devaluation. The relative rise in the costs of imported energy and raw materials also results, by contrast with earlier times, in a further loss of position in the world market.

An important reason why an international consensus exists on austerity policy as an anti-crisis strategy can be found in the political content of the political–economic strategy. The aim is to liberate market forces and reduce the government's role in the economy in order to enhance the power of the strong and to reorganize the domestic and international division of labour entirely according to the principle of competitiveness. On the domestic–political level, this strategy reduces the influence of organized interests of the population, i.e. trades unions, and causes disorientation and disintegration among the classes and strata affected. It dissolves integrative, corporative, political structures and is therefore capable of neutralizing social problems, such as unemployment and poverty, which intensify as a consequence of the policy. In effect, the austerity policy atomizes the potential for resistance. The classic model of the 'war of all against all' prevails in the austerity policy's approach to politics. It is based on confrontation and consequently on the use of force to repress the conflicts which occur when the strategy of atomizing resistance fails.

At the international level, there is no single authority which could impose a consensus and/or ensure respect for the implementation of national strategies. Even international political–economic agencies such as the International Monetary Fund which make possible common interventionary measures are losing their importance as a consequence of austerity policy. It may be the case that intensified competition is a means of restructuring the world market and a long-term way out of the crisis. Nevertheless, austerity policy intensifies the short- and long-term contradictions. In spite of their professed faith in free international trade, the less competitive nations are forced to make increased use of protectionism, especially in the form of non-tariff trade impediments and government export subsidies. This has led to an escalating rivalry between national economic policies in order to improve their respective international competitiveness.

This international 'beggar-thy-neighbour' policy of austerity, therefore, necessarily implies a *confrontational* type of international politics. As a result, concrete agreements on political–economic measures are in constant danger and, in individual cases, become impossible. Managing the unequal consequences of the austerity policy again and again gives rise to the danger that confrontational policies escalate, while the basic principle of finding compromises falls apart if the common interest in preserving world market integration can no longer be maintained. By contrast, *integrative* strategies try to minimize the negative consequences of a confrontation policy by balancing interests, so that costs and benefits correspond to existing relations, i.e. are distributed unequally, and try to achieve any agreement which is possible.

The relative decay of American productive capacities in the medium term provides the background to President Reagan's confrontational global strategy – domestic and foreign. The aim is to enable the United States to regain its position as the absolutely dominant power. At the same time, the United States still has considerable political–economic margins of manoeuvre because of its still-existing relative dominance. Therefore, it can impose a specific model for reorganizing the entire complex of economic, political and military relations in the crisis and so in the long term establish its hegemonic role. The mere fact that the austerity policy is essentially a monetary and currency policy, and that its execution is supposed to increase the pressure on the foreign governments to pursue similar policies, expands the United States' margin of manoeuvre because it can reap advantages from its dominance in the currency and credit sector. This policy provokes greater domestic–political resistance in Western Europe than in the United States. If the competitors of the United States do not succeed in persevering with such a policy because of domestic–political problems, then their international competitive positions will worsen unless they adopt protectionist measures, thereby violating the premises of an unlimited integration of the world market.

This danger of escalation through West European countermeasures, which could challenge world market integration itself and thereby remove the foundations of the American hegemonic strategy, can be countered by the United States via the politico–military elements of its global strategy, which it possesses as a result of its dominance within NATO. The thesis concerning 'military strength as compensation for economic weakness' can thus be advanced in this context; namely, how the United States manages the consequences of its economic hegemonic strategies, and what significance the military dimension possesses within the political and social model of austerity policy.

THE MILITARIZATION OF AUSTERITY POLICY

The militarization of American global strategy is not merely a reversion to more or less 'normal' forms of pursuing American interests after the 'Vietnam shock'. There is more to it than this. The revitalization of the military instrument of foreign policy assumes a specific economic and social importance in the context of the international economic crisis and the austerity policy. The tendency to use military instruments to guarantee an open world market is increased because of the confrontational character of the austerity policy. Moreover, the growth of protectionism escalates this tendency because the consequences of protectionism are managed through additional confrontational policies.

The militarization of austerity policy can also influence the reorganization of the structure of production in the world economic crisis. The Reagan administration's attempt to utilize the arms build-up to revitalize the economy, to subsidize certain areas in the 'sunbelt' and to promote new growth branches (electronics and aerospace), also contributes to the formation of new political power structures. It may be that, in the long term, a military–industrial policy retards economic development and does not contribute to prosperity. However, such a policy may help, politically, to stabilize the New Cold War policy. This is evident in the political shift away from the East Coast and the way in which the New Right has succeeded in militarizing domestic politics; they are able to fortify their social basis through the war economy.

Nevertheless, it is obvious that the arms build-up at current levels is inconsistent with the austerity policy, because it leads to deficits which hinder the prospects of a restrictive monetary policy. The change in the Reagan administration's economic policy, whereby the consolidation of the budget was considered to be secondary to the arms build-up, has thus come up against growing domestic resistance. At the same time, the arms build-up is undermining, in the long run, the goal of restoring international competitiveness via austerity policy. Military expenditures, after all, have contributed to the relative economic decline of the United States by hindering capital formation in the civilian economy, raising the inflation rates and reducing the spin-off effects of technological innovations.

Even though there are limits to the militarization strategy, it still has a function in weakening Western Europe in international economic competition and in exploiting the leverage of the security guarantee to impose the reorganization of the model of economic growth on a world scale. If the United States pursues this strategy consistently, a militarization of international economic and political relations can actually help the United States regain its hegemonic position, in that it can define by its policy the criteria according to which the hierarchy of the international division of labour is structured. The United States weakens the Western European economies with its arms build-up (especially its conventional aspects) by drastically redistributing the burden of spending. It can also try, as a result of the associated arms exports, to regain a dominant position in new technological areas, and thus attempt both to improve its foreign economic situation and to utilize civilian production. The experience of history tends to cast doubt on the possibility that such a political–economic strategy can be successful. However, such a strategy can exert considerable influence on the political–economic prospects of the West European countries, and can sharply constrict their margin of manoeuvre. The military instrument also serves to manage the contradictions and consequences of the austerity policy through the arms spiral. The model of Cold War society is being consolidated both internally and externally. This includes the social consensus which sustains this, which is based more upon the hostile image of Communism in foreign policy, and the restoration of national greatness via expanded 'power', and less upon 'prosperity'. A certain stability of this model is quite possible via a negative feedback process, i.e., anti-Communism and the militarization of society reinforce a foreign policy strategy of safeguarding of interests through military means and vice versa. Thus, militarization becomes a self-legitimizing principle of society in a comprehensive sense.

As confrontational strategies escalate, however, countervailing forces are called forth. The domestic American critique of the Reagan administration's policies, and even more so the West European opposition to its arms build-up, apply not only to single elements of the global strategy but include elements of a different economic and social model which is linked to 'detente' and promotes integrative conflict resolution in terms of both domestic and foreign policy.

The fundamental difference between the confrontational and the integrative type of political strategy is to be found in the importance and meaning of the military instrument, in terms of all its social and economic functions within the overall framework of political strategy. The failure of Keynesian economic policy in the present crisis indicates the objective limits set to integrative variants of this type. Concrete alternatives to the militarization of austerity policy have to encompass broader political and economic strategies concerning foreign economic expansion and dependency in particular, in order to overcome the premises of global trade liberalization and *laissez-faire* economic policy. In this context the West European countries have to decide on whether the formation of a regional bloc – together with parts of the Third World – and a common industrial policy can de-escalate the contradictions of different national austerity policies, at least in Western Europe, and thus neutralize the American 'compensation' strategy.

The distinction between confrontational and integrative conflict-solving models is important for the development of political alternatives for peace. Alternatives to the militarization of the austerity policy are only feasible as overall social strategies: countering the 'armament spiral' with a 'disarmament spiral' consists above all in carrying out a civilian reorganization of productive capacities in the economic crisis. The way to do this is first of all to reduce military expenditure; this must involve an active industrial policy to maintain international competitiveness and to finance a 'cushioning' of its social consequences.

A long-term anti-militarist strategy must also find an alternative to the fundamental problem of austerity policy, the contradiction between internal political–economic reorganization and the degree of international interdependence and competition, in order to reduce international confrontation in economic policies. An alternative economic strategy represents the prerequisite for an alternative policy for peace and security, not only in the direct sense of arms conversion as an alternative to the arms economy, but also in a comprehensive sense of an alternative economic model and a strategy to implement it.

The Reagan administration's confrontational global strategy does not only imperil the formulation of concrete compromises in transatlantic relations, as shown by the complex differences over military burden-sharing, economic policy, East–West trade, Middle East policy, policy *vis-à-vis* the Third World etc. Beyond this, more fundamental elements of the consensus are being jeopardized: by using its security guarantee to achieve leverage for its militarization austerity policy, and thereby questioning the compromise which led to the transatlantic consensus on NATO strategy, the United States is provoking confrontation over the character and the reliability of this security guarantee itself.

THE REORGANIZATION OF THE SECURITY GUARANTEE AND SECURITY DEPENDENCY

Differences in security interests between Western Europe and the United States exist as a result of different geostrategic locations and different global–political orientations. However, over a long period, there existed a consensus in NATO that the US security guarantee was to be understood as a strategic–nuclear guarantee. Since the mid-1970s, however, the reorientation of US global strategy and increased pressure on NATO to accentuate war-fighting elements in its military posture, have shaken the foundations of this consensus. The present controversy about the shape of transatlantic relations must be seen as an attempt by the Americans, under changing global and political conditions, to reduce the nuclear risk to American territory. This new emphasis on nuclear war-fighting by the United States is often considered to be a 'decoupling' of the United States from the nuclear risk of a European war between East and West.

This development is not the same as a withdrawal of the security guarantee by the United States, which would not be in its interest – if that were to happen, the security dependence of Western Europe would disappear and with it the American opportunity for influence. So, seen from the US perspective, it is a question of changing the nuclear form of the security guarantee in such a way as to permit Washington to maintain its dominance in security policy, while at the same time minimizing the territorial risks to the United States. Thus, one can speak of a 'one-sided decoupling'. President Reagan's Strategic Defense Initiative (Star Wars) takes this one-sided decoupling to its logical conclusion.

ESCALATION VERSUS WAR-FIGHTING INTERPRETATIONS OF FLEXIBLE RESPONSE

Since the strategy of 'flexible response' was formulated towards the end of the 1950s in the United States and was finally accepted by the Europeans as official NATO strategy in 1967, there have coexisted within NATO two basically irreconcilable interpretations of this strategy: according to one interpretation, flexible response is an escalation strategy, which is primarily orientated to West German security interests; according to the other, it is a war-fighting strategy, which conforms more to the American security interests.

Assuming that any extended, mobile war fought in Central Europe, even a conventional one, would destroy West Germany, the interpretation of flexible response as an *escalation strategy* is aimed at achieving the fastest possible termination of a military engagement once started. The political leaderships of the aggressor must be compelled to cease its aggression before extensive damage is done. This is only possible through an early demonstration of the defender's own determination to climb the nuclear escalation ladder ('selective use of nuclear weapons' in the course of 'deliberate escalation').

This interpretation of flexible response emphasizes the deterrent effect of a politically controlled threat of annihilation – even on the separate rungs of the escalation ladder during war. The preservation of the nuclear first-use option by NATO is vital for this conception. It is also vital to threaten the Soviet Union credibly with the 'full nuclear risk', that is, the willingness of the United States if necessary to use its full-scale nuclear–strategic potential against the Soviet Union in the defence of Western Europe. This is the keystone of the deterrent shield; without it the deterrent effect would be removed at the lower levels of the escalation ladder, since the Soviet Union would be able to calculate its risks and keep them under control. In this understanding only the demonstrative will to escalate to all-out nuclear war would deter smaller, limited wars. Accordingly, in this orthodox way of thinking, the US security guarantee only maintains a continued durability as a strategic–nuclear guarantee.

In contrast, the concept of flexible response as a *war-fighting strategy* involves the capacity to fight a protracted war at lower rungs of the escalation ladder and the development of a diverse range of military options to suit all military situations. An effective conventional war-fighting capacity is essential for this. Moreover, tactical nuclear weapons are to be used on the battlefield to defeat the opposing forces, and not for political purposes (demonstration of the escalation risk). For this reason, however, their function as a link to the strategic nuclear weapons is undermined. The imperative of preventing escalation replaces the will to 'deliberate', and raises the spectre of geographically limited war. Accordingly, instead of terminating a war by emphasizing the preservation of deterrence also during war itself (compelling a political decision), there emerges the concept of terminating a war because of the incapacity of the opponent; the threat of total annihilation is replaced by deterrence through the threat of military defeat.

Flexibility in this interpretation of the strategy means the ability to defeat the opponent on every level it chooses. The contradictory dual function of the American intercontinental strategic nuclear weapons in the escalation strategy (on the one hand to deter an attack on US territory – national function – and on the other to make an attack more probable by integrating these weapons into the escalation ladder of a European battlefield – alliance function) is thus resolved. The more the war-fighting conception is put into practice, the more clearly the United States is avoiding the risk of war in Europe.

CONSENSUS THROUGH AMBIGUITY IN NATO'S MILITARY POSTURE

How were these differing interpretations of NATO strategy – escalation and coupling on the one hand, war-fighting and decoupling on the other –

able to coexist in the Alliance for such a long time? Essential to the explanation is the fact that the NATO posture was not unambiguously organized according to one or other of the interpretations. The consensus was defined *politically*, on questions of both military strategy and armaments.

The masking and temporary suspending of military–strategic differences via political consensus is made simpler by the fact that the connection between concrete arms decisions and military–strategic concepts does not have to be clear-cut. One and the same arms decision can be made and promoted jointly, although it might be linked to controversial military options. In this way, a margin of manoeuvre is won, which can be used to build up a relative consensus on the principle of transatlantic consensus.

The INF weapons called for in the NATO decision from December 1979 are an example of this. From a narrow technical military–strategic perspective it can be shown that – as intended by Helmut Schmidt – NATO's new INF weapons were clearly intended to couple the European battlefield to the US strategic potential by extending the strategic triad to a kind of 'quadrad', adding intermediate range missiles in Europe to the triad of long range bombers, intercontinental ballistic missiles and submarine launched ballistic missiles. This new third step was supposed to close the escalation gap to intercontinental weapons. The use of INF weapons from NATO's European territory is beneath the threshold of the American strategic nuclear systems but nevertheless possesses strategic effect in the Soviet Union because these weapons can hit targets that used to be covered only by intercontinental missiles. This corresponded to the logic of deterrence and war-preventive notions based on the threat of escalation; the territory of a potential aggressor is drawn early into the battle and confronted with the threat of annihilation. But it can also be demonstrated that Helmut Schmidt was mistaken and that the NATO decision constitutes a decoupling. For it also created new war-fighting options enabling the United States, in theory, to stop the vertical escalation and to gain a 'victory' below the level at which this word loses its meaning for the United States as well.

After developing both arguments and considering the technical parameters and the integration in the whole NATO posture, there indeed remain in *both* cases some inexplicable contradictions. The fact that these could be papered over indicates the *political* compromise within the alliance, which permitted both sides to feel their security interests had been taken into account in the case of the INF decision.

THE EROSION OF CONSENSUS

Fifteen years after the strategy of flexible response was officially introduced into NATO, Washington is no longer willing to maintain a NATO posture which permits both interpretations of flexible response, i.e., as an escalation and as a war-fighting strategy. The United States is purposefully putting NATO strategy into practice in terms of the war-fighting interpretation, and thus decoupling further the American strategic nuclear potential from the defence of Europe.

The changes that have occurred in America's global strategy have to be seen as a reaction to the relative weakening in the course of the 1970s of the American capacity to promote its interests globally and to maintain its unchallenged position as the dominant world power. The decoupling of US territory from the risk of nuclear war as reflected in the reformulation of the NATO strategy towards a war-fighting concept and in SDI corresponds to the changed balance of power in two ways: the threat and intervention capabilities are being strengthened to offset the weakening global position, while the risks resulting from the relative weakness and greater danger of confrontation are being limited.

The alliance's previous compromise formula has become a fiction as a result of changed global–strategic conditions. Its basic assumption, a common evaluation of the global situation despite structurally different security interests between Western Europe and the United States, has been undermined. Thus, the specific concept of flexible response formulated and promoted by the United States right from the beginning, because of its different global situation and role, has come to dominate, i.e., the war-fighting interpretation.

However, it is important to point out that there are two quite different ways in which the United States could insulate itself from the risk of nuclear war:

1 The *confrontational* policy of the current Reagan administration, which has initiated the Star Wars project, while building up the conventional and nuclear war-fighting capabilities – especially those pertinent to first use.
2 The more *integrative*, oppositional, no-first-use conception, subdividing NATO strategy into both a conventional war-fighting and a nuclear retaliatory strategy (second-strike capability).

REAGAN'S CONFRONTATIONAL POLICY

At the present time a confrontational brand of global strategy is dominant in Washington. To simplify matters, it will be referred to as 'Reaganism'. In military–strategic terms, the policy could still be presented as a compromise – new doctrines could be interpreted in terms of escalation. However, this is not true for the overall political–strategic conception. The confrontational course with the Soviet Union, that is, the tendency to deny the Soviet Union the right to exist, to restrict its margin of manoeuvre by using threatening rhetoric, condemnations, boycotts and an excessive arms build-up (with the clear goal of gaining a first-strike capability and military superiority), to perceive the North–South conflict in terms of confrontational East–West relations, and to emphasize again the use of military means as a political instrument to be brought to bear in the East–West conflict and the Third World, conflict with West European security assessments and strategies more than the military–strategic aspects of the policy do. Within this global confrontation course, NATO's INF weapons, which constitute a qualitatively new threat to the Soviet Union, acquire significance as a political instrument, and thereby exacerbate conflict and increase the risks of war world wide.

It is primarily the political dimension of current American policy which causes the administration's endeavour to reorganize alliance security relations to produce more dissensus than consensus in NATO. That current policy is not only confrontational *vis-à-vis* the Soviet Union, but also *vis-à-vis* the allies.

In view of the American dominance in NATO, the allies cannot reject this policy totally. However, bringing it into harmony with their understanding of their own security interests is also not without problems. By moving away from the willingness to settle or eliminate conflicts and antagonisms by political means, the dangers – especially for those suffering higher risks – of basing a nuclear security guarantee on the war-fighting deterrent concept have become more evident. The overall political–strategic conception of American security policy progressively undermines the military–strategic elements.

CONVENTIONAL BUILD-UP AND RAISING OF THE NUCLEAR THRESHOLD AS A NEW CONSENSUS?

Paradoxically, it seems to be the risky element in Reagan's policies which provokes a reaction on the part of West German politicians, a reaction which conflicts with their customary interpretation of the deterrence doctrine and security guarantee and which reflects the exposed situation of the West German state. On all sides of the political spectrum, the same alternative has been articulated, the demand for raising the nuclear threshold.

In earlier times, the 'necessity' for strong conventional armed forces was justified on the grounds that a low nuclear threshold would entail an unacceptable nuclear risk to American territory and therefore the United States would be unwilling to keep its nuclear–strategic potential available for the defence of Europe. The deterring/war-preventing escalation chain would then be broken. Today the argument is the other way round and is military rather than political in character. In order to limit the damage, the use of atomic weapons must be delayed as long as possible. The old argument made by the advocates of an escalation strategy that even a conventional war between East and West would leave West Germany in ruins probably has even greater justification today (and is still continuing to be put forward by defenders of a nuclear orientation for NATO strategy).

This turnaround in the arguments used in the West German strategy debate is only comprehensible as a response of politicians who see that (*a*) the risk of war has increased, (*b*) in the event of war a war-fighting concept will be used, and (*c*) atomic weapons would be used in a war-fighting role. In other words, a nuclear guarantee based on escalation and orientated towards a quick political termination of a war no longer exists or has become shaky. If the only choice that remains is between fighting a war using nuclear weapons or fighting without them, it is quite logical to delay the use of nuclear means of destruction as long as possible. For consistency, this concept presupposes the removal of short-range nuclear weapons (especially nuclear artillery), which tend to give an incentive to first use. A conventional arms build-up is also considered necessary to realize this concept.

The concept of raising the nuclear threshold is an inadequate attempt to solve militarily a political problem, namely the growing danger of war evoked by the Reagan administration's overall political–military strategy. Because it is assumed that war prevention is not possible without American nuclear weapons, the West Germans submit themselves out of alliance loyalty to the fundamentals of nuclear strategy as they are predetermined by the United States, and at the same time try to limit the worst outcomes. This policy would maintain the security/dependency of Western Europe, which is attractive to the United States, in the framework of a strictly conventionalized strategy of offensive war-fighting. In particular, it is planned to apply this concept through the new highly accurate, long-range conventional arms and personnel back-up.

The concept of the 'high nuclear threshold' requires a comprehensive change in thinking on the part of West Germany, and it could unwittingly contribute to certain aspects of Reagan policies. These policies also involve greater emphasis on conventionalizing NATO military posture, and on a more mobile and offensively organized war-fighting strategy, which represent a departure from the traditional NATO concept of forward defence which is so important for West German domestic politics.

The problem for the Americans is the instability of the military threat. A strategy which makes a Pyrrhic victory the only likely outcome is not very credible as a political instrument. In order to pursue an offensive and confrontational political option, it is important to minimize the apparent escalation risk, and to make a strict distinction between conventional and nuclear war-fighting strategies in order to show that the military instrument can be used with reasonable cost–benefit and risk calculations. The so-called 'Rogers Plan' and 'AirLand Battle' correspond with this aim. They allow wars, in political terms, to be thinkable, fightable, limitable and thus more probable. The military can thus be used for political objectives.

THE INTEGRATIVE TYPE OF POLITICS: NO-FIRST-USE

The no-first-use proposal gained new importance in the current security debate when four distinguished US experts from the Democratic camp (Bundy, Kennan, McNamara and Smith) seized upon it at the beginning of 1982. They put the no-first-use concept up for discussion as a way of working out the intra-alliance differences about the future orientation of security policy. The four advocates of no-first-use also demand a conventional build-up and a conventionalization of NATO strategy. Atomic weapons are retained, although on a reduced and reorganized scale, and first use is clearly renounced. This concept is very different from the Reagan concept. It is integrative rather than confrontational. Although the proposal is organized around a military core, its logic is primarily political. Consequently, the four authors generally speak about the *politics* of renouncing first use.

The goal is to create the foundation for a stable long-term consensus on transatlantic security relations. It is recognized that a continuation of current American policy will jeopardize the NATO alliance – and thus, essentially, American interests – by giving rise to growing resistance in Europe and by eroding the legitimacy of NATO. The no-first-use policy is presented as a strategy for avoiding 'destructive mutual accusations', and 'the prospect of conflicts among the allies', as well as a contribution to 'cohesion' and 'the inner vitality of the Western Alliance'.

The four authors openly concede the relative weakening of the American position because the credibility of the Atlantic connection, upheld by the threat to engage in strategic nuclear war, no longer exists. The Europeans are politely but unambiguously informed that a security guarantee in terms of war prevention by means of a threat of deliberate, extensive nuclear escalation does not exist, and this situation is not new. Given this condition – and here again the four make no bones about it – any form of nuclear security guarantee which retains the first-use option is only feasible within a strategy of limited nuclear war-fighting. But a security guarantee, reformulated to mean fighting a limited nuclear war, is also not credible as a deterrent strategy. This is because it is unlikely that a nuclear war can be limited and because it threatens the West Europeans with nuclear self-destruction.

Under these conditions, political resistance against NATO and the United States is likely to grow further, say the four authors, both among the general public and within governments. Since the introduction of tactical nuclear weapons in Europe, alliance cohesion has been maintained only by the general ignorance about the hypothetical plans for their use. Under the current conditions (decoupling of strategic weapons, war-fighting concepts, growth and diversification of nuclear weapons arsenals, expanding public debate) this way of maintaining an alliance consensus is rapidly becoming impossible. NATO is politically jeopardized if it does not turn away from the first-use option and with it the nuclear war-fighting strategy. Nuclear war-fighting plans cannot plausibly enhance NATO and the United States, but lead rather, in the long term, to political erosion.

The no-first-use policy with its declaratory renunciation of first use, denuclearization of the NATO posture and massive conventional build-up conflicts with the customary West German military–strategic notions of security even more than President Reagan's conception. Atomic weapons would merely deter an opponent's first use of atomic weapons by using the threat of retaliation on the basis of a survivable second-strike capability, but they would not deter a conventional attack through the threat of escalation. A conventional attack would be solely deterred by conventional forces in terms of an unambiguous conventionalized strategy of victory through war-fighting. This has been developed in the no-first-use concept in pure form by a clear-cut distinction between nuclear and conventional weapons.

The proposal of the four US politicians was repudiated by a coalition of four high-ranking West German experts from the Conservative Party and the right wing of the Social Democratic Party (Kaiser, Leber, Mertes, Schulze): they argued that the application of this concept would allow

Western Europe to be blackmailed by the Soviet Union, who could then calculate the risks of a limited conventional attack.

However, the domestic pressure in Western European countries to reduce the reliance of NATO strategy on nuclear weapons is likely to grow. In the short or long run this will prompt politicians to change their positions. The policy of no-first-use is preparing the way for this eventuality. It offers an alternative conception of the security guarantee still in the hands of the United States – the extensive build-up of the United States' conventional engagement in Europe (financed from savings in the nuclear programmes) and a new definition of the *nuclear* security guarantee as a guarantee of retaliation against the first use of atomic weapons by the Soviet Union. This reformulation of the security guarantee is said to be more credible and less controversial than current policy, and at the same time can maintain the Western European security dependency, minimize the risks for the United States and integrate the NATO alliance.

Moreover, the no-first-use policy contains an additional 'offer' for European politicians. This is related to the political dimension of security policy. The no-first-use policy does not set out a comprehensive blueprint for American global strategy. The integrative model of formulating a political strategy on which the no-first-use policy is based also represents a non-confrontational approach to the East–West conflict. The renunciation of the first-use option alters political relations with the Soviet Union by toning down the Western threat, which currently consists of a nuclear posture optimized for war-fighting and first use. In addition, the no-first-use policy implies a recognition of Soviet security interests, the opening up of arms control and arms reduction efforts (above all in the realm of nuclear weapons), and a stronger emphasis on confidence-building measures.

Hence, the no-first-use proposal also offers an essential starting point for a reformulation of the transatlantic consensus with regard to the East–West conflict. Although it presupposes a changed military–strategic way of thinking by the European allies, above all by West German strategists, it does offer the prospect of continuing detente policy. Thus the no-first-use proposal potentially allows West Germany an expanded margin of manoeuvre *vis-à-vis* the West. This, in turn, touches on political power relations within West Germany and is decisive for the peace movement if it wishes to design an alternative foreign policy.

EXPANDING THE POLITICAL MARGIN OF MANOEUVRE THROUGH DETENTE

From the point of view of the United States, the East–West conflict appeared as a global rivalry between itself and the Soviet Union, with the partitioned Germany representing a geographical focal point. For American foreign policy, therefore, it followed that no regional conflict could be politically autonomous. This perception has shaped the context in which European–American relations have been organized, and especially the way in which conflicts are resolved and compromises are reached. The policy of detente which began in the early 1960s did not fundamentally change this perception. The East–West conflict continued to be viewed as the antagonism between fundamentally different social systems. The agreement on the rules of discourse between both hegemonic powers presupposed the acceptance of the balance of power, their respective interest spheres and mutual non-interference in these spheres and it thus expanded the United States' manoeuvring space in foreign and domestic policy. The idea was to reduce the most immediate confrontational elements of US–Soviet relations rather than to remove the *source* of the conflict. From the American viewpoint, the existence of the Soviet Union threatened the international status quo because of its alleged expansionist tendencies. Thus, the Soviet Union carried the seeds of potentially unbounded violence. However, as a result of the changed military balance of power, it was necessary to establish a new relationship. The principle of linkage, which signified the coupling of American concessions in one region of the globe to Soviet behaviour in another (Kissinger), assumed that all regional conflicts were instigated by Moscow.

American detente policy came into conflict with official West German policy not least because the Americans moved to recognize officially the territorial status quo in Germany which resulted from World War II. However, Bonn's eventual settlement of the border problem and recognition of the territorial status quo marked a fundamental change in West Germany's view of itself, and its role in the Western alliance and at the international level. Bonn overcame the contradiction between its westward orientation and its aim of reuniting both Germanys, and thereby transformed its view of itself as a provisional state and instead saw itself as a member of the Western alliance, possessed of its own unique identity and a claim to equal rights.

The relaxation of tensions on the Central European 'front' created a greater margin of manoeuvre for West Germany *vis-à-vis* the United States, as did increasing West European economic power under West German leadership. Because the so-called revanchist ally of the United States, West Germany, no longer posed a threat to its Eastern neighbours, the threat emanating from the Soviet Union (for example to Berlin) was also reduced.

One difference between American and West German detente policies is the German concern to remove conflicts that are rooted in the German question. The Eastern treaties and subsequent cooperation in political, economic and cultural spheres were embedded in an ideal foreign policy concept, which was supposed to lead to a European Peace Order. This (Social Democrat) concept, carrying the names of Brandt and Bahr, was supposed to reduce the threat to both sides by creating a web of mutual treaties and dependencies. Thus, it was aimed at changing certain structures both in East–West as well as in alliance relations. It was linked to the hope that a reduction of confrontation in East–West relations would help to temper the hostile perceptions on both sides and thereby widen the margin of manoeuvre on both sides for domestic reforms. The concept of a European Peace Order was supposed to reduce security dependence on the United States, and thereby create a greater freedom of action for all West European countries, which, especially in the context of North–South relations, was becoming more and more important. However, the Eastern treaties which were the hallmark of Brandt's Ostpolitik, were not capable, on their own, of calling into question the security dependence on the United States.

The margin of manoeuvre won by West Germany *vis-à-vis* the United States as a result of the reduction of tensions and conflicts in the course of detente policy was not utilized to propel detente policy further towards realizing a European Peace Order. The United States could have restricted Bonn's manoeuvring room in foreign policy, but no attempt was made to expand the space for manoeuvre by making use of broad popular support for detente. Schmidt's government did not advance Brandt's Ostpolitik positively but rather presided over what had been achieved in order to portray West Germany in the West as a 'Central European power'. It became evident that West Germany would not translate economic strength, in the short term, into political influence, but rather flirt with the role of remaining a political dwarf, and make the best of the situation. Thus, West Germany could use its strong position within the European Community to advance its own interests in the European context. At the same time, Bonn's special relationship with the United States enabled it to promote understanding of West European concerns and to urge that West European interests ought to be respected.

Reagan's politics of confrontation have magnified the West German dilemma. On the one hand, West Germany must oppose the United States and its confrontation course – especially in the economic sphere in Europe where Germany is dominant. On the other hand, it is probable that the Reagan administration will be able to transplant at least partially its confrontational policy to West Germany; this is because of the fixation on the war-preventing function of nuclear weapons, which necessarily requires the threat of first use, and because of the absence of a positive debate on the political dimension of the national security policy which is being pursued by President Reagan. By considering the nuclear first-use option (even if it is the 'late-first-use' option advocated by General Rogers) to be *sine qua non* of its national security policy, West Germany restricts its margin of manoeuvre *vis-à-vis* the United States, upon whose decision this option depends.

A change in the premise underlying West German national security policy (the first-use option) would, therefore, be a pre-condition for the continuation and revitalization of detente policy. The no-first-use proposal is offered as an alternative to the current crisis in NATO which is supposed to make possible the integration of differing interests in the Western alliance into a new consensus without challenging the basic structures. Implicitly, the proposal plays down the Western, especially the German, threat analysis and could redefine the meaning of security. A reorganization of West German dependency on the American nuclear security guarantee could potentially expand the West German margin of manoeuvre within the West–West relationship. This would affect policy towards the Eastern bloc as well as the Third World. From the West German point of view, a detente policy means a non-confrontational relationship with the Eastern bloc and the developing countries. Concealed in the no-first-use concept is the fear that Reagan's confrontation course and the growing crisis of consensus with NATO could lead the West European allies to alternative security policies that are not entirely in the American interest. The four authors of the no-first-use proposal obviously impute considerable domestic influence to the West European peace movements (without ever mentioning them by name), which go beyond the immediate threat seen in the deployment of Pershing and cruise missiles and could potentially undermine the legitimation of nuclear weapons and the arms race as such. Although this signifies a rejection of Reagan's confrontational policies, the four do not advocate a policy of disarmament; on the contrary, they link the renunciation of first use of nuclear weapons to a conventional build-up, i.e., a conventionalization of NATO strategy.

CONCLUSION

If one wants to understand the dynamic of transatlantic relations and examine alternative policies for peace, one cannot reduce transatlantic relations to relations between autonomous governments, but rather must interpret them in terms of their dependence on domestic–political conflicts. The domestic–political dimension of foreign policy has up to now been largely ignored and/or mentioned in passing. In conclusion, we would therefore like to put forward a few thoughts on the connection between domestic and foreign policy and on the interpretation of the crisis of transatlantic relations as a starting point for an alternative policy for peace.

We have argued above that the United States' confrontation strategy in the economic, military and political spheres is aimed both at reorganizing international relations and establishing a corresponding model of society: militarization and arms build-up; austerity policy and human misery; confrontation and New Cold War. This social model stands in opposition to that which was implied in the concept of a European Peace Order. The connection between foreign and domestic policy becomes evident in considering West German detente policy at the end of the 1960s, which expanded the domestic and foreign–political margin of manoeuvre for reform, and was only capable of being carried out by mobilizing the population and thus changing the pattern of politics. The mobilization occurred outside parliament and the delicate ratio of representation in the Bundestag was maintained by the motto 'risk more democracy'.

The abrogation of the transatlantic consensus by the United States was followed by the rejection of the transatlantic consensus by the peace movement on the domestic level. In the course of the controversy surrounding the NATO decision of December 1979, fundamental assumptions about the alliance's security policy were questioned. These included the national circumstances under which the security policy is decided, and at the same time the overall social consensus on which economic, security and arms policy is based.

The anti-nuclear protest and the peace movement as a whole have become a political force, mainly within domestic politics. But this domestic debate does have an impact on the way in which individual nations manage the crisis of transatlantic relations. The controversy surrounding the confrontational American global strategy is not only between Western Europe and the United States, but also within these countries. Bringing its hegemonic position to bear in executing its confrontation policy, the United States inevitably had some influence on the consciousness of the European population. The stationing of cruise and Pershing missiles also had a symbolic significance. At the domestic level, the rockets represent a symbol of the dominance of the United States and the willingness of the West German government to accept this, and the United States' resolve to impose its will regardless of the explicit opposition of the majority of the West German population and considerable reservations on the part of established politicians and military people. Deployment of the missiles demonstrates that the crisis of transatlantic relations has a domestic–political impact on the political system which will not end with that deployment.

The peace movement has gained some political influence. That does not mean the peace movement has actually expanded the margin of manoeuvre in foreign policy for West Germany. It has, however, changed the way in which the current arms build-up is legitimized. (SDI, for example, was justified by claiming that we could get rid of nuclear weapons as such.) This is the case in three respects:

1 With the subjects it addresses and the forms by which it articulates itself, the peace movement has been able to attract a surprising amount of attention in the broad population within West Germany and abroad. This is surprising for all concerned, because the peace movement is distinguished by having hardly any organization, by a non-hierarchical heterogeneous mode of operation at many different levels. This is true at least for West Germany.
2 The peace movement has publicized the crisis of transatlantic relations in such an unconventional way that it is being debated not only within the circle of experts but also among the general public. The problems have become comprehensible for large portions of the population and this puts pressure on the established politicians to explain and justify their policies. The explosive nature of transatlantic relations can no longer be hidden; security policy loses its domestic–political powers of integration, because 'foreign policy' is being debated now by the peace movement in loosely organized groups that are difficult for the prevailing powers to control and integrate. These groups of people, who never before considered themselves to be political activists, are now making demands, denouncing current foreign policy and proclaiming the immobility and inhumanity of the political structures in such a way that the established powers (the media, unions, parties, churches, etc.) feel compelled to respond.
3 The peace movement undermines the transatlantic authorities' monopoly in giving interpretations and information on the question of security, and thus their ability to shape political consciousness and action.

It can hardly be denied that the peace movement plays a role in the crisis of transatlantic relations. But what active influence can the peace movement exert in order to ensure that reorganization of transatlantic relations contributes to a new European Peace Order? The capacity to attract attention, to keep up-to-date, to provide analysis and provoke reactions are all prerequisites for this. For the peace movement to be able to play an active and decisive political role, however, changes are necessary in domestic–political structures and categories.

The political system (of West Germany) is like international relations: nothing statistical but rather a dynamic functional relation. The following points are to be emphasized with reference to the current political situation in West Germany.

1 The loss of the Social Democratic Party's capacity for domestic and foreign–political integration, of its governing mandate and its change to the opposition role. This change was caused not only by the world economic crisis and the United States' strategies of austerity and confrontation, but also by the SPD's own political perspective, which expressed itself in terms of a movement away from internal party democracy and a separation from extraparliamentary opposition movements.
2 The appearance of new social movements and alternative parties (especially the Greens) and the peace movement. These movements have become a power to be reckoned with, having formulated a political perspective with content and forms contrary to those of the SPD. They have succeeded in mobilizing and bringing together large sections of the population, thereby overcoming social–structural and ideological boundaries.
3 The disintegration of socially integrative institutions and assumptions that have bound individuals to the political system: the welfare state, growth, full employment, control of nature, orientation to the future and notions of security in which peace seems achievable via the United States' nuclear guarantee, and also the 'faith' that these questions can be solved in the framework of the existing political structures, or that these can be changed in accordance with demands. (There is also a danger of an internal polarization of society and of military solutions to integration.)

How can political forces inside and outside the parties succeed in formulating alternative policies for peace, which not only have points in common with established policy (no-first-use), but also function integratively? First, they must make possible cooperation between the parties (SPD and Greens) and the extraparliamentary movements (especially the peace movement). Secondly, they must address the discontented population which is presently forced into passivity, apathy and submission to authority, but which represents the political basis for demands to democratize the decision-making process in the international area of foreign and peace policy.

The long-term domestic political possibilities for influencing foreign policy depend not only on establishing a more adequate form of security policy but also on making the mechanisms for carrying it out and the chances of shaping it clear to every individual. This is why democratization is so important. It helps to overcome the conflict between, on the one hand, the conservative function of military security policy and, on the other, the need for social transformation. And it ensures that the peace movement remains a political force in the area of foreign policy.

BIBLIOGRAPHY

Altvater, Elmar, 'Die Zeitbombe auf dem Weltmarkt tickt', *Probleme des Klassenkampfs*, 42 (1981), pp. 6–24.

——, Kurt Hubner and Michael Stanger, *Alternative Wirtschaftspolitik jenseits des Keynsianismus* (Opladen, 1983).

Bielfeldt, Carola and Peter Schlotter, *Die militärische Sicherheitspolitik der Bundesrepublik Deutschland-Einführung und Kritik* (Frankfurt, 1980).

Brauch, Hans Günther, Security Options for the 1980s – New perspectives for a policy of detente and arms reduction in Central Europe. In Louis Herrera and Raimo Väyrynen (eds), *Peace, Development, and the New International Economic Order* (Tampere, 1979), pp. 104–121.

Bundy, McGeorge, George F. Kennan, Robert S. McNamara and Gerard Smith, 'Kernwaffen und das Atlantische Bündnis'. *Europa-Archiv*, 7 (1982), pp. 183–98.

Czempiel, Ernst-Otto (ed.), *Amerikanische Aussenpolitik im Wandel – Von der Entspannungspolitik Nixons zur Konfrontation unter Reagan* (Stuttgart, 1982).

——, 'Die Zukunft der Atlantischen Gemeinschaft. Kooperation und Konflikt zwischen den Vereinigten Staaten und Westeuropa in den achtziger Jahren'. *Aus Politik und Zeitgeschichte*, 13 (1983), pp. 10–21.

Falk, Richard, *The End of World Order* (London, 1983).

Frank, Andre Gunder, *Die europäische Herausforderung. Friede und Arbeit durch europäische Entspannung* (Stuttgart, 1983).

Haftendorn, Helga, Lothar Wilker and Claudia Wörmann, *Die Aussenpolitik der Bundesrepublik Deutschland* (Berlin, 1982).

Hanrieder, Wolfram, *Fragmente der Macht. Die Aussenpolitik der Bundesrepublik* (Munich, 1981).

Holthus, Manfred and Diana Winkler, 'EG–USA. Probleme der atlantischen Partnerschaft'. In Hajo Hasenpflug (ed.), *Die EG–Aussenbeziehungen. Stand und Perspektiven* (Hamburg, 1979), pp. 119–61.

Jacobsen, Hanns-Dieter, 'Asymmetrien und Interdependenzen in den transatlantischen Wirtschaftsbeziehungen'. (Ebenhausen, Stiftung Wissenschaft und Politik, 1981), p. 287.

Kaiser, Karl, Georg Leber, Alois Mertes and Franz-Joseph Schulze, 'Kernwaffen und die Erhaltung des Friedens. Stellungnahme zu einem amerikanischen Vorschlag über den Verzicht auf Ersteinsatz von Kernwaffen'. *Europa-Archiv* 12/1982, pp. 357–68.

——, Winston Lord, Thierry de Montbrial and David Watts, *Die Sicherheit des Westens – Neue Dimensione und Aufgaben* (Bonn, 1981).

Kaldor, Mary, *The Disintegrating West* (London, 1978).

——, *Rüstungsbarock. Das Arsenal der Zerstörung und das Ende der militärischen Techno-Logik* (West Berlin, 1981).

Kissinger, Henry A, 'The future of NATO'. In Kenneth A. Myers (ed.), *NATO – The Next Thirty Years. The Changing Political, Economic, and Military Setting* (Boulder, Col./London, 1980), pp. 3–20.

Krell, Gert and Hans-Joachim Schmidt, *Der Rüstungswettlauf in Europa. Mittelstrecken-systeme, konventionelle Waffen, Rüstungskontrolle* (Frankfurt/New York, 1982).

Kuper, Ernst, 'Der Wandel der westdeutschen Entspannungskonzeption während der sozialliberalen Koalition'. In Helga Haftendor et al. (eds), *In Verwaltete Aussenpolitik Sicherheits – und entspannungspolitische Entscheidungsprozesse in Bonn* (Cologne, 1978), pp. 241–62.

Lubkemeier, Eckhard, *Probleme, Voraussetzungen und Chancen einer Konventionalisierung einer NATO–Strategie* (Bonn: Forschungsinstitut der Friedrich–Ebert–Stiftung, 18 February 1982).

Lucas, Michael, 'Die Vereinigten Staaten von Amerika und die Krise des Kalten–Kriegs–Systems'. *Probleme des Klassenkampfs* 48 (1982), pp. 119–55.

McNamara, Robert S, 'The military role of nuclear weapons – perceptions and misperception'. *Foreign Affairs* (Fall 1983), pp. 59–80.

Noelke, Michael, Robert Taylor and Wolfgang Hager, *Protektionismus in der Europäischen Gemeinschaft und im Welthandel*, Band 2. *Handels – und industriepolitische Strategien in und ausserhalb der EG* (Brussels, 1982).

Mechtersheimer, Alfred, *Rüstung und Frieden. Der Widersinn der Sicherheitspolitik* (Munich, 1982).

Mutz, Reinhard, 'Das Sicherheitsproblem der Bundesrepublik und die Bundesrepublik als Sicherheitsproblem'. In Wolf-Dieter Eberwein and Catherine M. Kelleher (eds), *Sicherheit – um welchen Preis?* (Munich/Vienna, 1983), pp. 75–102.

Paris, Rainer, 'Soziale Bewegung und Offentlichkeit'. *Probleme des Klassenkampfs*, 43 (1980), pp. 103–28.

Rattinger, Hans, 'Strategieinterpretationen und Rüstungskontrollrezepte. Anmerkungen zum NATO–Doppelbeschluss'. *Aus Politik und Zeitgeschichte*, 28 (1981), pp. 21–37.

Stratmann, K. Peter, *NATO–Strategie in der Krise? Militärische Optionen von NATO und Warschauer Pakt in Mitteleuropa* (Baden–Baden, 1981).

Scheffler, Thomas, 'Aussenpolitik und Hegemonie in der Bundesrepublik Deutschland'. In *Sozialliberalismus oder rechter Populismus? Hegemonie und Politik in der Bundesrepublik Deutschland*, Argument–Sonderband 51 (West Berlin, 1980), pp. 31–44.

Sklar, Holly (ed.) *Trilateralism. The Trilaterial Commission and Elite Planning for World Management* (Boston, Mass., 1980).

Schwarz, Klaus-Dieter, 'Amerikanische Militärstrategie 1945–1978. Eine Analyse zum aussen– und innenpolitischen Problem strategischer Politik'. In *Sicherheitspolitik. Analysen zur politischen und militärischen Sicherheit*, 3. Aufl. (Bad Honnef-Erpel 1978), pp. 345–72.

Union of Concerned Scientists, *No First Use* (Cambridge, Mass., Union of Concerned Scientists, 29 December 1982).

Wellmann, Christian, 'Konventionalisierung der NATO–Strategie – weder neu noch ein Grund zur Beruhigung'. *Antimilitarismus Information*, 7 (1983), pp. Y-65 – Y-78.

Ziebura, Gilbert, 'Die Krise des transatlantischen Systems und die Zukunft der deutsch-amerikanischen Beziehungen'. *Weltpolitik* (Jahrbuch für Internationale Beziehungen) Band 2 (Frankfurt/New York, 1982), pp. 15–42.

7

The Atlantic Technology Culture

MARY KALDOR

Atlanticism can be described as a culture. It combines a philosophy, a view of the world, with a set of international arrangements and domestic styles and politics, entrenched in a set of social, economic and military institutions. Atlanticist philosophy derives from a bipolar model of the world, characterized by a permanent confrontation between Western democratic and Eastern totalitarian systems. Within this model, the West's cohesion and stability is thought to reside in economic and military strength which in turn derives from supposedly superior technological dynamism.

The concept of 'dealignment' is based on an alternative world view. Dealignment means withdrawing from the culture of Atlanticism as much as from its formal structures. One aspect of Atlanticist culture is the faith in 'high' technology, especially military technology. This chapter will explore the role of 'high' technology in the Atlantic relationship and put forward the argument that 'dealignment' must entail an alternative approach to technology. The argument, which is an ambitious one, is set out somewhat schematically.

STATE STRUCTURES, ECONOMIC DEVELOPMENT AND TECHNOLOGY

I shall start by detailing a set of propositions about the relationship of state structures to stages in economic development, within which it is possible to situate an analysis of 'high' technology.

There has been a good deal of recent interest in the idea of long waves in economic history. The existence of fifty-year-long waves in economic history was first identified by the Soviet economist Kondratiev in the 1920s.[1] Whether or not one can be precise about long waves, I believe the concept is useful, especially when combined with Schumpeter's notion of bunching of families in technology.[2] The idea of long waves associated with certain technologies or industries is somewhat akin to theories about stages of economic development.[3] There is now a considerable literature on long waves with a number of different types of explanation.[4] In what follows, I shall summarize what seems to me to be the most convincing description of the phenomenon.

It has often been observed that technologies follow an S-shaped trajectory – increasing returns in the early phases as technologies become established, diminishing returns in the later phases as it becomes harder to improve the technology.[5] This idea of a technological trajectory can be applied to whole families of interrelated technologies. These families have been variously described as a 'technology regime' or 'culture', a 'technological style' or 'paradigm' or 'pattern'. I shall use the term 'technological paradigm'. A technological paradigm has been described as 'a kind of "ideal type" of productive organization or best technological "common sense" which develops as a response to what are perceived as the stable dynamics of the relative cost structure for a given period of capitalist development'.

> As long as the expected pattern of evolution of the relative costs of various types of material inputs, various types of equipment and different segments of labour skills follow the expected trends, managers and engineers will apply what becomes the 'technological common sense' to make incremental improvements along the natural trajectories of the technologies in place, or radical technological changes in those branches or production of goods or services which have not yet achieved the 'ideal type' of organization.[6]

The technological paradigm is linked with particular families of products, geographical concentration of investment, forms of transportation, particular skill mixes, patterns of consumption and so on. Perez, in particular, identifies a key factor of production as the core of a technological paradigm. For the first Kondratiev this was cheap and abundant labour associated with the introduction of the factory system; for the second, it was low cost and steam transportation; for the third, it was low-cost steel; for the fourth, it was abundant oil and low-cost energy; and for the fifth, it is the micro-chip.

Technological paradigms extend from peak to peak. The stagnation and depression phases can be treated as competition between the old and new paradigms. The old paradigm has, during the previous boom phase, begun to reach the limits of its potentiality. Profit rates in the dominant industries fall, labour is shed, prices may rise because of the slow growth of productivity. The new industries exhibit higher profit rates and perhaps falling prices due to rapid productivity increases, but their growth is constrained by the continued existence of the older industries. The predominance of the old paradigm is reflected in material and social structures; the location of factories and markets, consumer tastes, education, patterns of finance etc. have not adjusted to the new paradigm.

In the recovery and boom phase, the new paradigm establishes its predominant role and rapid diffusion of the new industries can take place. 'A particular form of growth stabilises; a particular way of life takes shape for the different segments of the population; a set of international investment production and trade patterns evolves; . . . the trajectories of a large cluster of technologies become "common sense" and seem to belong to the "nature of things" . . .'.[7] But as technological possibilities are explored, as the technological experience is transformed into factories, hardware and expensive machinery, and as markets become saturated, growth may begin to slow down and profitability decline, providing the opportunity for the emergence of a new paradigm, thus provoking a new crisis and a new phase of structural dislocation.

In this process, the state or perhaps, more accurately, a set of global and domestic institutions, play an essential role. The state is the guarantor of the social and material framework within which technological change takes place. The capitalist state guarantees the free movement of resources within a set of social and material parameters. Through its purchasing policies, tax systems, education priorities etc. the state establishes what might be described as a partiality for a particular paradigm.

Since the capitalist economy is a global economy, moreover, one particular state tends to take on the role of a global state guaranteeing the world-wide diffusion of a particular technological paradigm on a global scale. It is interesting that paralleling the literature on long waves is a literature on war cycles and on cycles of world order.[8] The world order cycles tend to fit the dating on long waves. Hopkins and Wallerstein, in particular, identify hundred year cycles for world order systems, each of which approximates two Kondratiev long waves. Their dating for the past 200 years is shown in figure 7.1.

Kurth has noted the way in which different industrial phases have been characterized by different state forms. He argues, for example, that there is an 'elective affinity' between the development of the textile industry and the liberal state, whereas the later iron and steel industries seem to have been associated with more authoritarian styles of politics.[9] In other words,

	Britain	United States
Ascending hegemony	1798–1815	1897–1913/20
Hegemonic victory	1815–1850	1913/20–1945
Hegemonic maturity	1850–1873	1945–1967
Declining hegemony	1873–1897	1967–?

FIGURE 7.1 World Order Cycles

Source: T. K. Hopkins and I. Wallerstein, *Processes of the World System* (Beverly Hills, Ca: Sage, 1980).

a partiality for a particular paradigm is institutionalized in the structure or organization of the state.

This should not be treated, however, as a deterministic argument. There may be any number of different state forms capable of nurturing particular technological paradigms. Rather, it is an argument about parallel developments in the political and economic spheres and how they interact.

The distinction between the state and the economy, the political and economic spheres of society, is a modern one. It emerged with the development of capitalism and is generally explained, at least in Marxist literature, in terms of the emergence of the labour contract, the notion of the 'free' labourer who can sell his labour power. Under capitalism, physical or moral force no longer plays a direct role in the acquisition of means of production – land or labour – and these activities therefore become institutionally and analytically separate. One way of distinguishing between political and economic spheres is empirical: a classification of outputs. The state produces political activities – legal machinery, military preparedness etc. The economy produces material goods. But in an era where state outputs extend into every social activity, it is perhaps more appropriate to develop an analytical distinction. Such a distinction could be based on mechanisms of adjustment; characteristic ways in which outputs and inputs are reconciled and how the direction of evolution is determined.

For the capitalist economy, the market, both for labour and for goods, is the mechanism for reconciling inputs and outputs and profit is a signal determining directions of change. The profit rate is a kind of arbiter of technological change, judging the competition between old and new paradigms. States do not adjust so easily. Mechanisms of adjustment tend to range from various democratic processes – elections or the voting process – which tend to be slow and cumbersome, to more extreme forms of political upheaval – revolution or war – which can provoke abrupt change. It is the different pace of political and economic evolution that can explain the different phases of economic cycles. Hence, stagnation and depression phases could be described as phases when state structures are inappropriate for new technological paradigms. A partiality for the older paradigm, on a domestic or international scale, may fetter the development of a new paradigm. In the recovery and boom phases, to put it simplistically, state and economy are working in harmony. Changes in the domestic and international structure of the state system are brought about, perhaps brutally through political crisis or war, and may eventually re-establish a harmonious relationship with the private economy.

It is in this context that it is possible to put forward an argument about the role of the Atlantic relationship in the post-war political economy. World War II (which is often treated as a continuation of World War I) finally destroyed the hegemony of the European empires and established the global role of the United States (and the Soviet Union). The American state had clearly shown a partiality for the technological paradigm of the fourth Kondratiev, based on mass consumer markets, mass production and Fordism, roads, airfields, automobiles and, above all, cheap oil. The Cold War, the military alliance system, the network of global inter-state connections, the various American-dominated economic institutions provided the framework for the diffusion of this technological paradigm, and provided the basis for the global boom of the 1950s and 1960s. It should be stressed that this was by no means the only framework that was possible. The Warsaw Pact and COMECON, also, to some extent, provided a framework for the diffusion of the technological paradigm, although, of course, this kind of long wave analysis is not appropriate for centrally planned economies where patterns of innovation and mechanisms of adjustment are so different.

The Atlanticist framework had the specific characteristic that it gave the United States an inbuilt competitive advantage. This can be illustrated with respect to many different aspects of Atlanticism. One important example is the role played by the military alliance and by high levels of military spending. Because the application of the technological paradigm of the fourth Kondratiev to military purposes had proceeded furthest in the United States, any global increase in military spending was bound to benefit the American economy. This would explain, for example, the important role of military Keynesianism in recent years, and why it can help to re-establish the dominant economic position of the United States.

The same framework which suited so well the technologies of the fourth Kondratiev, it can be argued, now provides a fetter on the emergence of a new technology paradigm, based on the spread of electronic technologies and geographically centred on Japan and Western Europe. The constraints imposed by present state partialities can be observed in many different aspects of society: the continued priority given to roads and airfields for transportation; to oil and nuclear energy which are no longer cheap rather than energy conservation and renewable energy sources which could be greatly facilitated through improved data processing; to military and private consumer markets rather than new collective health and environmental demands which could also be facilitated by the new technologies; it can also be seen in patterns of education, in trades union structures etc.

The Atlantic alliance entrenched institutional and elite interests that favoured the technological paradigm of the fourth Kondratiev, in both the United States and Western Europe. Nevertheless, there was, in Europe, partly as a legacy of World War II, to a greater degree than in the United States, space for alternative interests. Most important, perhaps, was the European commitment to the welfare state. In present strained circumstances, one can identify two ongoing conflicts: one between American and European elites for shares of the declining markets for the technologies and thinking of the fourth Kondratiev, and one within European society between the Atlanticist elites and those who favour alternative thinking about state priorities which could amount to a partiality for the new technological paradigm, within a more progressive political framework.

In what follows, I shall elaborate this argument with respect to 'high' technology.

THE ROLE OF 'HIGH' TECHNOLOGY

When we talk about 'high' technology we mean technology embodied in equipment that is complex, sophisticated, 'clever', based on the most advanced techniques available, generally involving large teams of designers, engineers and scientists. The main examples of 'high' technology are military technology, civil nuclear technology and civilian aerospace. 'High' technology could be described as a hybrid, determined simultaneously by the prevailing partialities of the state and the prevailing technological paradigm of the economy. By and large, 'high' technology is produced in the private economic sector and purchased by the state. Of course, this is not strictly true in the case of civilian technologies. Airline companies, electric utilities or communications enterprises that purchase aerospace and nuclear technologies may or may not be in the public sector and these differences do affect the role of these technologies – nevertheless, they do share many of the characteristics of military technologies. We can start by considering the role of military technology.

In the military sector, the main mechanism for adjustment is war. The 'ideal' type of military organization that prevails in any given period can be described as the military paradigm. This extreme competitiveness of war, a life and death struggle in fact, what Clausewitz describes as the tendency for Absolute War,[10] necessitates the use of the most efficient techniques available and the adaption of military doctrine and organization to those techniques. Failure to adapt may lead to defeat. In between wars, the military sector tends to be characterized by inertia. Military missions and military units associated with those missions appear to be remarkably resistant to change. This can be explained at a number of levels. Victorious states have an interest in preserving the memory of their victories, which may well be symbolized in particular military roles. Notions of military utility are necessarily drawn from military experience; it is difficult to change those notions without some new experience. And finally, vested interests in institutional survival develop in the absence of external stimuli. The old adage that 'generals always like fighting the last war' is, in fact, based on ideological and institutional realities.

Cycles of military technology can thus be analysed as a mismatch between military paradigms discontinuously established in war and technological paradigms perpetually adjusted by profit. How this has occurred in practice over the past 100 years is shown in fig. 7.2. In the last quarter of the nineteenth century, a number of successful engineering, shipbuilding and steel companies offered radical improvements in military technology based on developments in civilian technology, the paradigm of the third Kondratiev – what we might describe as 'spin-in'. Prevailing military doctrine and organization had been largely shaped in the Napoleonic wars, at least in Britain, which at that time was the hegemonic global power. British military doctrine and organization strongly influenced military doctrine and organization in other countries. Naval power was viewed as the base of British imperial power and British naval hegemony derived, above all, from the naval victory at Trafalgar. Battleships were a symbol of British imperialism. 'On them as we conceived' wrote Churchill 'floated the might, majesty, dominion and power of the British Empire'.[11]

What, in effect, happened was that the navy adopted some of the new technologies but forced them into a mould shaped by longstanding navy traditions. The military technology of the Anglo-German naval arms race could thus be described as the technological paradigm of the third Kondratiev incorporated into the military paradigm of Trafalgar. As the private companies became increasingly dependent on military orders, they competed to offer technological improvements that would secure new contracts and so developed an autonomous pressure for continued naval spending, which was particularly important in times of civilian recession. Indeed, it can be argued that a kind of naval Keynesianism played a role in upholding the partialities of the British state and the dominant British role within the international system in much the same way as military Keynesianism does for the American state today.[12]

But, by the same token, it can be argued that those same partialities inhibited the diffusion of the new technologies of the fourth Kondratiev. Except in war, there is no measure of saturation of military technologies. In the private economy, the saturation of older technologies is expressed in falling profit rates, thereby providing space for the new technologies. The dominance of the naval sector closed off some of that space, helping companies that would otherwise have gone bankrupt or shifted to new technologies. Although the concentration of military effort yielded new inventions – like automobiles that were originally manufactured in Britain and Germany as Army staff cars – the integration and diffusion of these inventions was resisted. Indeed, there is some evidence that growing expenditure on naval technology was linked to the relative stagnation of the British economy after 1870.[13] The army was never able to incorporate or assimilate the technologies of the third Kondratiev. John Ellis vividly describes World War I as a tragic conflict between the military paradigm of the late eighteenth century and the technological paradigm of the late nineteenth century.[14]

World War II established a new military paradigm which matched the technological paradigm of the fourth Kondratiev. Mass production, the internal combustion engine and oil brought about the American and Soviet victories. Air power in particular, both aircraft and missiles, came to represent for the American state what naval power had represented for Britain in the nineteenth century. Aircraft companies of the 1930s became the prime aerospace contractors of the postwar period, establishing an autonomous momentum for the arms race. And to some extent this happened with automobile companies too, or more specifically those divisions responsible for the manufacture of tanks. In the 1950s and 1960s high military spending facilitated the diffusion of the prevailing technological paradigm and, indeed, could be described as a particular

Dates	*Stage*	*Dominant Civil Technology*	*Key Factor*	*Military Technology*	*Comment*
1874–1893	Stagnation Depression	Heavy engineering Railway construction	Low-cost steel	Development of guns, and troop transportation, especially railways and warships. Invention of Maxim machine gun challenging prevailing military organization and doctrine.	Growth of inter-imperial rivalry. 'Spin-in' from engineering, shipbuilding and steel industries.
1894–1914	Recovery, Boom	,,	,,	Anglo-German naval arms race.	'Spin-off' as arms companies develop motor cars and electricity technology but do not apply it.
1914–1939	Stagnation Depression	Electricity, Automobiles	Oil, cheap energy	Early development of tanks and aircraft challenging prevailing military organization and doctrine.	World War I and economic nationalism. 'Spin-in' from aircraft and automobile companies.
1940–1966	Recovery, Boom	,,	,,	US–Soviet arms race based on aerospace and automobile technology	'Spin-off' as arms companies develop electronics, tele-communications etc, and new materials.
1967–	Stagnation	Electronics	Micro-chip	Development of PGMs, challenging prevailing military organization and doctrine.	Increased international tension. 'Spin-in' from electronics industry.

FIGURE 7.2 Long Waves and Military Technology

feature of the fourth Kondratiev. Although cycles of military technology may be relevant for all Kondratievs, it is the case that military spending was absolutely and relatively much higher than in previous periods. Even at the height of the Anglo-German naval arms race, military spending was only about 3.5 per cent of GNP for Britain and Germany. In the postwar period, military spending has amounted to around 6 or 7 per cent of the American GNP (and is much higher for the Soviet Union). Military and consumer demand is considered to be a characteristic of the fourth Kondratiev, just as the demand for capital equipment was characteristic of the second and third Kondratievs.

Just as in the nineteenth century, the concentration of scientific and technological effort in the military sphere yielded 'spin-offs' – the transistor and the integrated circuit – which contributed to the technologies of the fifth Kondratiev. New military electronic technologies were demonstrated in Vietnam and the Middle East but they were incorporated by the military only within the framework of the prevailing military–technological paradigm – crammed into ever more complex and sophisticated aircraft, tanks or long-range missiles. The debate about whether 'smart' weapons, i.e. precision-guided munitions (PGMs), imply more decentralized and dispersed military organization and more numerous, small and cheap platforms or whether they implied bigger, more expensive and more complex weapon platforms with greater protection and countermeasures etc,. seems to have been determined by the institutional structure of the military sector. The 'emerging technology' or ET espoused by General Rogers or the Star Wars plan of President Reagan could be analysed as theoretical (for they have yet to be shown to work) compromises between the military paradigm of the 1940s and 1950s and the new technological paradigm of the 1980s.

NATO'S TECHNOLOGICAL CRISIS

NATO provided a framework for the geographical diffusion of the military – technological paradigm. The NATO treaty contained no automatic and specific obligation to use armed force as a means of giving aid in the event of attack. Instead, an elaborate system of integrated commands was established. Although West European countries retained national commands, the bulk of their armed forces was assigned to NATO and placed under the command of an American, in the form of the Supreme Allied Commander Europe (SACEUR). Theoretically, the command system comes into effect only in crisis, but in practice it necessarily means that strategic conceptions and military missions are determined collectively within NATO headquarters and that NATO has to involve common infrastructure as well as peace time cooperation in training and practice. This, in turn, profoundly affects the choice of military technology. As Keith Hartley puts it, NATO's 'membership "fee" consists of a direct contribution to financing NATO's common infrastructure (airfields, communications, radar warning, pipelines) plus other costs in the form of a collective defence obligation with its general commitments and constraints on the level and composition of defence expenditure'.[15] In other words, NATO established a collective military paradigm for all of Western Europe, shaped by the conceptions of its most dominant partner, the United States.

By and large this military paradigm drew heavily on the World War II experience. The scenario of a Soviet blitzkrieg across the North German plains and West European dependence on American reinforcements and American technology, especially aircraft and missiles equipped with nuclear weapons, the US strategic nuclear forces, served as a confirmation of the results of World War II. And the scenario was built into the organizational structure of the NATO armed forces; NATO strategy based on this general scenario was effected through a series of military missions and roles which in turn were associated with particular military units and their interrelationships. The continued emphasis on armour, deep interdiction, or sea-based air power can be best explained in terms of the military partialities established during World War II.

Among European NATO members, only the British defence industry survived World War II. Elsewhere, armed forces were dependent on imports from the United States in the immediate postwar period and arms industries were gradually rebuilt, largely with American help. It was not merely that European arms production tended to be based on various forms of transfers of American technology, especially licensed production. Even where an indigenous design capability was developed, as was the case in France and Britain and for certain categories of equipment in other West European countries, these indigenous efforts had to fit, nevertheless, the conceptions of military utility contained in the Atlantic military paradigm. Hence, membership of NATO also meant a shared military – technological style.

This military–technological style is characterized by rapidly increasing costs. The military technology of the postwar period is typical of technologies that are approaching the end of their trajectories. It becomes harder and harder to improve on a given set of performance characteristics (speed, payload, range, protection etc.) defined by the military paradigm. Precisely because there is no test of military utility, there is no mechanism for determining at which point further improvements are no longer worth while, that is to say, at which point military technology is saturated. Hence military technology has become elaborate, sophisticated and extremely expensive, despite diminishing improvements to a given set of performance criteria. The British Ministry of Defence estimates that the cost of individual weapon systems increases at 6 per cent a year. For military aircraft the increase is even higher.[16] One well-known American estimate suggests that if present trends continue, the US Air Force will only be able to afford one plane in the year 2020.[17]

The increase in costs reflects an increase in the resources, the physical capacity, required to develop and produce individual weapons systems, individual examples of military technology. Even in the United States the military budget is not growing fast enough to ensure full employment of military industrial capacity. In Europe various schemes have been adopted to slow the growth of industrial capacity and to supplement military budgets. In the 1950s and 1960s there was a spate of defence industry mergers with the result that no European country any longer has more than one or two aerospace companies. During the 1970s European arms producers greatly increased their exports to the Third World. European countries export between 20 and 30 per cent of military output, and, in some cases, the proportion of exports is much higher. Dassault–Breguet, the French aerospace company, exports over 75 per cent of its output. The share of exports is much higher in Western Europe than for the United States and the Soviet Union.

But domestic concentration and exports have not proved sufficient. During the 1960s and 1970s most European countries participated in major collaborative projects jointly to develop and produce weapons systems so as to spread the costs and increase the size of the market. With the exception of Britain and France, collaborative projects now account for the major portion of European procurement budgets. But these projects merely seem to accelerate the growth of unit costs. This is partly because of duplication and waste, partly because each country insists on incorporating its own national requirement, which generally corresponds to a national manufacturing capability, and partly because work shares are distributed according to the political and financial bargaining position of the partner governments and not according to efficiency. The classic example is Tornado, the Multi Role Combat Aircraft (MRCA), developed and produced jointly by Britain, West Germany and Italy. Tornado at its peak accounted for 40 per cent of the RAF procurement budget. Its cost to Britain alone was greater than *all* the Spitfires developed and produced before and during World War II.

Now European countries are planning a follow-on to Tornado. It is known as the European Fighter Aircraft (EFA), with Britain, West

Germany, Italy and Spain all participating. Disagreements about the specifications of the plane led the French to withdraw from the programme; even so, the plane's weight is still a subject of controversy and the schedule has slipped. At present, and early estimates are always far too low, the programme is expected to cost at least 15 billion pounds. To rationalize this and other collaborative projects, such as the Italian–British helicopter or the French–British–West German family of anti-tank missiles, many in Western Europe are pressing for the creation of a West European arms procurement agency.

On and off, political leaders have been pressing for greater European arms cooperation for the entire postwar period. Since the mid-1970s, however, these calls have become increasingly insistent. Lord Carrington, for example, now Secretary General of NATO, has argued:

> . . . we have developed a new political consciousness in Europe, through the mechanisms of political cooperation. We now need to build, equally cautiously, but equally purposefully, a European security consciousness too. Not as an alternative to the Atlantic Alliance, but as a complement to it.[18]

There are various institutions within which cooperation for military technology takes place and which could be extended.[19] Within NATO the Eurogroup was founded in 1969 and, in 1970, the European Defence Improvement Programme was established to coordinate the European contribution to NATO, especially NATO infrastructure. EDIP now has seven sub-groups. France is not a member of EDIP and has been pressing for revitalization of the Western European Union (WEU). The WEU was formed after the failure of the project for a European Defence Community in 1954. Its main purpose, at that time, was to provide a framework within which West Germany could be rearmed. The WEU Treaty has a much stronger mutual defence commitment than NATO; parties to the Treaty are committed to use force in the event of an armed attack. As part of the process of revitalizing the Western European Union, many of the restrictions on West German arms production have been lifted, and France has reactivated the Franco-German defence commission, established under the 1963 Treaty of Friendship.

A third framework for arms cooperation is the European Economic Community, which includes neutral Ireland but not NATO member Norway. A series of resolutions and reports in the European Parliament have recently advocated greater arms cooperation as an essential element of a common industrial policy. The most important of these are the Klepsch Reports of 1978 and 1984, and the Fergusson Report of 1983.[20]

Yet another institution is the Independent European Programme

Group, formed in 1976 at the active instigation of the United States. The group includes European NATO members and France. IEPG seems to be the group most favoured by Britain. In May 1984, Michael Heseltine, the then British Minister of Defence, proposed through IEPG simultaneous adoption by Europe of ten new projects which included transatlantic collaborative projects as well as purely European ones. He also proposed that there should be IEPG meetings at ministerial level. The list of ten projects was viewed as Western Europe's collective response to SACEUR General Rogers' proposal for ET, which would be primarily based on American technology.

Finally, a new form of technological collaboration is the Eureka programme. Eureka was initially proposed by France's President Mitterand as Europe's answer to Star Wars. Originally, the French wanted cooperation on the kind of technologies demanded by President Reagan's Strategic Defense Initiative – super fast computers, lasers, etc. – so as to reduce the temptation for European companies to participate in Star Wars and to raise the level of Europe's technological efforts. Other European countries insisted that Eureka be purely civil, and now the programme includes neutral countries such as Sweden, Finland and Austria as well as projects that have to do with environmental protection or health care.

Alongside these European proposals have gone proposals for greater transatlantic collaboration in military technology. The American proposals for a Two Way Street, expanding the arms trade between Western Europe and the United States, and for a 'transatlantic partnership', as proposed in the 1983 Currie Report, are widely regarded in Europe as ways of increasing the market for American-produced military equipment. More recently, collaboration is thought to be increased through European participation in the Strategic Defense Initiative. A major current debate is whether the benefits to the United States from control over the direction and end-use of European Star Wars technology outweighs the so far limited financial and employment advantages obtained by Western Europe.

The difference between these various institutional frameworks is a difference in the terms under which Western Europe and the United States compete in the market for military technology *within the prevailing military–technological paradigm*. The NATO groupings, Eurogroup, EDIP, the Two-Way Street or the transatlantic partnership and the SDI programme, tend to favour the American arms industry. The EEC, Eureka and WEU proposals tend to be more protectionist, hence improving the competitive position of Western Europe. IEPG seems to be somewhere in between.

But institutional changes in favour of European military technology can never improve Western Europe's overall long-term competitive position. This is because the military–technological paradigm derives from a world view and a set of institutions within which the American state is predominant. The conceptions of what constitutes advanced military technology are drawn from an imaginary war which the United States has already won. By setting up institutions to encourage the development of European military technology, West Europeans are expressing a belief in the utility of current styles of military technology, a belief which upholds US global power. Moreover, precisely because of the partialities of the American state, such institutions are unlikely to be capable of seriously challenging the inbuilt US competitive advantage. On the contrary, they serve to expand a market in which the United States has a comparative advantage and this fact can explain why the US government does not oppose, indeed seems to favour, these European initiatives. They are, as it were, creating a Europe in America's technological image.

There is, moreover, an even more fundamental problem. If indeed the military–technological paradigm is one aspect of a set of state partialities that inhibit the diffusion of new technological paradigms, then such European initiatives could close off new possibilities for economic development in Europe. There is growing evidence to suggest that high spending on military research and development has contributed to slow productivity growth and declining industrial competitiveness in both the United States and Britain.[21] A major reason for this is the style of military technology – the emphasis on cost and complexity, the partiality for aerospace, automobiles and intensive energy use. An increase in expenditure on military technology within the Atlantic region as a whole is a way of re-establishing the American competitive position at the expense of overall economic well-being. Hence such an emphasis is likely to foster inward-looking protectionist tendencies in Western Europe, fettering the emergence of alternative technological paradigms that could be of global benefit.

CIVILIAN NUCLEAR AND SPACE TECHNOLOGY

A parallel story could perhaps be told about current developments in nuclear and space technologies. Both these technologies are closely related to military technology and were fostered because of the beliefs about what constituted 'advanced' technology generated by the arms race. In the case of nuclear energy, there has been growing collaboration among West European countries during the 1970s. In particular, the French Super Phoenix Fast Breeder and the La Hague and Windscale (Sellafield) reprocessing facilities involve European participation. Because of the general recession in the civil nuclear industry, there is pressure for increased collaboration and exports. Differential attitudes towards the non-proliferation regime can also be explained as ways of changing the terms on which the United States and Western Europe compete within the nuclear technology market. The United States has always favoured a much stricter non-proliferation regime than have the West Europeans. This could in part be explained in strategic terms – the American concern to maintain the United States' dominant position in the production of nuclear weapons. The argument of Third World countries, sometimes echoed in Western Europe, that the non-proliferation regime is discriminatory only makes sense in the context of a belief about the utility of nuclear technology which itself derives from the predominant American influence over technological conceptions. The American insistence on the non-proliferation regime might also be explained in commercial terms. Since the United States has few dual-purpose reactors, a strict non-proliferation regime would be more likely to favour the light water reactor, which produces very little plutonium in which the United States has a competitive advantage. Alternatively, it could be argued that because US civil reactors are not dual-purpose, the US civil industry is weaker relative to the European industry in times of recession and therefore pressures for a weakening on non-proliferation controls are less great.[22]

In the case of space technology, European cooperation through the European Space Agency (ESA), which was established in 1975 to replace the European Space Research Organization (ESRO), has greatly increased in recent years. Although there has been considerable participation in NASA projects, especially the American Space Shuttle, in recent years the Europeans have developed their own independent projects.[23] One of the most important of these is Ariane, Europe's own launch capability for the commercial launch of satellites. Other projects include the Giotto science satellite which intercepted Halley's Comet in 1986. Currently, there is some controversy between West Germany and France about whether to focus on a European contribution to the American Space Lab programme or whether to develop Europe's own space station with its own space tug – a short of shuttle – known as Hermes. The French see this project as part of the general technological competition with the United States.

Nuclear technology and space technology differ from military technology in that the partialities of the United States are less rigidly entrenched. In the case of civilian nuclear technology, the customers are electrical utilities and, in the long term, nuclear reactors have to demonstrate an economic method of generating electricity. The fact that this has not occurred, combined with public concerns about safety, has led to a major recession in the United States. There have been no new domestic orders since 1975. In the case of space, it is possible that launching satellites could prove commercially viable, but up to now the success of space projects has depended on state commitments, generally linked to military concerns.

This is evident in France, where the commitment to nuclear and space technology is quite clearly part of an ideology of technological chauvinism which is linked to conceptions of military strength which stem from the postwar military paradigm. General Jean Thiry, for example, the adviser to the Managing Director of the French Atomic Energy Commission, CEA, wrote of the Super Phoenix Fast Breeder programme:

> France will be able to build atomic weapons of all kinds and within every range. At relatively low cost, she will be in a position to produce large quantities of such weapons, with fast breeders providing an abundant supply of the plutonium required. Lucky Europe and lucky France – at long last in a position to engage in an enlarged deterrent of their own thus guaranteeing their security.[24]

Likewise in a speech at La Hague, President Mitterand outlined his vision of a new technological Europe:

> One element of this future would be a European space station as a military observation post in the first place, but one that could also carry laser and other Star Wars weaponry for the defence of Europe.[25]

TECHNOLOGICAL DEALIGNMENT

Despite the French emphasis on independence and European autonomy, France remains committed to the Atlantic culture. By opting for Europeanization of the military–technological paradigm, France has fundamentally accepted the bipolar model of the world, the military definition of political power and the strategic conceptions that go with this military definition, namely notions of 'balance' and 'deterrence'. It is acceptance of Atlanticist culture that fundamentally limits the internal room for manoeuvre, politically entrenching the elites committed to that culture and reducing the economic space for technological alternatives. The constraints on French policy are dramatically illustrated by President Mitterand's wholehearted support for the deployment of cruise and Pershing II missiles and his readiness to intervene on the side of right-wing parties in Belgium, Holland and West Germany in order to ensure that deployment went ahead.

Genuine dealignment would have to entail a shift towards a state framework that is more likely to favour a new technological paradigm. The problem is not so much to adopt a set of new partialities for the new paradigm. Rather, it is how to develop more flexible state structures so that harmony between state partialities and technological paradigms can be more or less maintained, thus avoiding future crises while allowing change. This problem, of how to develop flexible state structures, is the central intellectual problem of our time, requiring intensive thought and practice. In this context, it is not possible to do more than to indicate some of the changes that technological dealignment would require.

First of all, it would entail a shift in world view, such as has been described elsewhere in this book. The bipolar model of international relations upheld by a particular military scheme would have to give way to a more diverse pluralistic conception of international relations in which the military dimension has a much less significant part to play.

Secondly, the partiality for military spending would have to diminish. It is not just that military demand is an important component of the technological paradigm of the fourth Kondratiev. It is also that by their nature, military partialities are more rigid than other kinds of partiality – they do not have to respond to the rationale of the market nor public political reactions as is the case for consumers of welfare or other public activities. Greater flexibility of state structures must necessarily mean less emphasis on military structures.

Thirdly, in so far as states continue to spend on military activities, there needs to be a change in the definition of military missions and the relationship with private enterprise. This is *not* an argument for the adoption of a new military–technological paradigm based on the technological paradigm of the fifth Kondratiev i.e. information technologies, as is, for example, proposed by the military reform movement in the United States. Such a shift could only effectively come about through war, with all the hideous consequences that modern war implies. Even if non-hegemonic or dealigned states were to adopt new military technologies, their utility would have to be demonstrated in war. If the purpose were to challenge the political preeminence of the hegemonic states, then this would depend on political perceptions of military power, which rarely change except in war. Even if it were supposed that the world could survive such a test of military utility, the new military–technological paradigm would entrench itself in new state structures, creating the conditions for future crises.

Rather, perceptions of power have to be changed through a diminution of the military element. Restricting military missions, for example to defensive roles, and controlling the competitiveness of arms manufacturers would be part of that process.

In other words, dealignment has to mean a responsiveness to need as popularly defined so that new technological paradigms can develop in response to need and not to artificial conceptions of what constitutes advanced technology. In effect, what has happened is that notions of what is advanced have somehow got separated from what is progressive, i.e. capable of satisfying human need, material or spiritual. Atlantic culture is imprisoned in a definition of what is advanced, based on cleverness, ingenuity, size and complexity, as well as on overblown memories of past achievements.

NOTES

1 Nikolai Kondratiev, 'The Major Economic Cycles', summarized in *Review of Economic Statistics*, 18 (1935).

2 Joseph Schumpeter, *Business Cycles* (New York: McGraw-Hill, 1939).

3 Walt Rostow, *The Stages of Economic Growth* (Cambridge: Cambridge University Press, 1960).

4 For a survey of different long wave theories, see Joshua Goldstein, *Long Waves and War Cycles* (Department of Political Science, MIT, September 1983).

5 See G. Dosi, 'Technological Paradigms and Technological Trajectories', *Research Policy*, 11(2) (June 1982).

6 Carlotta Perez, 'Structural Change and Assimilation of New Technologies', *Futures* (October 1983).

7 Ibid.

8 See T. H. Hopkins and I. Wallerstein, *Processes of the World System* (Beverly Hills, Ca: Sage, 1980); George Modelski, 'The Long Cycle of Global Politics and the Nation State', *Comparative Studies in Society and History*, 20, (April 1978).

9 James R. Kurth, 'The Political Consequences of the Product Cycle: industrial history and political outcomes', *International Organization* (Winter 1979).

10 Clausewitz, *On War*, first published 1832, (London: Pelican Books, 1968)

11 Quoted in Philip Noel-Baker, *The Private Manufacture of Arms* (London: Victor Gollancz, 1936), pp. 411–12.

12 According to an article in the *Iron and Coal Trades Review*, March 1895, the effect of Admiralty programmes was to 'enable firms to tide over without disaster periods of depression that would otherwise have been extremely trying; and, naturally, we have seen that the same policy has stimulated local and provincial interest in naval affairs to a much greater extent than was formerly the case' (quoted in Kurth, 'Political Consequences of the Product Cycle', p. 17).

13 See Mary Kaldor, *The Baroque Arsenal* (London: André Deutsch, 1982), ch. 2.

14 John Ellis, *The Social History of the Machine Gun* (New York: Pantheon Books,

1973).

15 Keith Hartley, *NATO Arms Cooperation: A Study in Economics and Politics* (London: George Allen & Unwin, 1983), p. 21.

16 Dr. D. L. Kirkpatrick and P. G. Pugh, 'Towards the Starship Enterprise – are the current trends in defence unit costs inexorable?', *Aerospace* (May 1983).

17 Norman R. Augustine, 'One Plane, One Tank, One Ship: Trend for the Future', *Defence Management Journal* (April 1975).

18 'The 1983 Alastair Buchan Memorial Lecture', *Survival*, 25 (1983), no. 4, pp. 149–50.

19 For a description of these institutions, see Trevor Taylor, 'European Defence Cooperation', *Chatham House Papers, No. 12*, Royal Institute of International Affairs (London: Routledge and Kegan Paul, 1984).

20 Robert McDonagh, *The Development of the European Parliament's Activities in Relation to Security and Armament* (Luxembourg: Directorate General for Research and Documentation, 27 February 1984).

21 See Mary Kaldor, *Military R & D. A Report prepared for the Swedish Reference Group of the UN Governmental Expert Study on Military R & D* (May 1984). Mary Kaldor, Margaret Sharp and William Walker, 'Military R & D and Industrial Competitiveness', *Lloyd's Bank Review* (October 1986).

22 For a discussion of this, see William Walker and Mans Lonroth, *Nuclear Power Struggles. Industrial Competition and Proliferation Controls* (London: George Allen & Unwin, 1983).

23 See John M. Logsdon, 'US – European Cooperation in Space Science: 25 year Perspective', *Science*, 223, No. 4631 (6 January 1984).

24 Quoted in Michel de Perrot, 'Commercial Fast Breeders: Towards an Integrated European Force?', in Groupe de Bellerive, *European Security. Nuclear and Conventional Defence* (London: Pergamon Press, 1984), p. 46.

25 Robert Walgate, 'French Visions of Europe and Space', *Nature*, 307 (16 February 1984).

8

Neutrality, Dealignment and Political Order in Europe

RAIMO VÄYRYNEN

INTRODUCTION

Neutrality has always been a social fact in Europe. It has been manifested in two different ways. First, some governments have opted, either by legal arrangements or by political declarations, to stay outside military alliances, while provisions on neutrality in wartime are firmly embedded in international efforts by the states concerned. Secondly, neutrality is an option that is favoured by smaller or larger segments of the population in states that are members of alliances.

The main benefit of neutrality is the low probability of being drawn into the confrontation between major powers, while the ability of countries that pursue such a strategy to resist foreign aggression or political infiltration is often considered to be weak. Strength through collective defence is regarded usually as the main benefit derived from membership of a military alliance, while more or less automatic incorporation into any war between alliances is its principal drawback. Popular reluctance to accept this risk has been a major motivation for neutralism within allied countries. Such a motivation is often dormant, but its prevalence is suggested by the fact that the spread of neutralist ideas tends to be associated with the increase in the danger of war and with the advent of more threatening weapons technologies. Yet it is those very same conditions that tend to increase the resolve of leading governments to consolidate the ranks of their alliance either by coercion or by reform.

The popularity of neutrality and its political feasibility are different things and may even vary in a disjunctive manner. Political tensions and arms races tend to increase the attractiveness of neutrality. However, in these conditions, the practical possibilities for neutrality are fewer because of the emergence of counteracting forces. Even the freedom of manoeuvre of existing neutral countries in international relations may decrease if major powers suspect the credibility of their policies. The Dullesian attitude towards neutrality is one that fears a shift in the balance of power, which might take place if neutral countries choose another side. A process of dealignment would involve depolarization and the relaxation of political tensions. This tends to enhance the acceptability of neutrality and the political opportunities which it offers.[1]

Neutrality and alignment stand in a complex and interactive relationship to each other. While neutrality and alignment exclude each other, the concept of dealignment is consonant with the continued existence of military alliance. This is possible for the reason that a military alliance is a strategic and institutional fact, a state of affairs, while dealignment is a process that gradually modifies this fact.

Neutrality should be properly seen as a European phenomenon, while non-alignment refers to a related political movement in the Third World. These two orientations have both common and distinctive features. Historically speaking, the Non-Aligned Movement was the outcome of a collective decision of certain Third World countries to opt for cooperation with their peers – defined by the same low level of development and by their colonial past – in order to disengage from, and protect against, colonialism and the alliance system of the Cold War. These countries pitted decolonization against colonialism and non-alignment against membership in military alliances. They aimed, in other words, to create more freedom for political movement and economic development.

In this respect the desired world order of the neutral, industrialized countries, or small powers in general, does not appreciably differ from that of the non-aligned countries. Both these groups of countries have a common interest in increasing political and economic equality in the world and establishing effective international institutions that would counterbalance the influence of the great powers. The stress on disarmament is also a common feature of the attitudes of neutral and non-aligned countries, as it would enhance their security and also contribute to greater equality between nations of different sizes. It is indeed often forgotten that the goal of disarmament is not only connected with international security, though it should be its primary objective, but has an emancipatory aspect as well.

Strictly speaking industrialized neutral countries and less industrialized non-aligned countries do not have an identical interest in development. Politically, however, this interest is recognized in debates in international forums as well as in the greater relative propensity of small and medium-sized countries, compared with major powers, to provide development aid to the Third World. In fact, cooperation in development may be partly derived from the common interest of these two groups of countries in greater economic equality in the world system. Furthermore, both have also developed political strategies aimed at the transformation of the present undesirable world order. A major difference, however, lies in their beliefs in the efficacy of various transformation strategies.

Neutral countries do not – perhaps because they are relatively small in size and few in number – believe they can bring about, even if acting *en bloc*, major changes in the structure and principles of international relations. They may cooperate to reduce the political tensions and pressures of the arms race in Europe, to bring about reformist improvements in the international economy or to strengthen the role of the United Nations, but most of them seem still to take the present international order more or less as given. Small West European countries and all neutral countries belong to that category, and advocate a liberal international economy together with reforms to ensure domestic stability and compensation for those affected by the internationalization of the national economy.[2]

The approach of the non-aligned countries is different in this respect. In spite of internal frictions and the insufficiency of national and collective resources, the Non-Aligned Movement seems to believe in its ultimate ability to transform the prevailing, great power orientated international order. It is this belief *versus* disbelief in the ultimate 'victory' of an alternative world order which is one of the crucial differences between the neutral and non-aligned countries. The difference may be partly explained by the fact that for industrialized countries, even for smaller ones, no prospect of 'victory' – in terms of freedom from want and oppression – exists in the same sense as for developing countries; they are already on the winning side. In addition, one has to recall that the security environment of most neutral countries in Europe gives rise to quite different problems from those faced in the Third World. There problems of socioeconomic stability and various forms of great power intervention are much more common and serious than in Europe.

THE EVOLUTION OF NEUTRALITY IN EUROPE

In global perspective, the neutral countries of Europe are a liberal force for both the maintenance and gradual transformation of the system. No major changes have taken placè during the postwar era, but neutral countries have continued to advocate a liberal, multilateral, international economy where disparities are reduced by international institutions and coordination of economic policies. In the East–West context, the role of neutral countries has been much more radical. Immediately after World War II neutrality and neutralism became popular in Europe. The prevailing mood was that if the great powers wanted to fight another war, which was widely expected, they would have to do it without the contribution of European people, who were disillusioned with military power and military alliances as methods of solving international disagreements.

The first wave of neutralism, however, lasted only until 1947–48. By a series of multilateral and bilateral arrangements Europe was assimilated into a great power order that came to dominate the continent. In the immediate postwar era neutrality and neutralism suited neither American nor Soviet purposes; in fact a major motive for concluding military ties between great powers and European countries was to contain tendencies in this direction. Neutrality was regarded as an unstable option that would potentially lead countries practising it to the adversary camp which would subsequently alter the balance of power in Europe. Neutrality was not only rejected by the great powers as a viable political strategy, but many of the smaller European countries, in particular Western Europe, approached the United States for support against alleged Soviet expansionism. In fact, the atmosphere changed very rapidly in Western Europe between 1947 and 1949 from neutralism to acceptance of alliances. A major political and psychological transformation took place which legitimized the military alliance system.

During the first phase of the Cold War from 1948 to 1955, neutralism was contained by military alliances and neutrality was pushed to the background. Switzerland was, of course, traditionally a neutral country. Sweden's neutrality was barely tolerated and often questioned, in particular by the Soviet Union. Yugoslavia was in the crossfire as a consequence of its decision in the late 1940s to opt for a 'third road'. Finland was gradually building up, as a defeated country, her relations with the Soviet Union, and no real neutrality was yet possible. Prospects for the neutral alternative in Europe were bleak indeed.

The first thaw in US–Soviet relations in 1954–55 started to change the situation. Austria's *Staatsvertrag* was concluded in 1955 and her neutral status was declared by parliament later in the same year. In Finland the Soviet Union ceded back her military base at Porkkala and the country started cautiously to build up her political and economic connections with the West. In a sense, the second half of the 1950s was a period when neutrality was consolidated in Europe. The political line of these countries was no longer considered 'immoral', to use Dulles' term, but both great powers came to accept the existence of neutral states as a permanent phenomenon. They were economically firmly anchored in the West, and most of them became members of EFTA towards the end of the 1950s. Politically, however, they tried to stay outside the conflicts between the great powers and to maintain a modicum of balance in their statements and actions *vis-à-vis* the United States and the Soviet Union. Most neutral countries emphatically rejected indifference in ideological issues: with the exception of Yugoslavia, they declared support for the market economy and a competitive political system.

In structural terms, the neutral powers of Europe were not in fact neutral; they were affiliated both economically and ideologically with the West. Their political orientation was, however, acceptable to both great powers to the extent that neutrality became a *legitimate* orientation in foreign policy. Some countries, in particular Sweden and Yugoslavia, developed a strong military capability to defend their neutrality by means of deterrence (Sweden even considered the acquisition of nuclear weapons). Austria and Finland relied, in their turn, primarily on political means to stabilize their neutrality by enhancing its credibility in the eyes of the major powers.

The legitimization of neutrality did not yet signify an opportunity to influence actively the development of the European system. Throughout the 1960s neutrality was still on the defensive, even though changes in Europe increasingly favoured it. Relaxation of tensions and structural depolarization in the East–West system enhanced the freedom of action for neutral countries. The relative scarcity of political channels between East and West provided almost an historic opportunity for neutral countries to start playing an intermediary role in Europe. The ice of the Cold War started to melt and neutral countries – especially Austria, Finland and Sweden, sometimes even in a competitive fashion – put forward constructive proposals on how to promote security and cooperation in Europe. Their *bona officia* were also welcomed by the great powers who saw these offices as a way to promote their mutual interest.

It is in fact justified to speak of an era of *bridge-building* that covers the last years of the 1960s and the early 1970s.[3] It was brought about by the combination of the active foreign policies of neutral countries themselves and the needs created by the changing structure of great power relations. In fact neutral countries were instrumental in stabilizing the status quo in Europe that was established in the late 1940s (at the same time they further stabilized their own position as well). This effort was codified in a concrete manner in the Final Act of the CSCE (Conference on Security and Cooperation in Europe) that was concluded in Helsinki in August 1975.

Bridge-building could be practised unilaterally, as Finland did in contributing to the convocation of the preparatory phase of the CSCE, but it could be institutionalized as well. Such a development started from the Geneva phase of the CSCE in 1973–5 when neutral and non-aligned countries, nine altogether, started to act as a loose but identifiable group in multilateral deliberations. Even before the Geneva phase, the neutral and non-aligned countries, the so-called 'N&N Group', had started to make procedural proposals in order to facilitate the work of the conference. In Geneva they were complemented by more substantial political proposals: the N&N Group acted as an honest broker to narrow the differences of opinion between major powers and to promote an agreement between them.[4]

The emergence of the group of neutral and non-aligned countries in the CSCE has to be seen as a process of coalition formation. The Warsaw Pact was, with the partial exception of Romania which tried to promote cooperation across the blocs, a coherent group, while NATO was much more fragmented at that time. It has to be recalled that this was the period of American extrication from the Vietnam War, when Watergate paralysed domestic decision-making and the after effects of the oil crisis plagued relations between the United States and Western Europe. At that time, the US administration put more emphasis on the bilateral relationship with Moscow than the multilateral framework provided by the CSCE. That is why the European Economic Community emerged as the main group of NATO countries in Geneva. Its activities within the CSCE framework were in fact the first concrete effort to implement the programme for European Political Cooperation (EPC) developed gradually by the European Community after its summit meetings in The Hague and Luxembourg in 1969–70.

It may be argued that the N&N Group and the European Community had *complementary roles* in the process leading to the conclusion of the CSCE Final Act. This was particularly true of the neutral countries, i.e. Austria, Finland, Sweden and Switzerland. They were able, being free of major foreign policy problems, to act as an homogeneous group which could devote itself to the CSCE process. (This was not true of the non-aligned countries, in particular Cyprus and Malta.) The complementarity of the N&N Group and the European Community meant a continuous feedback process on substantial issues between these two groups in order to develop formulations that were acceptable to the great powers and to the countries most closely associated with them.

Cooperation between neutral countries in the CSCE was most efficient in the formulation of security principles and in developing the confidence-building measures embodied in the Final Act. This was partly associated with the fact that neutral countries had in this respect common interests due to the similarity of their security postures. Thus the neutral countries, and to some extent the non-aligned countries as well, did not only function as intermediaries, but also aimed to articulate their *common security interests* and to promote measures of confidence and security-building that would assure their survival. In matters concerning economic cooperation between the CSCE countries, the interests of neutral countries as small market economies were more similar, while in humanitarian issues their attitudes tended to be more at variance.[5]

In a way, it may be argued that neutral countries had a more united perspective on how the security system of Europe should be structured than on issues pertaining to intra-bloc or intra-national conditions in East and West. This is natural as neutral (and non-aligned) countries tend to benefit from arrangements that stabilize and regulate relations between military blocs and that enhance the space for action of non-bloc members of the European system. To put it another way, neutral and non-aligned countries benefited from the *multilateralization* of European politics that was associated with the CSCE.

The activity of the N&N Groups continued in the CSCE follow-up meetings in Belgrade and Madrid, though in a somewhat different context which tended to reduce the group's relative impact. The NATO grouping was strengthened as the United States and European Community started to coordinate their policies more effectively from the late 1970s. This development coincided with the reimposition of the bloc barrier in international politics and the resurgence of political and military tensions between the great powers. In such circumstances the European Community and the N&N Group could not play complementary roles in the way they had done in Geneva. The stress on humanitarian issues in Belgrade also tended to reduce opportunities for action by neutral and non-aligned countries as they did not have a real mutual agreement on them. In spite of a large number of proposals put forward, more than 100 altogether, the Belgrade conference accomplished very little and contributed to a rather widespread disillusionment. It is reflected in a comment by Karl Birnbaum who observed that the CSCE process 'should be viewed less as an instrument for promoting pan-European integration than as a forum where the effects of the forces shaping intra-European developments but operating largely outside the CSCE framework proper can be consistently assessed'.[6]

From these remarks one should not conclude, however, that the N&N Group has not had any real impact after the Geneva phase of the CSCE. It has continued to work actively both in the Belgrade and Madrid follow-up meetings. Especially in the latter the Group had a key role, together with Spain, in resolving the longstanding stalemate. In fact, the compromise by which the Madrid conference was finally saved in September 1983 was proposed by the neutral and non-aligned countries as early as December 1981.

At the Stockholm conference which began in January 1984, the N&N Group submitted two sets of proposals on 9 March 1984 and on 17 November 1985. These proposals were said to reflect only the national efforts and interests of neutral and non-aligned countries. In fact, they did serve to bridge the difference of perspectives between the members of NATO and the Warsaw Pact; the former stressing communication and confidence, the latter more tangible measures of arms control. The military blocs expected the core of the N&N Group to act as an intermediary between them. This has indeed been the case. Some of the neutral countries, in particular Finland, were instrumental in resolving the disagreement on the mode of work in the Stockholm conference. By proposing a division into two working groups it was possible to get negotiations moving in early 1985. This achievement was complemented by a 'gentlemen's agreement' of 14 October 1985 in which it was decided to focus the conference on informal work in five issue areas. Four neutral countries of Europe were appointed to coordinate the activities of these five groups. Switzerland would coordinate two groups (dealing with the exchange of information and constraints on military activities); Austria (non-use of force), Sweden (advance notifications) and Finland (exchange of observers), would be each in charge of one group.

It is often said that continuation of the CSCE process is the result of pressure by the smaller European countries, both aligned and non-aligned. It is to their advantage to continue the multilateral dialogue in Europe, even though the great powers may not always be interested. The commitment of small and medium-sized powers to the CSCE makes it inconvenient and even costly, for example in terms of political complications in intra-alliance relations, for the great powers to let the multilateral European process of security and cooperation break down. This point was recognized by Christoph Bertram in his remark that the Stockholm conference is a '*Komplott der Kleinen*', i.e. an effort of small powers to keep the great powers at a negotiating table and to utilize this fact for their own purposes.[7]

In the joint Soviet – American statement from the Geneva summit in November 1985 the American and Soviet leaders, referring to the Stockholm conference, stated 'their intention to facilitate, together with other participating states, an early and successful completion of the work of the conference'. They also reaffirmed the need for a document that would combine mutually acceptable confidence and security-building measures and the principle of the non-use of force. This statement reflects, on the one hand, the bilateral effort of the great powers to reach some concrete agreements in the multilateral forums and a potential compromise on which the conference document can be based. It is not, on the other hand, too far-fetched to argue that the political expectations of other participants in the CSCE process have induced the great powers to stress the need for progress.

An interesting issue is to what extent the neutral countries or the N&N Group meet the requirement for an intermediary in inter-bloc relations in the CSCE context and to what extent they articulate and promote their own security interests. As pointed out earlier, in the Geneva phase of the CSCE, members of the N&N Group advocated their own interests and did not only act as an honest broker between the blocs. In Belgrade and Madrid, probably due to the character of the meetings, this effort was lesss manifest. In the Stockholm conference individual members of the N&N Group seem to have emphasized these two objectives to somewhat different degrees. Trade-offs may indeed exist in the desire of neutral and non-aligned countries to reach concrete and positive results and the need to find compromises and proposals to ease the negotiation process in the working groups.

The role and impact of the neutral and non-aligned countries in the CSCE process should be neither over- nor under-estimated. Their impact has varied from one phase of the process to another and from one issue area to another. An empirical study of the Geneva phase concluded that neutral and non-aligned countries plus France and Romania contributed substantially to the negotiations, but could only to a limited extent influence the final shape of the text. The two great powers exerted considerable asymmetric influence, amounting to a kind of veto, over what was *not* included in the Final Act of the CSCE. Such a situation indicates 'a strong degree of asymmetry based on threat potential, on structural position within the international system and on resources to back up influence attempts'.[8]

NEUTRALITY AND THE BLOC STRUCTURE

Neutrality has become a legitimate and permanent political option in Europe. It is difficult to believe that the present neutral countries could opt for an alliance membership in any peacetime conditions. On the contrary, it has been suggested that, in conjunction with the depolarization of the European system, the proliferation of neutrality will accelerate. This may not mean, however, that new neutral countries relying on a traditional model of neutrality will emerge in Europe. Rather, the *substance of neutrality will change*, and the very concept will become more blurred. As one observer has put it, 'the borderline between the more indeterminately neutral countries and the more loosely aligned ones will become increasingly indeterminate and shifting. Partial neutrality which follows a specific factual line will increase. A growing share of activity in the field of neutrality policy will diverge from the institution and norms of permanent neutrality.'[9] This is, in a sense, what is involved in a process of dealignment.

This forecast implies that the formal bloc structure of Europe will remain intact in the foreseeable future. The norms and substance of behaviour within military alliances, as well as the nature of commitments, will, however, gradually change. New forms of partial, and often indeed very partial, neutrality will emerge from within the military alliances. These are primarily manifestations of lack of confidence in and satisfaction with the present alliances as a way of providing real security. This lack of confidence in the official security doctrines may be called neutralism. In other words, popular pressures to change security policy can lead to greater pluralism and sometimes to partial erosion of alliance commitments that favour neutralist tendencies. Alliances are expected to produce 'security'; because people feel that the level of 'security' is declining, they start to explore alternatives (such as no-first-use of nuclear weapons and nuclear-weapon-free zones) either by voicing their grievances or by seeking an exit.[10] Various forms of neutrality provide an exit option from the bonds of military alliances whose nuclear weapon component in particular has become increasingly unpopular over the past few years.

The position and policy of the neutral countries of today is not likely to change in any drastic manner during this century. There are naturally external pressures that gradually change the policies of neutral countries in Europe, but the outcomes are obviously dependent on such factors as geopolitical position, economic interests and affiliations with the major powers. Neutral countries mix political and military means of security policy in different ways. In this respect Sweden and Switzerland tend to stress the significance of deterrence based on military capabilities in the protection of neutrality while Austria and Finland rely more on political relations of trust with other countries. Yugoslavia has a mixed strategy in the sense that its defence conception comes closer to that of Austria and Finland, while in terms of financial outlays devoted to defence it is closer to Sweden and Switzerland.[11]

The rise in international tension since the late 1970s has tended to enhance the importance of the military component in the security policy of neutral countries, though domestic economic pressures have counteracted this tendency. One reason for this may be that the diplomacy of neutral countries has not been capable of extracting sufficient security assurances and building up stable relations with the major powers in a conflict-ridden Europe. In a sense the development of international relations since the middle of the 1970s has weakened the diplomatic efforts of neutral countries in the pursuit of security. The active and even central role of neutral and non-aligned countries has been significant, yet at the same time a minor achievement in the wider framework of security policy. In such circumstances the advocates of military strength and deterrence can more easily influence policy-making. Neutral countries have not yet become significantly more militarized than before, but there is certainly a tendency to strengthen the military component of their security policies. Ultimately, however, the military approach cannot assure the security of neutral countries because of their limited resources.

In this bind many neutral countries increasingly appear to stress the need to prevent military threats from materializing in advance. For major powers *preventive diplomacy* is a form of containment by which they try to steer confrontations to their own benefit. For them preventive diplomacy means the manipulation of conflicts in a manner that would not threaten the core values of foreign policy. Neutral countries have fewer opportunities to manipulate international conflicts and can hardly ever resort to force, which major powers customarily threaten to do in their preventive diplomacy. Neutral countries must try to develop rules of behaviour and institutional arrangements that reduce the possibilities of conflict escalation in their sub-region.

Preventive diplomacy, used as a comprehensive term here, can pursue several objectives at different levels of generality. At the most general end of the continuum, detente, disarmament and collective security enhance the stability of international relations and in that way reduce the likelihood of confrontations into which neutral countries might be drawn. More specific forms of preventive diplomacy by neutral countries include negative security assurances, advocacy of the various types of spheres of absence by great powers, and – related to the previous approach – zones of disengagement. In fact the strategy of *disengagement* has become, as shown by the interest in nuclear-weapon-free zones in Northern Europe and in the Balkans, a central ingredient in the policy of most neutral countries. The disengagement strategy aims at preventing by preemptive measures the spill-over of great power confrontations to the sub-system in question.[12] The idea is, in other words, to decouple these sub-systems to the greatest extent possible from the strategic rivalry between the great powers, and in this way to enhance their security.

In fact, disengagement is a central issue in any analysis of neutralist tendencies in Europe. Disengagement is a concrete strategy by which countries may try to keep themselves neutral in a military confrontation, i.e., try to avoid becoming a belligerent. Being basically a political strategy, disengagement tends to blur the distinction between neutral and allied states, as both types of country can pursue such a security strategy. It is, however, more of a problem for allied countries, because a partial disengagement from the alliance strategy – primarily from the nuclear-weapon strategy – raises the question of whether they are going to remain loyal to the alliance in other respects. Is disengagement, in other words, a stable security solution for an allied state or just a first step towards neutrality? This is a crucial issue which is extensively pondered, within NATO in particular.

Aspirations to keep their territory free of nuclear weapons are visible in such NATO countries as Norway, Denmark, Belgium, The Netherlands, Spain and Greece, and some of these countries have already taken measures to implement that objective. Similar tendencies can be discerned in Romania and Hungary within the Warsaw Pact, and in a way in both German states as well. In all of them there are predilections to leave the nuclear umbrella of their alliance leader, yet to stay otherwise as members of the alliance. Such plans are usually resisted by bloc leaders; a decision of one or more members to opt out of the nuclear strategy would curtail their freedom of military action in crises. Equally important is the fact that such 'renegades' from nuclear strategy would set a political precedent that others might follow. In the longer run such a process would lead to the fragmentation of the strategic basis of an alliance.

The advocates of nuclear-weapon-free zones often point out that inclusion in such a zone would not otherwise alter the security commitments of that country's allied members. Formally this is true, but the point should not be generalized too far, and one should pay attention to the underlying political dynamics as well. A decision to opt out from a central tenet of today's military alliances, i.e. their nuclear weapons strategy, may be based on a domestic coalition of interests that is also prepared to redirect the country's external policy in other ways. Changes are seldom abrupt, however, but rather partial and gradual; they may take 30–40 years to mature. The relative slowness of such changes is due to their intrinsic nature in which power structures and institutional arrangements interact. In the course of three or four decades the distribution of power within and between nations usually changes to the extent that intergovernmental institutional arrangements, such as specific types of military alliance, start becoming outdated and their desirability is questioned. The *legitimacy* of old institutional arrangements is eroded by new political coalitions and ideas as well as by a new distribution of power within and between alliances. The restoration of legitimacy requires the establishment of new institutions and rules of behaviour that better correspond to the new political reality.

The present political fermentation within military alliances is a manifestation of their legitimacy crisis. In more concrete terms, the resurgence of a movement towards nuclear disengagement is a sign of dissatisfaction with the outdated and even dangerous character of military arrangements within alliances. This may lead us to expect further shifts in the external policies of alliance members. Indeed, Europe seems to be heading towards the establishment of disengagement zones and opting for various types of partial neutrality; in other words, a dealignment process. As a matter of fact there seems to be a degree of consensus that this is a probable future alternative. Attitudes towards the desirability of this alternative vary, however. A considerable number of people support the objectives of disengagement and even of neutrality. In an opinion poll conducted in March 1981 in West Germany, Great Britain, France and Italy 27–39 per cent of the respondents in the age bracket of 18–34 years favoured neutrality to membership in NATO. In the age group of 35–49 years 18–34 per cent, and finally in the group of 50 years and older, 5–18 per cent supported the neutral alternative.[13]

Desire for neutrality is not just a spectre but a political force, though still largely unorganized. Those opposing the development towards neutrality among alliance members tend to paint a dark picture of disengagement, stressing how it would lead to reduced security and even to a loss of sovereignty. For example, the West German Defence Minister, Manfred Wörner, has uttered the following words of caution: 'The Soviet Union wants to disentangle the non-nuclear-weapon countries of Western Europe in a crucial area from the protection of nuclear weapons by the United States and to convert her Western foreground in Europe to a status of lesser security'.[14]

The erosion of military alliances, which is also a result of political and economic depolarization in Europe, may be counteracted in different ways. One possibility is the attempt to re-erect the old hegemonic structures under the aegis of the great powers to ensure the compliance of other members of the alliance. This option is not very effective, however, as the wheel of change in international structures cannot be turned back. Another possibility is transformation of the doctrines and institutions of the alliances so as to better correspond to the new realities without changing the basic premises. Within NATO the Reagan administration has relied on the former strategy, while such retired policy-makers as Henry Kissinger and Helmut Schmidt have supported institutional rather than doctrinal reforms. Doctrinal reforms such as the renunciation of a central tenet of NATO's nuclear strategy, the first use of nuclear weapons, have also been proposed by Robert McNamara and others. In spite of differences between various reformist proposals there are, however, two common features: the stress on conventional armaments as the mode of management of Soviet power, and the effort to stem the spread of neutralism in Europe by making NATO strategy less reliant on the use of nuclear weapons.

Within the Warsaw Pact problems of legitimacy are not so much due to nuclear weapons, even though they are also gradually becoming an issue; more immediate are the problems of managing social and political change in socialist countries. Successful management of change while retaining some degree of public legitimacy requires at least some innovation and flexibility in order to assure sufficient political and economic performance. This is hardly possible without some autonomy in decision-making that may, in turn, be perceived as a potential source of instability and insecurity by the Soviet Union. Recent events in Poland show how difficult it may be to operate in such a cross-pressure of conflicting internal and external demands. Ultimately the legitimacy of the institutional and military arrangements embodied in the Warsaw Pact hinges upon the ability to encourage, and, at the same time, control social change within the member countries.[15]

Neutrality as an orientation of security policy is often misinterpreted. It does not necessarily mean 'pacificism' as feared by its opponents. Neutrality, partial or total, can certainly be combined with military capability and there is even, as pointed out above, a certain predilection for it. Nor do neutrality and disengagement necessarily lead to the erosion of nation states, and hence they are consonant with a number of alternative futures for Europe. These alternatives include, for example, Europe des Etats, Fragmented Europe and, in Western Europe, a more independent Europeanist future.[16]

POLITICS AND COUNTERPOLITICS FOR NEUTRALITY

Traditional neutrality has become a stable and legitimate part of international relations in Europe. Hardly anybody questions the orientation of Austrian, Finnish, Swedish or Swiss foreign policy. The same can be said of most of the non-aligned countries on the outer edges of Europe and their foreign policies. Neutralist tendencies within military alliances are, however, a hotly contested issue which gives rise to wide-ranging political debates.

Finland's international position has, for instance, often been converted or relegated to the metaphor of 'Finlandization' that is quite stereotyped in its nature. Through this metaphor, usually conservative politicians or authors have tried to convey a warning to Western European countries. Finlandization is identified with the loss of the ability to decide independently about one own's affairs. Very few observers want to criticize Finland's foreign policy as such; on the contrary, there is no shortage of people who try to convince their audience that they feel the deepest sympathy with the past heroic struggles waged by the Finns and with the predicament in which they now live. The present policy, i.e. coexistence with the Soviet Union, may even be regarded by them as the only real alternative. The 'Finnish model' should, however, never become a model for Western Europe. What is good for Finland is not good for Western Europe. The latter has a different geopolitical location and more economic resources to thwart any Soviet encroachments, if it has the political determination to do so.[17]

On the other hand, this very differentiation of Finland from West European states has tended to increase its attractiveness as a model of inter-state relations, especially for countries located in the vicinity of Soviet borders. Finnish neutrality has been regarded, particularly in academic and political opposition circles, as a model by which stable relations with the Soviet Union can be established, while at the same time avoiding complications in relations with major Western powers. Interest in the 'Finnish model' was, it is true, higher during the era of detente and has tended to decline with the rise of international tensions. The neutral alternative may become again more common now that the alliance members have realized that the price they have to pay for the security provided by the collective defence arrangement may be higher than the expected gains.

The counter-reaction to military alliances has occasionally been baptized 'Hollanditis', a 'Dutch disease' leading to neutralism and pacifism.[18] It differs from the concept of Finlandization in that the metaphor is chosen from within NATO. This is, in itself, a sign of the erosion of the alliance system. Hollanditis is, like Finlandization, a myth that generalizes certain features of policy-making into an all-encompassing stereotyped pattern. Politics and in particular counter-politics appear to need such myths, however, in order to manipulate public opinion.

In a sense Hollanditis and other similar myths, derived for example from the Danish situation, have released Finland to some extent from her previous role as a cautionary example. Instead, in political debates in Western Europe and North America, Finland's foreign policy has been used as a model for socialist countries bordering the Soviet Union in

Europe and Asia. 'Finlandization' is suggested for Afghanistan and Poland in particular, as a method of moving from an alliance with the Soviet Union to a neutral status more acceptable to the West. This partial shift in allegiances is considered an ingredient in the resolution of conflicts in which these countries are involved.[19]

Such a strategy of transition from alliance membership to neutrality/non-blocism is recommended for the reason that it would cause less disturbance to the prevailing political and military order than an outright jump from one alliance to another (which is, of course, a highly unlikely event). If the country deserting a military alliance is, however, willing to follow a 'benevolent neutrality', taking into account the security concerns of its former ally/allies, the transition from one role to another is conceivable. This is the background of the idea of 'Finlandizing' Afghanistan, Poland or some other similar countries. It is, however, a poor strategy as it neglects some important differences in the international position and domestic structure of Finland and her would-be imitators.

Finland is a capitalist country with a competitive political system which distinguishes her from the countries allied with the Soviet Union. Soviet cooperation with Finland is a form of collaboration between *different* social systems which recognizes the possibility of neutrality. The socialist political system and neutrality have, at least so far, been incompatible with each other (Yugoslavia and, in a sense, Albania are partial exceptions). This is due to the prevailing definition of membership in the Warsaw Pact, as an obligation by socialist countries to those with *similar* social systems and to the entire socialist community. This underlying fact is reflected in a comment by the Deputy Prime Minister of Poland, Mieczyslaw Rakowski, that the term 'Finlandization'

> suits Finland well, but not Poland, because our geographical situation is completely different. Our social system is similar to the Soviet Union's. The transfer of status corresponding to that of Finland to Poland is not an idea that can be taken seriously. Our task is to create good neighbourly relations with the Soviet Union and our entire history shows that our relations cannot be based on neutrality. Our relationship to the Soviet Union can only be an alliance, and it corresponds also to Polish interests in the longer run.[20]

This conclusion is valid for all the socialist countries. There is, in other words, only a meagre political basis for changes in foreign policy by socialist countries of Europe. On the contrary, they have tended to pursue almost singlemindedly the Western recognition of their borders as well as the power structure that emerged in Europe after World War II. Socialist countries are a part, and nowadays a legitimate part, of this structure.

Deviation from this pattern would lead to uncertainties in relation not only to the Soviet Union but to the overall structure of the European system as well. Pressures towards dealignment in Eastern Europe are contained by at least two factors. The experiences of Hungary, Czechoslovakia and Poland indicate that open or disguised efforts at neutrality are an effective way of halting any progress towards domestic economic and political reform. Furthermore, a breach of the status quo would yield little, if any, advantage in terms of ability to influence international relations.

Thus constraints on a partial neutrality in Eastern Europe are formidable. There are pressures, however, for a greater autonomy in East–West relations. Such pressures surfaced in an interesting manner in 1984 when a coalition of Hungary and Bulgaria emerged to support the efforts of East Germany to advance her relations with West Germany. This search for autonomy was, however, rapidly contained by the Soviet Union and it has not been manifested since. To repeat an earlier observation: the probability of dealignment in Eastern Europe by political choice is low.

The socialist countries are facing increasing challenges to make their economies more dynamic and flexible. These challenges originate both from the capitalist world economy and from the new Soviet leadership. The Soviet objective is obviously to induce a managed process of change by which both the economic relations within the Council for Mutual Economic Assistance (CMEA or COMECON) would be reorganized on the basis of new technologies and, as a consequence, a new kind of political solidarity would be mobilized to strengthen the alliance commitments. Such a project is both timely and, to a degree, unpredictable. It is not entirely inconceivable that the policy of economic modernization could unleash new sociopolitical processes that would increase the indigenous nature of socialist societies and hence make their alliance ties more pluralistic and flexible. The Warsaw Pact is, however, a political fact which will retain its basic character in the foreseeable future.

In Western Europe the prospects for dealignment may be somewhat greater, because the role of nuclear weapons in NATO strategy is currently resisted to the point of disengagement by several member governments, not to speak of the people. Tendencies towards disengagement in Europe continue to persist and even mature, but the changes are unlikely to be rapid or abrupt.

It is often claimed that tendencies towards neutrality are brought about by the adversary great power in order to undermine the power base of its opponent. There is, however, little evidence that such a process of 'encouragement' would have worked in Europe during the postwar period. In fact, NATO has restrained its support to socialist countries that have challenged the leadership role of the Soviet Union in Eastern Europe. In Soviet policy 'there has been a change from ideologically motivated opposition towards conditional support and flexible search for areas of common international interests with neutral tendencies within NATO but almost invariably without any tangible results'.[21] This further suggests that neutral tendencies are internally caused, i.e. they are fostered by domestic and intra-alliance conditions rather than by the policy of the opposing alliance.

Neutrality and neutralist tendencies are sometimes regarded as a source of instability and disorder in the European system. The supporters of power politics and deterrence consider bipolarity and the ensuing politico-military stalemate as a major precondition for stability. This kind of interpretation ignores at least two beneficial effects that neutrality has injected into the European system. First, neutrality has added a new political category to the European system and has hence diluted the impact of overlapping divisions which have been created by exclusive military and economic blocs and segregated sociopolitical systems. The degree of polarization in the European system would be further reduced if smaller countries in both military blocs could cooperate more frequently and effectively with each other. Thus the non-nuclear-weapon countries of Europe could institutionalize their contacts and jointly ponder their common security problems.

Secondly, neutral countries have had a geopolitical function in the continent. In addition to criss-crossing the European system in a positive manner, particularly in northern Europe and southern–central Europe, they have separated the military blocs from each other. This geographical separation has prevented a competitive arms build-up by the great powers in these areas. As a consequence political tensions have also been curtailed. Neutral countries have, in other words, formed a kind of disengagement zone in Europe.

A NEW ROLE FOR THE NEUTRAL COUNTRIES?

So far, the neutral countries have primarily striven to build bridges between the two military blocs and their leaders. If circumstances have allowed, the neutral countries have proposed potential compromises between the great powers and offered the means to achieve them. With the partial exception of economic relations, their mutual cooperation has not been very profound. Rather they have formed a kind of political community which has relatively similar views on disarmament, development and global cooperation. Together with some smaller members of the Western alliance the neutral countries have formed a club of like-minded states on these and related issues.

All the neutral countries oppose the idea of establishing a neutral bloc in Europe. Their foreign policies are, on the contrary, rather individualistic in the sense that self-determination on matters of national security and economic well-being have a high priority. An autarkic policy is, however, impossible and hence the production of military hardware, for example, has to be based on transnational cooperation. In a sensitive area such as military production the dependence on allied powers easily undermines the credibility of neutrality in the eyes of the opposing power. This has been experienced by Sweden, which has received almost continuous criticism from the Soviet Union because of her extensive cooperation with NATO countries in the development and production of aircraft and other weapons systems.

This is a political factor which encourages more cooperation between the neutral countries of Europe. It may not lead to military–industrial cooperation, but may be confined to arms transfers. In fact, Sweden is becoming an 'arsenal of neutrality' which is prepared to equip the air forces of other neutral countries with modern military aircraft. Austria and Finland, in particular, have shown interest in Swedish aircraft. Such purchases may also satisfy criticism, expressed every now and then from NATO, that neutral countries are a military vacuum and cannot defend themselves against the Soviet threat with their own means.

Political consultations between the neutral countries may intensify in the future. Already such consultations regularly take place within the CSCE framework. There are signs that a similar, though less intense and frequent system of consultation might evolve in such matters of security policy that do not directly touch upon national defence. This kind of system could also contribute to a rapproachment between NATO and the Warsaw Pact if it were able to create some new arrangements. An example is the proposal made by Switzerland in February 1985 on the launching of a joint verification satellite by the neutral countries to observe the compliance of major powers with arms control treaties.

Such an idea may not be feasible for several reasons, but on a more modest scale the neutral countries could indeed contribute to the verification of arms control. Austria has made a proposal to the Stockholm conference that would create a role for the neutral countries in the process of verification. They could, for instance, prepare a list of observers from which the great powers could choose in order to help verify alleged breaches of international treaties. According to the proposal the neutral countries could also establish a data base on military issues to facilitate participation in verification.[22]

The Final Document of the Stockholm Conference in September 1986 did not give, however, any special role to the neutral countries in the verification of confidence- and security-building measures. The decision to use the facilities of target countries, instead of the equipment provided by neutral countries, was resented in particular by Austria and Switzerland. A lesson of the Conference is that there are limits to the influence of neutral countries in the European security diplomacy. It does not eliminate, though, the future possibilities that neutral and non-aligned countries will make a difference to the competition between detente and tension. Such a role would ensure a more active continuation of detente in Europe. An aspect of such activity would be to extend cooperation over the bloc barriers, and draw smaller allied countries into political contact with neutral countries. The common aspiration for denuclearization would form a foundation for such a cooperation.

NOTES

1 See Harto Hakovirta, 'The International System and Neutrality in Europe 1946–1980–1990', *Yearbook of Finnish Foreign Policy 1980* (Forssa: Finnish Institute for International Affairs: 1981).

2 See Peter J. Katzenstein, 'The Small European States in the International Economy: Economic Dependence and Corporatist Politics', in John Gerard Ruggie (ed.), *The Antinomies of Interdependence. National Welfare and the International Division of Labor* (New York: Columbia University Press, 1983), pp. 91–130.

3 See Raimo Väyrynen, 'Prospects for Arms Limitation Talks: Negotiations, Asymmetries and Neutral Countries', *Co-existence*, 9 (1972), pp. 1–15.

4 On the early stages of cooperation between neutral and non-aligned countries in the CSCE see Hanspeter Neuhold, 'Die neutralen Staaten Europas und die Konferenz über Sicherheit und Zusammenarbeit in Europa', *Europa-Archiv*, 13 (1973), pp. 445–51.

5 Many of the insights into the role and operation of the N&N Group have been gained from an interview with Mr Jaakko Iloniemi on 15 March 1984. Ambassador Iloniemi was the Head of Finnish Delegation to the Geneva phase of the CSCE.

6 Karl E. Birnbaum, 'Alignments in Europe: the CSCE Experience', *The World Today*, 37 (1981), pp. 219–23.

7 See Christoph Bertram, 'Ein Anfang, noch kein Durchbruch', *Die Zeit*, 39 (1984). On the background of the Stockholm conference see, for example, Raimo Väyrynen, 'Mot en europeisk nedrustningskonferanse', in Thorbjorn Jagland and Sverre Bergh Johansen (eds.), *Før det blir for sent. Atomkrig eller nedrustning* (Oslo: Tiden Norsk Forlag, 1982), pp. 346–61.

8 See P. Terrence Hoppman, 'Asymmetrical Bargaining in the Conference on Security and Cooperation in Europe', *International Organization*, 32 (1978), pp. 141–77.

9 See Hakovirta, 'The International System', pp. 47–8.

10 See Raimo Väyrynen, 'Military Alliances, Nuclear Deterrence and Nuclear-Weapon-Free Zones', in Kari Möttölä (ed.), *Nuclear Weapons and Northern Europe*. (Forssa: Finnish Institute of International Affairs, 1983), pp. 47–52. The concepts of voice and exit come naturally from Albert O. Hirschman, *Exit, Voice and Loyalty. Responses to Decline in Firms, Organizations, and States* (Cambridge, Mass.: Harvard University Press, 1970).

11 For a useful overview see Annemarie Grosse-Jütte, 'Profile neutraler/blockfreier Sicherheits-und Verteidigungspolitik', in Dieter S. Lutz and Annemarie Grosse-Jütte (eds.), *Neutralität – Eine Alternative? Zur Militär – und Sicherheitspolitik neutraler Staaten in Europa* (Baden-Baden: Nomos Verlagsgesellschaft, 1982), pp. 215–55.

12 On recent tendencies see articles in Möttölä (ed.), *Nuclear Weapons and Northern Europe* and Helmut Hübel, 'Präventive Krisendiplomatie der nordischen Neutralen', *Europa-Archiv*, 4 (1984), pp. 119–26.

13 See Kenneth Adler and Douglas Wertman, 'Is NATO in Trouble? A Survey of European Attitudes', *Public Opinion*, 6 (1981), p. 10.

14 Interview with Defence Minister Wörner in *Der Spiegel*, 24 January 1983, p. 41.

15 Cf. Ronald H. Linden, 'The Security Bind in East Europe', *International Studies Quarterly*, 26 (1982), pp. 155–89.

16 For an early analysis of various future models of (Western) Europe, see Christoph Bertram, 'Models of Western Europe in the 1970s – The Alternative Choices', *Futures*, 2 (1968), pp. 142–52.

17 See, e.g., George F. Kennan, 'Europe's Problems, Europe's Choices', *Foreign Policy*, 14 (1974). See also the discussion in Raimo Väyrynen, 'Stability and Change in Finnish Foreign Policy', *University of Helsinki. Department of Political Science, Research Reports*, ser. A, no. 60 (Helsinki, 1982), pp. 11–17.

18 Walter Laqueur, 'Hollanditis: A New Stage of European Neutralism', *Commentary*, 19 August 1981, pp. 19–26. A careful survey of polls on Dutch opinions indicates that its pacifism and neutralism is usually exaggerated: 'if the Netherlands is unique, it would seem it is in the impact of opinion rather than in levels of support and denial', see Richard C. Eichenberg, 'The Myth of Hollanditis', *International Security*, 8 (1983), pp. 143–59.

19 See, e.g., Selig S. Harrison, 'Dateline Afganistan: Exit through Finland', *Foreign Policy*, 41 (1980–81), pp. 163–87.

20 An interview with Mieczyslaw Rakowski in *Suomen Kuvalehti* (Helsinki) 4 (1984), p. 52. Cf., for example, Dieter Senghaas, 'Die Ostproblematik eines europäischen Systems kollektiver Sicherheit', *Vierteljahresschrift für Sicherheit und Frieden*, 2 (1984), pp. 37–40. Senghaas argues that the implementation of 'Finlandization' in Eastern Europe would mean considerable social progress and would reduce Soviet military influence there. The author has, however, some doubts on whether this goal can be reached in Eastern Europe.

21 See Harto Hakovirta, 'The Soviet Union and the Varieties of Neutrality in

Western Europe', *World Politics*, 35 (1983), pp. 563–85 (the quotation is from p. 582).

22 For details, see *Die Presse*, 16 February 1985, and, on a more recent development, Raimo Väyrynen, 'The European Cooperation and Security Process, Security Dilemmas and Confidence-Building Measures', *Bulletin of Peace Proposals*, 16 (1985), pp. 349–61.

9

From Third World Non-alignment to European Dealignment to Global Realignment

A.W. SINGHAM AND SHIRLEY HUNE

THE NON-ALIGNED MOVEMENT

Despite efforts by the opponents of the Non-Aligned Movement (NAM) to either discredit or minimize its importance, non-alignment has become a permanent feature in world politics. More importantly, since World War II, the NAM has also become a creative initiator and mediator in the world arena. This is a remarkable achievement, especially since the NAM does not have an institutionalized structure or a deliberately precise ideological framework. Non-alignment is nothing more than a coalition of countries that share common concerns and come together to promote certain global issues. At the Seventh Summit Conference of heads of state in New Delhi, 7–12 March 1983, 101 members attended from Asia, Africa, the Arab World, Europe, Latin America and the Caribbean. This collectivity of leaders from the Third World represented countries from every continent and the majority of the world's population. There was, on the one hand, the head of state of the Republic of India, with a population of more than 700 million and, on the other hand, the leader of the People's Revolutionary Government of Grenada, representing less than 100,000 people.

The summit conference provides an opportunity for all members, regardless of size and level of development, to participate as equals and determine the policy of the movement. Members may differ in language, religion, culture and social, economic and political forms, but they share a common commitment to the basic principles of non-alignment:

1 Support for political independence, self-determination, and racial equality.

2 A commitment to peace, especially disarmament.
3 The restructuring of the existing international economic order to reduce the inequality between rich and poor nations.
4 A need for cultural equality through restructuring the existing information and communications order.
5 The democratization of international relations, primarily through the utilization of the United Nations as the most appropriate organization to deal with global issues.

In its efforts to promote these principles, the NAM represents the only international social movement in world politics.[1]

The First Summit Conference of the heads of state of non-aligned countries was held in 1961 in Belgrade, but the origins of the movement can be traced to a number of earlier meetings of colonial peoples. The concept of the NAM goes as far back as the 1927 International Congress of Oppressed Nationalities Against Imperialism, held in Brussels. Its more immediate origins are in the various regional meetings of Asian states in the late 1940s and early 1950s which culminated in the Colombo Powers Conference of 1953 where the concept of an Afro-Asian meeting – subsequently the Bandung Conference – was developed.

Non-alignment began as an anti-colonial movement seeking the right of self-determination for all colonial peoples. Its formal beginning as an organization took place during a period of acute tensions between the United States and the Soviet Union. Thus the movement has tried throughout its history to bring an end to the Cold War and to reduce conflict between these two major powers. Self-determination and peace remain two of the fundamental objectives of non-alignment. They are, however, closely linked with a number of other issues, including the eradication of racism and the creation of a New International Economic Order (NIEO) and a new information order.

At all NAM meetings since 1961, the non-aligned countries have sought to change existing international relations by advocating certain universal global values that transcend the narrower values of earlier empires, continents, regional organizations, or nation states. This emphasis on universal values has meant that non-aligned countries have self-consciously sought to submerge their own national interests in the interest of the larger international community. It is precisely for this reason that non-aligned countries have ardently supported all international organizations, especially the United Nations, and argued that international relations should be expanded from the narrow concept of state-to-state relations to the creation of a multi-state system. They have also been pioneers in multilateral diplomacy through such concepts as collective self-reliance. As a global social movement, the NAM has sought greater equality between nations (independence, democratization of international relations and disarmament), between peoples (race), between cultures (information) and between economies (the NIEO). This emphasis on egalitarianism at the international level has led the member nations to challenge seriously the existing world system in all its political, economic and social spheres.

The search for a new world order by the non-aligned countries is fraught with major difficulties and contradictions. International peace and the creation of the modern nation state are often in contradiction with one another. The struggle for peace is a universal and international goal, but nationalism has, in many instances, accelerated the division of the world into geographical, political, social and cultural units known as the modern nation state.

The expansion of Europe into Asia, Africa and the Americas resulted, as we know, in the creation of empires which arbitrarily divided the peoples of the world into a variety of administrative units. The struggle for political independence meant that these arbitrary administrative units now took on objective realities as nation states. In each of these administrative units a number of cultural groupings were integrated into a national unit which upon independence from the empire acted as autonomous members of the family of nations. This gigantic process of decolonization was a monumental step in the world system which was undertaken with a great deal of suffering. In some instances there was a peaceful transfer of power. In others, where colonial powers refused to give up their territories, some peoples have had to take up arms in wars of national liberation to obtain their right of self-determination. Such changes also often led to massive movements of population resulting in the relocation of indigenous peoples. Furthermore, this entire decolonization process was undertaken at a time when the world was seeing another major revolution in the global system, the consolidation and growth of the world's socialist system which then found itself in antagonism with the capitalist system.

There are two stages to the anti-colonial revolution. The first was the emergence of the European-type model of the nation state in the era dominated by world capitalism. In the second stage we find nations of Asia, Africa and the Caribbean coming into being during the period of confrontation between socialism and capitalism. This antagonism has been complicated by yet another major revolution in the global system, a revolution in the technology of warfare where nuclear weapons and now even the possibility of space wars have replaced conventional weapons on the ground. The independence movement was thus born in the nuclear era, which radically transformed relationships between major powers, and more importantly, relationships between these new states, which are non-nuclear, and the nuclear powers.

Non-aligned countries have also been acutely aware of the contradictions of being politically independent while remaining economically dependent on former colonial masters and transnational corporations, a condition which seriously jeopardizes their sovereignty. In entering the world arena at this time, these nations have been primarily concerned with preserving their fragile and newly won independence. To do so, it has become imperative that they pursue a policy of seeking peace between the major world actors while at the same time becoming economically independent and viable. Most importantly, non-alignment was the one form of political organization in the world system that self-consciously expressed its support for the right of a people, whatever its size, to seek independence and to choose its own path of social, political and economic development. This policy of support for self-determination and national liberation was largely responsible for the process of decolonization since the 1960s and was to a considerable extent the work of the non-aligned countries.

Throughout the history of the NAM, the heads of state have sought to link two contradictory objectives – i.e. preserving nationalism in an era calling for internationalism. The problem has been complicated by secessionist movements in a number of nation states, an outgrowth, in part, of the colonial legacy. Consequently, fragile nation states were often forced to call upon the international system and, in some instances, their colonial masters for assistance, including military support to maintain existing state structures. Nationalist movements which had undertaken the arduous task of bringing about independence now faced a dual threat externally and internally. Internally, divisive secessionist movements which made alliance with the international system threatened to further Balkanize fragile states. Externally, the international system, wrought with disunion and distrust, reacted by interfering in the internal affairs of these nations, often with force. Thus the NAM was formed not only to advance the right of self-determination, but to preserve and protect their member states' national sovereignty.

This transnational organization is qualitatively different from the United Nations, which was designed primarily as an arena for inter-state relations. The NAM came into being because non-aligned countries felt the need to have an organization to develop their political strategies as small, weak nations in a world of large, powerful nations. Non-alignment has provided a structure and platform where joint global, social, political and economic objectives could be worked out by these states prior to their participation in international organizations.

There was another major structural reason for the unity between non-aligned countries. The majority were not only weak in economic and military terms but were often small or middle-sized states. The scale and size of nations greatly affected their capacity to participate as equal members in the global system. A large number of the non-aligned countries were among the least developed in the world system, and were also either island or land-locked states. They were thus especially vulnerable to the vicissitudes of world politics and economics, compounded by the continuing presence of their former colonial masters within their economic and social structures. Nor were they anxious to become objects of competition for larger neighbouring countries which were also, in some instances, developing countries. Non-alignment, by stressing the doctrine of non-interference in internal affairs, was in effect trying to guarantee further the political independence of small states.

Finally, questions have been raised in the international community concerning the right of small or middle-sized developing nations to participate as equal partners. Suggestions have been made to reduce the number of these states and fuse them into larger units. This would continue to leave global decision-making in the hands of the major powers. The importance of the NAM is that it thus enables small and middle-sized states to play a decisive role in world politics as members of a coalition sharing common concerns and promoting specific objectives.

The following section will discuss in greater detail the NAM in practice, through an examination of the New Delhi summit of 1983 as a reflection of the movement's view of the global situation and its role in world politics.

THE NON-ALIGNMENT MOVEMENT IN PRACTICE: THE NEW DELHI SUMMIT

The NAM is unique in that it is an international social movement consisting of nation states. The movement has grown fourfold in membership from its original 25 members at the First Summit in 1961 to the 101 members who attended at the Seventh Summit in 1983. It is also unique in that it self-consciously resists institutionalization and has developed an organizational form to enable it to function coherently in world politics. Most importantly, it is not a single issue movement, but a multi-faceted one that insists social, economic and political problems are structurally linked and hence any solution must deal with all these issues simultaneously. For this reason, inequality in the world is viewed as not merely political, economic or social, but as an institutionalized structure that keeps nations permanently stratified in the global hierarchy.

The movement also self-consciously tries to minimize conflicts between its members through a series of decision-making mechanisms which negate tension-building and withdrawal. By developing the consensus mechanism of decision-making, non-aligned countries have tried in their final declarations to cultivate issues that enjoy broad international support and reduce potentially divisive ideological concerns. However, member nations, if they wish and feel strongly, do have the right to dissent on any specific item by filing a reservation after the conference. Thus this movement has been able to remain a force in world politics for the past twenty-five years without disintegrating from ideological and philosophical differences, something which tends to happen in most transnational organizations. (There has only been one resignation, Burma, since the founding of the movement.)

When members of the NAM met at their Seventh Summit in New Delhi, they were convinced, like their predecessors at their previous summits, Belgrade 1961, Cairo 1964, Lusaka 1970, Algiers 1973, Colombo 1976, and Havana 1979, that the world was in a deep political, social and economic crisis. Non-aligned countries have made it abundantly clear that they are not another power bloc, nor an emerging military/social–economic alliance, but a movement of the world's dispossessed. The question of whether the leaders themselves have been drawn from the dispossessed classes of their own countries has become the focus of many Western analysts, both from the Left and the Right. This, however, ignores the simple fact that in spite of the oil wealth, mineral deposits and large granary areas of their nations, the representatives of the NAM are indeed the spokespersons for 'the wretched of the earth'. These heads of state cannot escape dealing with the fundamental issue that confronts their societies, namely, that their peoples are the victims of poverty, disease and war. It is this vantage point that has conditioned their diagnosis of the current global crisis.

In their efforts to address the critical issues which face the world, non-aligned countries periodically engage in a review of global events. The heads of state meet every three years for their summit meeting to assess the current international situation. The foreign ministers meet during the mid period and undertake a similar analysis. The Co-ordinating Bureau meets to examine specific crises as they emerge and, in addition, the ambassadors meet regularly at the United Nations to respond to specific issues. Thus the movement has devised, in spite of its insistence on not developing an institutional framework, a mode of operation to respond to and review global events and to call for specific changes.

The most important gathering is the summit conference. It provides an occasion for states to conduct bilateral diplomacy, but within the multilateral framework of the non-aligned. For example, in New Delhi, India and Sri Lanka met bilaterally to sort out their differences over the Indian Ocean and yet the final resolution reflected the multilateral concerns of the non-aligned. Most importantly, the summit enables heads of state to develop a joint strategy to deal with issues that come before the United Nations, making that institution a more viable venue for multilateral diplomacy. It is precisely this strategy of collective agreement before meeting at the United Nations that has led a number of Western countries to criticize the NAM strongly. For them, the non-aligned, having worked out their contradictions prior to an international gathering, have an advantage that is difficult for the major Western powers to exploit.

Since the Sixth Summit in Havana in 1979 the world had seen the widening of regional conflicts and experienced several years of stagnation in the global economy with serious consequences for developing countries. The tone and focus of the Delhi conference was set by the outgoing Chair of the non-aligned countries, President Fidel Castro of Cuba, and the new Chair and host for the Seventh Summit, Prime Minister Indira Gandhi of India. Both were determined to make the global economic crisis the central issue of the 1983 summit.

One of Cuba's contributions as Chair had been its ability as a Caribbean nation to bring Latin America fully into the movement. Indeed it was Cuba's role as a Latin American country that led most of Asia and Africa to accept Mr Javier Perez de Cuellar as an authentic representative of the Third World, helping him to become the Secretary-General of the United Nations. Latin American coutries have also been able to inform the rest of the non-aligned world of the long tradition of resistance on the part of their people to absorption by the dominant Euro-American culture. It was Cuba which, from the founding of the movement, warned the Asian, African and Arab countries of the new imperial power, the United States. It was also the Latin Americans who helped alert the Third World to the hollowness of political independence without economic independence and demonstrated how economic dependency too often leads to the creation of fragile political structures where military juntas frequently govern and destroy the democratic aspirations of the people.[2]

Thus, in his last act as outgoing Chair, President Castro, recognizing the magnitude of the global crisis and, as a Latin American, acutely aware of the problems of neocolonialism, dependency and the debt problem, prepared a report entitled *The World Economic and Social Crisis* which describes in detail the impact of the crisis on underdeveloped countries.[3] This volume was presented to the heads of state and provided the basis for much of the analysis and debate during the conference.

Prime Minister Gandhi, in her opening speech, also called for the Seventh Summit to deal with this global crisis. She stated:

> Humankind is balancing on the brink of the collapse of the world economic system and annihilation through nuclear war. Should these tragedies occur, can anyone of us, large, small, rich or poor, from North or South, West or East, hope to escape? Let us analyse the economic crisis. We of the developing world have no margin of safety. We shall be the first and worst sufferers in any economic breakdown. In this interdependent world, where you cannot 'stir a flower without troubling a star', even the most affluent are not immune to such disturbances.[4]

She went on to point out matters that the movement should take up in the next three years:

> In spite of Ottawa, Cancun and Versailles, the dialogue between the developed and developing has not even begun. Only a few in the North realize that the sustained social and economic development of the South is in its own interest. Thus we ask not for charity or philanthropy but sound economic sense. Such cooperation between North and South will be of mutual benefit.
>
> The Non-Aligned Movement has stood firmly for a thorough going restructuring of international economic relations. We are against exploitation. We are for each nation's right to its resources and policies. We want an equal voice in the operation of international relations. We reiterate our commitment to the establishment of a New International Economic Order based on justice and equality. Long-range solutions need time and preparation. Immediate problems brook no delay.[5]

At the end of each summit conference, the heads of state adopt a final declaration explaining in detail why the world is facing a particular crisis. The non-aligned countries firmly concluded in New Delhi that the present global crisis was not of their making. According to their analysis, the malaise was, and is, a result of institutionalized political, economic and social inequality. The central problem of the post World War II era was the emergence of a political, economic and social system that had an inbuilt pattern of inequality not only between nations, but concomitantly, between all peoples of the world. Inequality, they argued, was the root cause of international tensions. And these tensions, they further argued, often resulted in violence and war.

The structured inequality thus identified is manifested in many ways. Throughout its existence the NAM has made recommendations to resolve such inequalities. The movement, in many ways, reflects the moods and changes of the global system. At the First Summit it was primarily concerned with peace and disarmament, especially reducing East-West tensions. In the late 1960s the emphasis was on supporting national liberation movements. In the 1970s the global economic crisis led them to call for an NIEO (New International Economic Order) and the Group of 77, originally created in 1963, expanded and became a permanent political grouping within the United Nations framework representing Third World economic interests. And now in the 1980s they have had to face interventions, destabilization and the twin problems of dealing with their internal contradictions, i.e., conflicts between member nations and the possibility of these internal contradictions becoming embroiled in the East – West conflict, creating an international situation with the potential of a nuclear war. In spite of these changing emphases, the movement continues to reflect one single concern – to engage in policies that reduce structural inequality in the global system. These manifestations and solutions are summarized in table 9.1.

Primarily, because it is attempting to restructure the global system, the movement recognizes that it has opponents and that these opponents have always been consciously ready to destabilize and dismantle it. One of the movements's greatest achievements has been its capacity to survive and remain a vital and viable force in world politics by developing the ideological framework of 'unity within diversity'.

At the New Delhi summit, it was possible to detect some basic shifts in the NAM's analysis of the global power structure. Reference was made to the dominant role of major powers in world affairs, especially the resurgence of big power politics and the emergence of a new international conservative coalition in the West consisting of the United States, West Germany, Britain and Japan. Concern over the consequences of big power politics was expressed in the following statement:

> The Heads of State or Government believed that international relations have entered a phase where decision-making on issues of vital concern to all countries of the world can no longer be the prerogative of a small group of countries, howsoever powerful they may be. The democratization of international relations is an imperative of our times which will lead to the realization of the unfettered development and genuine independence of all States. The peoples of the world increasingly recognize the futility of basing national security on theories and doctrines which, if implemented, would result in the annihilation of humankind . . . People all over the world, in both the developed and the developing world, who are concerned with questions like employment, economic planning, environment, public health, etc., are mobilizing public opinion on armament-related issues. Peace movements around the world are increasingly challenging the cogency of decisions to intensify the arms race, particularly in the nuclear field. World solidarity on the vital questions of human survival is today not merely a lofty ideal, it is an overriding necessity.[6]

TABLE 9.1 Global inequality – problems and NAM solutions

	Manifestations	*NAM solutions*
Political inequality	Colonialism Military alliances (bloc politics) Neo-colonialism Major power dominance	Democratization of international relations Support for national liberation (including armed struggle) Reduction of East–West tensions
Economic inequality	Price system (markets) Monetary system (debts) Monopoly of the transnational corporations and transnational banks	New International Economic Order Collective Self-reliance
Armaments inequality	Arms race	Zones of peace Disarmament Denuclearization
Technological inequality	Dominance of industrial technology (including warfare) Dominance of industrial nations in research and development Monopoly of scientific information and training	Transfer of technology
Information inequality	Domination and control of the world's information system and all forms of communication technologies	New International Information Order
Social inequality	Racial, gender, cultural stratification	Restructuring the world's cultural and educating systems of exchange Campaigns against racial, sexual and cultural discrimination
Global structural inequality	All of the above	Multilaterial diplomacy and conflict resolution under the auspices of the United Nations

The fundamental issue of political sovereignty was also raised, but in a different manner than on previous occasions. This time the movement was quite convinced that political sovereignty could be destroyed either by economic destabilization techniques, especially through the world monetary system, or by direct military intervention. Hence they argued that since World War II a number of independent Third World countries had had their sovereignty challenged. Furthermore, the heads of state noted that the global arms race had severely compromised the political independence of non-aligned states.

President Castro laid the groundwork for the major debate over political sovereignty with his detailed empirical study on the global social and economic crisis. Firstly, he linked the arms race to economic development and suggested how this might have an effect on political stability and sovereignty. He stated:

> In 1979–82, the amount spent on the arms build-up has continued increasing, especially by the great powers. Between 1979 and 1981 military expenditures averaged $505 billion a year. It was higher in 1982. The United States and other developed capitalist countries, and the Soviet Union and the European socialist countries, accounted for over 70 per cent of all military expenditures.
>
> Recently, the contrast between the underdeveloped countries' financial requirements and the potentially suicidal squandering of world resources on the arms build-up has been ever more paradoxically highlighted by the fact that such squandering has yearly equalled, and even surpassed, the total external debt of the countries of Asia, Africa and Latin America, a debt that has forced them to cut back – if not cancel – their development programs and introduce restrictions that have severely affected their people's income, employment and living standards.[7]

Secondly, he explained how transnational corporations at the end of the 1970s controlled close to 40 per cent of the industrial production and approximately 50 per cent of the foreign trade of the underdeveloped countries. Not only did this effectively compromise the sovereignty of non-aligned countries, but it threatened to turn a number of countries into client states of global corporations.[8] In addition, the militarization of the economies of the Third World had resulted in the non-aligned world becoming a series of war zones.

A great deal of attention was given to the militarization of the globe. In their analysis of international events, the non-aligned countries found their members at the centre of major conflicts on all continents. Internal as well as international conflicts had involved their peoples in civil wars, wars of national liberation and wars between nations, especially border conflicts. These conflicts had resulted in the militarization of not only individual countries, but whole regions. Once again, as outgoing Chair of the NAM, Castro succinctly explained in his report why the Third World was becoming militarized and how the transformation of large areas of the world into war zones has serious social and economic consequences for a number of Third World countries.

> The international climate of tension and violence generated by the aggressive policies of the imperialist powers and their regional gendarmes, the aggressions and direct or indirect pressures aimed at destabilizing or destroying revolutionary processes and defending neocolonial interests, the regional conflicts often encouraged by those very interests: these are the major factors that have contributed to Third World involvement in the arms race.
>
> Over 30 countries of the underdeveloped world today produce weapons. In 1979, military industrial output in these countries amounted to $5 billion. More than 15 million people make up the regular armed forces of the underdeveloped countries, i.e., about 60 per cent of total world regular military personnel.
>
> Parallel to the arms race, the arms trade is growing by leaps and bounds with a turnover in 1980 of approximately $26 billion annually. Close to three-quarters of this total is imports of weapons and war material by underdeveloped countries. Recent estimates put the value of weapon exports to Third World countries, at 1975 constant prices, at $3 billion in 1970 and almost $9 billion in 1980, i.e., a 200 per cent increase for the decade. At current prices, in 1980 the underdeveloped world imported weapons for $19.5 billion, that is, according to FAO, more than twice the total amount spent on cereal imports by the lowest-income countries that same year.
>
> The arms trade constitutes a considerable burden on weak economies of the underdeveloped countries. It is the most sterile, unproductive and unequal exchange for those countries. The arms trade deprives the importing country of resources that could be used for productive activities. Arms imports expenditures do not generate increased consumption or production, or future production to pay for its costs, nor do they promote public health, education or culture.[9]

The militarization process has additional consequences. Countries, once they become dependent on the weapons purchase system, quickly find that their internal institutions are also transformed: civil politics give way to military politics. These states often become police states. Furthermore, even the newly wealthy countries, especially those who have benefited by oil prices, have found that military ventures have consumed much of their surplus. In the Middle East, for example, the permanent war between Israel and the oil-producing Arab countries has meant the curtailing of the benefits of the OPEC strategy. The war between Iran and Iraq has devastated these two potentially rich industrial giants of the Middle East. In Southern Africa, Mozambique, Angola, Zambia, Zimbabwe and Tanzania are involved in a permanent war with the Republic of South Africa, which has again depleted their resources. The wars in South-East Asia, in turn, have had a debilitating effect on the already war-torn economies of Vietnam and Kampuchea. Similarly, the war in West Asia, including conflicts in Afghanistan, between Pakistan and India, and Bangladesh and India, has meant that all states in the area have had to divert their resources away from social and economic development. The most important recent war, however, is in Central America. The effects of the transformation of this region into a massive war zone have been felt dramatically within the economies not only of Nicaragua and the surrounding countries, but indeed as far as Mexico and Venezuela. Finally, the American invasion of Grenada in 1983 has set in motion a new military process in the English-speaking Caribbean, where small disparate islands are beginning to arm themselves, turning themselves into garrison states.

THE NON-ALIGNED MOVEMENT'S RESPONSE TO THE CREATION OF WAR ZONES

The final declaration at New Delhi noted that the world not only faced the dangers of many concurrent war zones, but that there was a conscious effort to transform wars of liberation in the Third World into testing grounds for the East–West conflict with the dangerous potential of a global war. Non-aligned countries were particularly alarmed by the existence of at least five war zones globally. In Asia, there are war zones in East Asia, continuing from the Korean War, and in South–East Asia, from the Vietnam War. In West Asia, there are the developments in Afghanistan. In the Middle East, there are the wars between Israel and the Arab countries and between Iran and Iraq. In Africa, there are wars in Southern Africa, including Namibia, and in the North, around the Western Sahara and the Horn of Africa. In the Americas, there is the growing war in Central America and the historic opposition to Cuba in the Caribbean. Finally, even in Europe, the Cyprus issue has resulted in the militarization of the Mediterranean region. These concerns were duly noted in the many resolutions relating to those crisis areas in the New Delhi declaration.

While fearful of the transformation of their societies into military zones and police states, the countries of the NAM have always made a distinction between the just struggle of a people to engage in a war for liberation and the efforts by certain nation states to manipulate those wars of liberation for their own private ends. They noted, for example:

> In this context, they [non-aligned countries] have expressed their determination to keep away from power blocs and groupings aligned against one another, the existence of which threaten the world with a major catastrophe. However, current trends in the international situation give cause for grave concern. There is increasing recourse to the use or threat of force, military intervention and interference in violation of the principles and purposes of the United Nations Charter. Forces hostile to the emancipation of peoples continue to infringe the independence, sovereignty and territorial integrity of countries and to impede the rights of peoples under colonial and alien domination to self-determination and independence. The attempt to erroneously characterize the struggles of people for independence and human dignity as falling within the context of East–West confrontation denies them the right to determine their own destiny and realize their legitimate aspirations.[10]

The declaration thus clearly attempts to distinguish between just and unjust wars in the non-aligned world. Wars of liberation, like those that took place in Algeria, Vietnam and Angola, are seen as just wars. Non-aligned countries set a precedent in international politics by treating these liberation movements as the official spokespersons for their people prior to independence. Thus the leaders of the MPLA (Angola), or the NLF (Vietnam) were treated as heads of state, and the movements they led became fully fledged members of the NAM prior to their countries' becoming independent. Indeed, this precedent established by the non-aligned countries ultimately resulted in the acceptance by the United Nations of these new states as legitimate members of the international community.

Two continuing struggles of liberation in war zones also remain central to the NAM – the war in the Middle East, especially the rights of the Palestinians to have their own state, and the war in Southern Africa, especially the struggle of the Namibian people. The NAM has given the PLO full status as a member and consistently elected it to its Co-ordinating Bureau.[11] The movement has also provided historic support for the struggles of the peoples of Namibia and their representative, the South West Africa People's Organization (SWAPO), for national independence and self-determination. The movement has played a major role in keeping the issue of Namibian independence before the global community.[12] This independence struggle is not only one of the oldest in existence, but is linked with the struggles against racism and apartheid within the whole of

Southern Africa. Indeed one could argue that as a result of the non-aligned strategy, the apartheid regime of South Africa is now encircled by independent African states, some of whom had to win their independence through armed struggle. Only Namibia remains as a colony in the region.

The Middle East and Southern Africa are old war zones. The most recent war zone is to be found in the Americas, most notably Central America and the Caribbean. This war zone is different from the others. It has been created out of the repression of the struggle against neocolonialism, whereby people have taken to arms, when necessary, to liberate themselves from dependent capitalist ruling classes as well as military and landed oligarchies. This war zone has grown ever wider with the United States' undeclared war against Cuba after 1959, the violent overthrow of elected leaders supportive of non-alignment, in particular Salvador Allende of Chile in 1973, the war in the South Atlantic involving the Falkland/Malvinas Islands in 1982, the ongoing Central American crisis provoked by America's secret war against the government of Nicaragua, and the military intervention in Grenada in 1983, a mere eight months after the Seventh Summit. The Grenada invasion illustrates as do the conflicts in Palestine and Namibia, how all the principles of non-alignment are intertwined and represented in these war zones. For the ultimate objective of the Non-Aligned Movement is to create zones of peace. It is ironic, and indeed tragic, that the murdered Prime Minister of Grenada had called at the New Delhi summit for a zone of peace in the Caribbean.

GRENADA AND THE POLITICS OF INTERVENTION

The invasion of Grenada was part of a military and security design developed with care after the Vietnam War. It was not a policy aberration of the Reagan administration, but part of a larger geopolitical strategy enjoying considerable bipartisan support in the United States, especially since its architects included Kissinger, Brzezinski and Kirkpatrick. A careful reading of the Kissinger Commission Report on Central America will illustrate succinctly the essence of this doctrine. It could be summarized as follows.

National liberation movements in the Third World are not authentic or indigenous political movements for social justice, but are part and parcel of the global Communist conspiracy whereby the Soviet Union, through its surrogates, influences the course of these revolutions. Consequently, liberation movements represent a military threat to the security of the United States, the Western world and its allies in the Third World. Since some of these revolutions do enjoy domestic support, because of the poverty and the problems created by underdevelopment, it behoves the Western world to follow a twofold strategy. The first would be to provide massive military assistance to all those governments, whatever their ideology, which are engaged in an armed struggle against national liberation movements. Secondly, since some of these movements exploit the economic deprivation of the people, it also behoves the United States and its Western allies to provide economic assistance to these faltering regimes. Thus, this doctrine synthesizes the mainstream ideology of the liberal–conservative coalition in the United States and the countries which participated in the Trilateral Commission.

This new liberal–conservative coalition is also designed to counteract one of the most important lessons from the Vietnam War. The architects of this doctrine are convinced that it was domestic American opposition to the war that resulted in the fiasco of Vietnam. Hence, they conclude that all future wars against national liberation movements must be quick and surgically precise. Project Fury was designed for Grenada, but was intended as a trial run for similar operations throughout the Third World. The Grenadian situation provided all the ingredients for success, both domestically (in Grenada and in the United States) and internationally (support from the Eastern Caribbean countries).

The juridical points of the invasion have been examined in a number of different contexts. Such action clearly violates two major treaties, the Rio Treaty and the Charter of the United Nations, both of which directly include the Latin American and Caribbean countries involved. The major arguments made by the Reagan administration to justify the invasion of Grenada were that it had the support of the Organization of East Caribbean States (OECS) and the Rio Treaty countries, and that the action was in conformity with the Charter of the Organization of American States (OAS) and the United Nations. However these claims are not based on a proper interpretation of the terms of the treaties which established these various organizations. On the contrary, it can be shown that according to these treaties, the action was unlawful.[13]

In reality, world politics is not necessarily governed by international law. Nations have always tended to violate laws in the name of their own security. The Grenada invasion, however, raises a fundamental issue in world politics, that of the concept of national security, and at the same time introduces a new interpretation of this concept.

The national security of the Caribbean and Central American states, for example, is now being integrated with the national security of the United States. This view of American national security is largely a result of the Kissinger–Brzezinski–Kirkpatrick doctrine which has insisted that all struggles or conflicts throughout the globe are structurally linked to the existing global power structure, i.e., the conflict between the United States and the Soviet Union. This linkage doctrine implies that all conflicts are structurally part of the East–West conflict. Thus there is very little room for nations to follow an independent path and in a world of power politics the national interest of smaller powers must be subsumed to the global interests of the major powers. The new doctrine is not necessarily a variation of the old Monroe Doctrine, but an expanded version of that doctrine which now includes Africa and Asia, as well as Latin America and the Caribbean.

The Grenada invasion also gave rise to a new phenomenon in world politics – the doctrine of regional security. Regional security ventures of the kind undertaken in Grenada imply that a new type of military alliance structure is emerging. The NAM began its history over twenty years ago by trying to dismantle military alliances of the first Cold War. While it was successful in dismantling some of these military pacts, such as SEATO and CENTO, it had not anticipated the evolution of a new type of alliance threat, namely, a regional alliance which subsumes the national interest of sovereign nations into regional military coalitions. The destruction of Grenadian sovereignty presented one of the greatest challenges to the movement since its inception. The Bolivian ambassador to the OAS and Chairman of the Permanent Council of that body said: 'Any intervention, regardless of the motives, would constitute a violation of the Charter of the OAS – this is Grenada; it could be any country tomorrow. It reminds us a little bit of the Dominican Republic'.[14]

The global crisis, including the threat of intervention, provides the NAM with new challenges. For example, how can it continue to support struggles for national liberation without creating conditions that would increase East–West tensions? The old dilemma persists, namely, how to maintain peace with independence. If this challenge seems almost insurmountable in the political sphere, in the economic sphere, it is catastrophic.

EUROPE, DEALIGNMENT AND NON-ALIGNMENT

Tito saw the importance of creating a movement that included Europe, and persuaded Nehru, Nasser, Nkrumah and Sukarno that they should move beyond an Afro-Asian concept of the movement. He was primarily concerned about the independence of Yugoslavia, but he also wanted to prevent Europe from becoming the epicentre of the East–West confrontation. However, with the exception of Yugoslavia, European participation in the NAM has been minimal. The only other European members are Cyprus and Malta.

The concept of non-alignment has had a long history in Europe. More recently, European interest in a non-aligned posture has grown. In Southern Europe Greece, under Papandreou, has insisted that it wants to dealign from NATO and cease being a European dependency of the United States. In addition, Papandreou has made definite links with non-aligned countries, especially in the Middle East and Central America. The major impediment, besides Greece's membership in NATO, is the thorny question of Cyprus. While the non-aligned have been quite vociferous in their support for Cyprus and critical of Turkey, the problem of a Muslim secessionist movement presents a major difficulty to the Islamic members of the movement. Papandreou's efforts to change the tilt from the United States to a more even-handed one between the superpowers has won him many friends in the non-aligned world. These policies have definitely been pro-non-aligned, but it is very unlikely that the internal situation in Greece, as well as the question of Cyprus, would result in its seeking membership in the movement. Portugal and Spain have also been paying new attention to non-alignment, but they too are unlikely to take any formal steps to join the movement for both internal and external reasons.

The Scandinavian countries have had a profound interest in the activities of the non-aligned group and have attended some of the meetings as guests and observers. However, they too have been reluctant to participate formally in the movement due to the contradictions this could produce in their stance towards the rest of Europe.

Non-alignment has also been a concern of Eastern Europe, with the most active participant being Romania. President Ceausescu has made a number of statements that show his interest in the goals of non-alignment, and at the Seventh Summit he sent a special message of support to Indira Gandhi, the Chair of the movement. In other international forums, he has often made reference to the fact that Romania is a socialist developing country and is anxious to join with the NAM in implementing the NIEO. Again, in spite of all these ideological claims, it seems unlikely that as a Warsaw Pact member, Romania would want totally to delink its relationship with the socialist world.

F. S. Northedge in a most interesting article on the future of non-alignment is quite sceptical about European participation in the movement. He explains:

> It could be argued that the even larger non-aligned world, which would be formed if European NATO members disengaged from the alliance and

> joined that world, would be in a stronger position to moderate the ideological conflict between the giant Powers. Nehru, in his hey-day, fervently believed that, by expanding the 'areas of peace', the Cold War of the Super Powers could be confined to a diminishing fraction of the world. One would imagine that any likely candidates for admission to such a club of 'independent' countries would think of Britain as having too many problems on its hands as it is to be able to contribute much to solving those of other countries. But, in any case, any such development would run the risk of driving the Super Powers into a form of isolation, all the more dangerous for being peevish and resentful. If that was not expressed in even sharper tensions between the United States and the Soviet Union, it might take the form of their joining together in opposition to a world which separated itself from them.[15]

A. J. R. Groom, however, seems to be more optimistic about the prospects of non-alignment in Europe and uses as his point of departure the political climate in Europe, especially the reaction of the peace movements to the missile question.[16]

While some of the Eastern European countries and Southern European capitalist countries have similar economic problems with the world capitalist system, the vast majority of Western European countries are the prime architects and beneficiaries of the existing global economic system. This structural contradiction between the economic interests of Western Europe and the economic interests of the dependent weaker capitalist states in the non-aligned countries makes it virtually impossible to envisage a genuine European non-alignment.

While there are European lobbies in the NAM, i.e. some Francophone and Anglophone countries, the political distrust of Europe in the Third World is a historical one and emanates primarily from colonial experience. European involvement in the arms trade has also created further tensions between the non-aligned and Western Europe. The transformation of a number of non-aligned countries into client neocolonial states of Europe and the extraordinary influence of transnational corporations and banks in the Third World have also led to major schisms within the movement.

It is because of these divisions that dealignment may be a more useful concept for Europe. It could be important to develop a new framework to foster dealignment and non-alignment globally. Falk is quite correct when he notes that 'state security' has become the dominant ideology in the modern world system which eventually leads to local wars with the prospect of their becoming regional wars, and eventually resulting in a nuclear confrontation.[17] However, an alternative strategy would be to develop links between transnational social movements within both the developed and the underdeveloped world. Such transnational movements could insist on a new concept of national and global security. The peace movement is the most advanced global social movement today. By linking the peace movement with movements for social justice, one can possibly begin to challenge the total hegemony of the modern national security state. The coalition of national security states has resulted in an international garrison state system. This international garrison phenomenon has created an international garrison society: the Grenada intervention is merely the latest example. The movements for non-alignment and dealignment have the major responsibility for challenging these garrison values and replacing them with new international social values for peace and justice. While the political success of such a movement seems far away, the process has certainly begun.

NOTES

1 For a detailed history of the development and role of the Non-Aligned Movement in world politics, see our larger work, *Non-Alignment in an Age of Alignments* (London: Zed Books; Westport, Conn.: Lawrence Hill; Harare: College Press, 1986).

2 A. W. Singham and Shirley Hune, 'The Non-Aligned Movement from Havana to New Delhi', *Man and Development* (*India*), 5 (March 1983), pp. 99–100.

3 Fidel Castro, *The World Economic and Social Crisis* (Havana, Oficina de Publicaciones del Consejo de Estado, 1983).

4 *Final Documents*: *Seventh Conference of Heads of State or Government of Non-Aligned Countries, New Delhi – March 1983* (New Delhi, 1983), p. 190.

5 Ibid., p. 191.

6 Ibid, p. 7, item 15.

7 Castro, *Economic and Social Crisis*, p. 20.

8 Ibid., pp. 144–5.

9 Ibid., pp. 203–4.

10 *Final Documents: Seventh Summit*, p. 5.

11 See A. W. Singham and Shirley Hune, 'The Non-Aligned Movement and the Internationalization of the Palestine Question', in *Palestinian Rights: Affirmation and Denial*, ed. I. Abu-Lughod (Wilmette, Ill.: Medina Press, 1982), pp. 161–81.

12 See A. W. Singham and Shirley Hune, *Namibian Independence: A Global Responsibility* (Westport, Conn.: Lawrence Hill, 1985).

13 Cited in *TransAfrica Forum Issue Brief* (November–December, 1983), p. 13.

14 Cited in Fitzroy Ambursley and James Dunkerley, *Grenada Whose Freedom*? (London: Latin America Bureau, 1984), p. 96.

15 F. S. Northedge, 'Has Non-Alignment a Future in Europe?', *The Nonaligned World*, 1 (October–December 1983), pp. 505–6.

16 A. J. R. Groom, 'Western Europe and the New Cold War: the Need for "Concerned Independence" ', *The Nonaligned World*, 1 (April–June 1983), p. 237.

17 Richard Falk, *The End of World Order*, (New York and London: Holmes & Meier, 1983).

10

Europe, the NATO Alliance and the Third World: Can They be Dealigned?

ROBIN LUCKHAM

THREE DEADLY CONNECTIONS

It is sometimes said that the NATO alliance has assured Europe forty years of peace, albeit a peace founded upon the unstable equilibrium of the arms race. In the Third World it is quite a different story. Whole regions have remained in a state of semi-permanent armed conflict. At the same time, Third World military spending has increased faster than that of the industrial North, although the increases took place from lower base levels and levelled off when the developing countries were hit by the full force of the global recession in the early 1980s. All but a handful of the developing countries are governed under authoritarian, unrepresentative regimes, almost half of which are of military origin.

The 'deadly connection' between conflict in the Third World and the nuclear arms race has become a major issue for the peace movement. It is equally a major concern of Western defence and policy-making establishments, where of course the arguments are couched in another rhetoric and are used to support quite different policies. Virtually all the standard strategic scenarios – works of fiction like Major General Hackett's *World War III*, planning documents like the US Defense Guidance, British Defence White Papers, or France's five-year military programmes – envisage that war in the Third World might, in combination with tension in Europe, escalate into global conflict.

There is a second deadly connection, or rather series of connections, between armament, armed conflict and underdevelopment in the Third World. War directly aggravates and feeds upon other man-made disasters – such as mass population movements, destruction of the environment and famine. Substantial resources are reallocated from development to the military sector. The purchase of complex and increasingly costly weapons systems aggravates foreign exchange scarcities and debt burdens. More important even than the effects of military spending on growth – which have yet to be conclusively demonstrated – is its tendency to support social inequalities and repressive strategies of development.[1]

A third set of deadly connections operates between the military activities of major powers of both blocs and the processes of militarization in the Third World. It is these linkages that will be examined in greater detail in this chapter, focusing in particular on the NATO alliance. The argument that will be spelt out is that the first deadly connection – the risk of conflict spreading *from* the Third World into a European and global holocaust – follows indirectly from the second, the relation between war and underdevelopment and directly from the third, the globalization of the military activities of the powers into the Third World.

This is the point, however, where peace research parts company with cold war analysis. Generally speaking, the latter does not accept that military intervention by the Western powers results in conflict spreading back from the underdeveloped South to the industrial North. Instead, it regards conflict and intervention as the products of the Third World's own 'turmoil' or 'instability' and of the Soviet Union's 'thrust toward globalism'.[2]

It is quite true that conflict in the Third World derives from local and regional as well as international contradictions. Nor can it be denied that the Soviet Union has increased its Third World strategic interests, expanding its arms sales, developing a 'blue water navy', and intervening decisively in Third World conflicts. However, the Soviet intervention is not of concern to Western policy-makers because there is a real possibility that the Soviet Union could replace the West in the Third World: rather, it is construed as a threat to the West's overall strategic and economic *superiority*. Soviet parity in the nuclear arms race could just about be tolerated, at least until the Reagan administration began its attempt to restore strategic superiority through the Strategic Defense Initiative (Star Wars); Soviet moves towards parity in the Third World could not. Or, to be more precise, the Soviet challenge has provided a convenient rationale for the United States to globalize the Cold War and attempt to reconstruct the Pax Americana. This policy, as we shall see later, has domestic as well as international roots, which are to a certain extent independent of the priorities of particular US administrations. One of the most crucial turning points, indeed, was the Carter administration's decision to create a new 'security framework' in the Indian Ocean and Persian Gulf around the US Rapid Deployment Force (established in 1980 and reorganized as

US Central Command, USCENTCOM, in 1983). As Zbigniew Brzezinski, President Carter's National Security Adviser, described discussions within the US administration in 1979:

> Schlesinger argued forcefully that American presence in the Indian Ocean – Persian Gulf area should 'balance' the Soviets, and when Vance and Christopher reacted negatively, I not only backed Schlesinger, but stated that in fact our objective ought to be military preponderance, since the area was vital to the United States, while not of equal significance to the Soviets.[3]

Under the Reagan administration, rolling back Soviet influence in the Third World has become an even more central goal of US policy. As Secretary of Defense Caspar Weinberger put it in 1984:

> We must be prepared to halt and seek to reverse the geographic expansion of Soviet control and military presence, particularly when it threatens a vital interest or further erodes the geostrategic position of the United States and its Allies.[4]

Despite the fact their hegemonic project is manifestly crumbling, US policy-makers increasingly assume that it ought to be shared by their NATO allies. This assumption was made when the US pressed for European cooperation in its bombing raid on Libya in April 1986 (Operation El Dorado Canyon). It has also surfaced in recent alliance discussions of the United States' Maritime Strategy, in the course of which Weinberger is reported as describing the restriction of alliance military operations to the NATO area as 'an outworn geographical tag'.[5]

The Pax Americana (although it has never been a peace) was superimposed in the course of the disintegration of the European colonial empires following World War II. Nevertheless, it could never have functioned – either in Europe or in the Third World – without the cooperation of the United States' partners, secured through the Western alliance. Thus the argument presented below is that although NATO's responsibilities were theoretically confined (under article 6 of the North Atlantic Treaty of 1949) to the territories of the signatories and to the Atlantic ocean north of the Tropic of Cancer, it was intended to be and has in practice operated as a *global* arrangement. It watched over decolonization, mediated the Pax Americana and coordinated the search for alternatives to the latter when, from the late 1960s, it began to disintegrate. Yet it has come under increasing strain from international rivalries during the 1980s, following attempts by the United States to enlist Europe in its pursuit of global military superiority.

NATO AND THE THIRD WORLD: THE MYTHS OF AN ALLIANCE

The North Atlantic alliance is a hegemonic arrangement, dominated by its largest partner (the United States), but also dependent on the consent of even its smallest members. Like other hegemonies, it operates through political myths, among which four are central. First, that NATO is primarily a military and political alliance, constructed to defend Europe from attack by the Soviet Union. Second, that this defence and forty years of peace in Europe have been assured by the nuclear deterrent. Third, that the alliance is a partnership between the United States and its West European allies, with the former acknowledged as *primus inter pares*. Fourth, that it is geographically limited to the North Atlantic area, being a regional rather than a global alliance. Each of these characterizations is seriously incomplete; each is not so much wrong as contradictory, concealing a Janus-face, that of imperialism reorganized in the era of superpower politics and transnational capitalism.

The Myth of a Purely Military and Political Alliance

NATO is a pact among the world's major *capitalist* powers (apart from Japan, which has its own special place in the Western security framework). The North Atlantic Treaty's immediate precursor was the Brussels Treaty of Economic, Social and Cultural Collaboration and Collective Self Defence, of March 1948, whose cumbersome title illustrates how economic and security concerns were interconnected from the start. It was signed in an historical matrix shaped by the Truman Doctrine and the Marshall Plan. Under the former, the United States gave priority to the containment of Communism and turned towards the construction of its own 'national security state'. Under the latter, it financed European economic recovery in an international economy already dominated by the dollar, whose rules of operation had been established under the Bretton Woods Agreement of 1944.

Within the United States, as Wolfe suggests in chapter 4, this helped to construct a bipartisan Cold War consensus, preserving the politics of the New Deal by linking it, through the Truman Doctrine and the Marshall Plan, to the containment of Communism. Within Europe, as Lowe points out in chapter 5, it coincided with and partly facilitated a decisive defeat of the Left, illustrated with particular clarity by the exclusion of Communist parties from the governing coalitions in France and Italy, and paralleled by a similar process of consolidation in what became the Communist bloc in Eastern Europe.

The complex interconnections between alliance politics and the management of the global economy persist to this day. The institutional arrangements – on the one hand those of NATO itself and on the other hand those of a multiplicity of overlapping economic bodies, including the Western economic summits, the IMF, the OECD, the EEC etc. – are quite distinct. But in practice, economic issues – like the oil crises of the 1970s, the effects of recession on defence spending, grain exports to the Soviet Union, defence production and technological progress – have inevitably come up for discussion within the alliance. Likewise, military issues have frequently been dealt with outside the formal bounds of NATO. In particular, recent Western economic summits have tackled a wide range of non-economic questions, including the deployment of cruise and Pershing missiles in Western Europe, the Geneva Peace Talks between the United States and the Soviet Union, the Strategic Defense Initiative and (in 1986) nuclear safety and the question of Libya and international terrorism.

This does not mean that members of the alliance have always been in agreement. Sharp conflicts of interest between the United States and Europe have been almost as common: as during the 1974 oil crisis, or in the dispute over the construction of a natural gas pipeline from the Soviet Union, or over the vexed issue of the transfer of military-related technology to the Eastern bloc. It is arguable, indeed, that it is precisely to contain the damage from such conflicts of interest that alliance politics has been kept formally separate from economic cooperation. Within the North Atlantic community itself interimperial rivalries seem to loom ever larger. Yet looked at from the outside, from the vantage point of the Third World, it is the underlying unity between the NATO alliance and Western capitalism that remains most visible.

The Myth of Deterrence

The United States has maintained military forces on European soil since World War II and is in principle still committed to defend Europe, if necessary, by launching its own strategic missiles against the Soviet Union. But its willingness to do so has been called increasingly in question, and Europeans have become correspondingly less enthusiastic about coupling their own defence to the US nuclear guarantee. Although it was originally envisaged that nuclear arms would permit reduction of conventional armaments in Europe, lowering the costs of defence, almost the reverse has happened. Successive versions of the doctrine of 'flexible response' – first formally adopted by NATO in 1967 – have legitimized the introduction of a panoply of high technology conventional armaments and of tactical and theatre nuclear weapons, in order to maintain the 'credibility' of the deterrent.

During the 1980s three crucial developments have crystallized fears that deterrence within the alliance may diminish rather than increase Europe's security. Firstly, it is widely believed that the deployment of cruise and Pershing missiles in Western Europe – and that of SS-20s in the Soviet Union – increases the risk that Europe might become a nuclear battlefield in a confrontation between the superpowers. The United States' Strategic Defense Initiative (SDI), secondly, has brought into question the ground rules of deterrence and the intra-alliance division of labour. And thirdly, the reassertion of the United States' right to intervene militarily in the Third World under the Carter and Reagan 'doctrines' has pushed the frontiers of deterrence beyond the NATO area.

In sum, both the arms race and the deterrent have been systematically globalized. Even previously the majority of the crises in which the use of nuclear weapons was threatened – notably the Korean War, the Cuban missile crisis, the Vietnam War and the 1973 Arab–Israel War – involved the Third World. In these conflicts the ambiguity shrouding the circumstances in which nuclear weapons might be used has been even greater than in Europe. Only in Korea (and arguably around the pre-1967 heartland of Israel) is there a clearly demarcated Cold War fracture, equivalent to that existing in Europe, where both sides clearly recognize that an attack could provoke nuclear retaliation. Hence it is widely recognized that the danger of horizontal escalation has increased as a consequence of Third World conflicts; and because of increased 'forward based' military and naval deployment by the major powers outside the NATO area.[6]

While the deterrent in Europe has, it is claimed, actually prevented armed conflict – though in fact producing that form of suppressed conflict we call the Cold War – not even this can be claimed in the Third World. The period when the Western alliance was pieced together after World War II coincided with a series of colonial and anti-Communist wars, in Indonesia, Indo-China, Greece, the Philippines, Korea, Malaysia, Algeria, Kenya etc. Since then, one part of the Third World or another has been more or less continuously in a state or war. It would be an exaggeration to say that the Cold War was responsible for all these conflicts. Nevertheless, in many cases they were intensified by outside intervention by the Western powers, by the Eastern bloc, or by both in competition with each other. It has been estimated that the United States has intervened in roughly a quarter of the wars in the Third World since World War II and the former colonial powers in more than a third.[7] And this does not include the conflicts fuelled indirectly by arms transfers or by covert intervention.

Deterrence has been refashioned as an instrument of global geopolitics through a series of shifting and ambiguous strategic concepts, including 'extended deterrence', 'linkage' and 'extended containment'. The first term is used to refer to the vertical coordination between nuclear threats and other forms of military and political pressure within the established geographical boundaries of the Cold War; but it has also been applied to the horizontal extension of deterrence beyond these boundaries into the Third World. 'Linkage' was introduced into the vocabulary of the Cold War by Henry Kissinger in the late 1960s, although its practice predates him. In effect it has mortgaged detente and arms limitation to American goals in the Third World. As Zbigniew Brzezinski sardonically put it when explaining the demise of detente in the late 1970s, 'SALT lies buried in the sands of the Ogaden',[8] a remark that gains salience from the current efforts of the Reagan administration to lay the SALT Treaty to rest in 1986. 'Extended containment' explicitly revives the Truman Doctrine of the containment of Communism to legitimize the present globalization of the New Cold War outside the European theatre.

Such concepts are not just doctrinal fig leaves for American intervention; they are also a logical outcome of 'flexible response'. As explained by a senior Pentagon official under the Reagan administration:

> What was needed for the 1980s and beyond was flexibility – in doctrine, in mobility, in responsiveness – rather than continued concentration upon the European theatre as a separate and dominant entity.[9]

The Myth of Partnership between Europe and the United States

By founding the alliance upon American hegemony, based on the consent rather than the outright domination of Western Europe, the myth of partnership ensured European acquiescence in the emergence of the United States as the major imperial power after World War II. Yet rivalry as well as cooperation between the United States and Europe was built into the alliance from the start, nowhere more so than in relations with the Third World.

The most explicit European challenge to American hegemony has emerged in the Gaullist policies pursued by successive French governments since the late 1950s. However, it should not be forgotten that General Charles de Gaulle had originally hoped to formalize an intra-imperial division of labour in which France and Great Britain would be recognized as guardians of the free world, on a basis of parity with the United States. As he put it in a memorandum to President Dwight Eisenhower and Prime Minister Harold Macmillan in September 1958, it was

> not the view of France that NATO in its present form can do justice either to the security requirements of the free world, or to its own. It therefore seems to France that an organization comprising the United States, Great Britain and France should be created and function on a world-wide political and strategic level. This organization would make joint decisions in all political questions affecting global security and would also draw up and, if necessary, implement strategic action plans, especially as regards the use of nuclear weapons. In this way, it would be possible to foresee and organize eventual theatres of operation which would be subordinate to the general organization (such as the Arctic, the Atlantic, the Pacific, the Indian Ocean, for example) and which could be subdivided into sub-regions, if necessary.[10]

The proposal was rejected by Eisenhower on the grounds that it would not be acceptable to the other members of the alliance, an extension of which beyond the North Atlantic area would cause manifold difficulties. In any case, the time for it had already passed. The colonial empires were on the verge of final disintegration and France had already fallen out with the United States over Indochina, Suez and Algeria. These humiliations, as well as the decisive rejection by the United States and Britain of the proposal for a global partnership, were among the events that prompted de Gaulle to veto Britain's first application to join the EEC in 1963 and to withdraw France from the NATO command structure (although France remained in the alliance).

As for Britain's 'special relationship' with the United States, it never was an equal partnership, and became more unequal as Britain's imperial star declined. Britain found it ever more difficult to sustain a military presence in the Third World because of economic difficulties and the restraints upon defence spending introduced in a series of defence reviews starting in 1957. Its defence industries were rationalized, and after the 1950s its arms exports to the Third World trailed behind those of the two superpowers. The retreat from empire culminated in Britain's 1968 decision to withdraw from its bases and most of its military responsibilities east of Suez.

The United States itself – though quite happy to make use of individual 'special relationships' with Britain and other European allies when it suited its purposes – has consistently encouraged European integration. It put its support behind the abortive attempt to establish a European Defence Community, abandoned in 1954 after the French legislature failed to ratify it. It promoted the formation of the European Coal and Steel Community and of the European Economic Community (EEC) and has consistently supported the enlargement of the latter – this despite coming into conflict with the EEC over a range of economic issues. Equally, it has encouraged efforts to establish a broader European approach to defence.

Such efforts have been pursued through a variety of ad hoc institutional channels. These include the West European Union (WEU), a political body created after the failure of the European Defence Community in 1954 to monitor German rearmament and recently revived as a forum for the discussion of defence and foreign policy. A framework for bureaucratic coordination has been established under the Eurogroup, a consultative forum for European defence ministers, established in 1968, whose members have recently pledged themselves to closer collaboration on defence issues, including the development of a competitive armament industry, as a 'fundamental aspect of Europe's contribution to the Atlantic alliance';[11] and under the Independent European Program Group (IEPG) formed in 1976 to encourage standardization and cooperation in arms production. The European Community has begun to take an active interest in security issues outside Europe under the rather amorphous framework of European Political Cooperation (EPC). The latter, for instance, was mobilized to secure European support for Britain during the Falklands/Malvinas war; and to coordinate European measures against 'international terrorism' following the American bombing of Libya in 1986. Under Article 30 of the Single European Act signed in February 1986, the members of the community have formally pledged themselves to 'coordinate their positions more closely on the political and economic aspects of security' and to 'maintain the technical and industrial conditions necessary for their security'.

None the less, such cooperation has not bridged the disparity between Europe's subordinate place in the alliance and its economic strength, slowly rebuilt following World War II. Disputes have arisen between the United States and its European partners over military and financial 'burden sharing' within NATO; over the 'one-way street' in the purchase of American weapons; about the deployment in Europe of new weapons systems like cruise and Pershing missiles and binary chemical weapons; concerning European interests in arms control negotiations between the United States and the Soviet Union; over the Strategic Defense Initiative; and about how to deal with 'international terrorism'. The Ostpolitik of improved relations with Eastern Europe pursued by some West European governments has come ever more sharply into conflict with the imperatives of the New Cold War and the reassertion of American military interests within the NATO alliance. As for the United States, its commitment to Europe has been weakened by shifts in the centre of economic and strategic gravity, towards the Pacific rim and Middle East.

Nor even has a common European approach yet emerged. European policy-makers have veered between three positions. Some have devoted their efforts to ensuring that European defence remains firmly coupled to the US strategic deterrent. Some adopt an 'Atlanticist position, which aims at constructing a firmer European pillar for the alliance. Others adopt a Gaullist view which would like Europe to take on a more autonomous role – although its principal proponents have never resolved whether this autonomy should be established on a European or a national basis. France herself under three successive presidents since de Gaulle has moved gradually towards a more Atlantic Gaullism:[12] whilst most of her European partners are more prepared than in the past to assert their independence from the United States.

What is crucial for our purposes is that all three approaches would still involve Europe militarily in the Third World. The United States expects cooperation from its allies out of the NATO area in return for its participation in the defence of Europe – and complains when it does not receive it, as after the bombing of Libya in 1986. Yet a more assertive European defence policy could lead to more rather than less European intervention in Third World affairs. After all, one of Gaullism's central objectives is to construct a global role for France, distancing it from the two military blocs by building military and economic links with the Third World. A European Gaullism would probably be no different.

The Myth of a Geographically Limited North Atlantic Alliance

Enough has already been said to indicate that NATO has never confined its interests solely within the geographical limits established by the North Atlantic Treaty. As a 1983 report of a subcommittee of the North Atlantic Assembly on 'Out of Area Security Challenges to the Alliance' has put it:

> Among the historical reasons cited for drawing the limit there, it was frequently noted that some Allies were still at that time with jurisdiction over territories south of the Tropic of Cancer. The line was intended, therefore, to mark a distinction between Alliance territory, on the one hand, and, on the other, national interests that did not fall automatically within the protection of the Alliance. It was not meant to demarcate the sole area of Alliance attention to international security challenges.[13]

This version of alliance history is of interest partly for what it reveals about the state of current NATO discussions concerning 'out of area' operations. If it is correct, one major purpose of the demarcation was to ensure that the alliance did not tie the hands of the colonial powers or indeed interfere with the United States' established sphere of interest in Latin America. However, it was the United States and Canada who were most insistent on geographic limits, to avoid an open-ended commitment to support crumbling colonial empires. On the other hand, their European partners pushed for extensions in these limits.[14] Members of the alliance still recognized an obligation to support each other where, to quote a communique of the North Atlantic Council's December 1952 meeting, 'resistance to direct or indirect aggression . . . is an essential contribution to the security of the free world'; and the same communiqué went on to express the Council's 'wholehearted admiration for the valiant and long-continued struggle by the French forces . . . against Communist aggression' in Indo-China.[15]

Indeed it was partly because their scarce resources were tied up in what remained of their colonial empires that European governments had been prepared to accept American military protection in Europe. For when the North Atlantic Treaty was signed in 1949, France and Britain were fighting major colonial wars in South–East Asia; Britain had already ceded power in India; both countries, along with Belgium and Portugal, were still entrenched in their African colonies, not to be seriously challenged until later; and Holland had recently been forcibly ejected from Indonesia. Not only did European governments count on American troops in Europe releasing their own to police their colonies, some of them even hoped for more direct alliance military support.

During the long and fiercely contested period of decolonization, however, a new system of global hegemony was gradually constructed, organized around direct investment in the Third World by international (many of them American) firms and protected by informal alliances between Western powers and the ruling classes of what became independent Third World states. The United States directly hastened this process by insisting that previously protected colonial markets be opened up and that decolonization be hastened under the principles of self-determination it had insisted on writing into the Atlantic Charter of 1942. Yet American support for decolonization was selective: both because it wished to reduce friction with its European partners and because the Cold War and defending the 'free world' from Communism soon took precedence. When it could be persuaded that colonial wars were anti-Communist, as in Indo-China, the United states was prepared to provide arms, finance and diplomatic support; even if its own troops did not fight alongside those of the colonial powers. Neither France, Britain nor later on Portugal could have maintained a military presence or fought their colonial campaigns without the Marshall Plan and American military aid. The United States frequently used force or threats of force on its own account, both where the authority of the European powers had already disintegrated (as in South-East Asia) and where it was itself the hegemonic power (as in Latin America).

It can be argued, in sum, that during the early Cold War there emerged a global division of strategic labour between the United States and its European partners, which persists in certain respects to this day. The Korean War of 1950 – 3, officially fought under the banner of the United Nations, but in reality on behalf of the alliance, had a formative influence on NATO's command structure. From the start, the alliance's formal responsibilities covered the Mediterranean and thus impinged upon North Africa and the Middle East. Turkey was invited (with Greece) to join the alliance in 1951, and is still regarded as vital to the containment of the Soviet Union in the Middle East and Southern Europe. It continued to be assumed that military bases maintained by individual allies outside the NATO area would be available for alliance use in emergency,[16] although the alliance's global reach was subsequently narrowed by decolonization, France's withdrawal from the NATO command structure and Britain's abandonment of its bases east of Suez.

The early Cold War also saw the formation of a series of parallel, regionally based pacts straddling the Third World, in which the United States participated by itself or in partnership with Britain and France. These included the Inter-American Defence Pact signed in Rio de Janeiro in 1947; the ANZUS pact covering Australia and the Pacific; the Baghdad Pact and subsequently CENTO in the Middle East; and SEATO in South-East Asia. Nevertheless, these pacts fell into disrepair when these regions began to assert their independence. SEATO was dissolved in 1977, although the Manila Pact calling for joint action against outside aggression, which SEATO was set up to implement, still remains in force. CENTO was wound up after the Iranian revolution, although it had been moribund for some time. There remains in force, however, a dense network of ad hoc arrangements and bilateral agreements between individual Western powers and Third World governments, which informally incorporate many of the latter within the strategic terrain of the Western alliance, discussed later in this chapter.

More formal arrangements than these would perhaps not have accommodated interimperial rivalries. During the early postwar period such rivalries stemmed largely from decolonization, coming openly to a head during the Suez crisis of 1956, when American pressure on the pound brought the Anglo-French invasion of Egypt to a humiliating halt. From the 1960s onwards, however, it was instead the United States' global domination that came into dispute after being asserted more explicitly than ever before under the Alliance for Progress and in Vietnam. It was in the latter that the transition from European colonization to American imperialism was most direct.

Vietnam's loss demonstrated the limits of American power almost as cruelly as France's earlier defeat at Dien Bien Phu had exposed the fragility of the latter's colonial empire. In combination with the decline of the dollar and the collapse of the Bretton Woods system of international payments, it forced the United States into temporary retreat from its global ambitions. Even in defeat, however, the United States remained economically and militarily more powerful than any other country on earth. American imperialism has gradually been reconstituted: initially under the 'Nixon doctrine' of arms sales and support for Third World client regimes; later, after the oil shocks and the fall of the Ethiopian Emperor and the Shah of Iran, under the more openly interventionist policies of the 'Carter doctrine'; and now under the 'Reagan doctrine's' open advocacy of global military supremacy.

This would-be reinstatement of American imperialism has added a crucial new dimension to the Cold War, forcing corresponding adjustments in relations with Europe. These adjustments are all the more difficult to make because since the 1950s the economies of the European members of the alliance have gained ground relative to the United States, as well as being integrated within an enlarged EEC. At the same time, the Europeans have remained more dependent on imported oil and international financial markets than the United States, even though the latter's energy dependence and external financial obligations have also increased. The European response to American global strategies has been correspondingly nuanced. Just as during the early Cold War the United States distanced itself from the colonial empires, during the New Cold War European members of the alliance have been reluctant to identify themselves too closely with the American intervention in Central America and the Middle East.

Nevertheless, the United States has continued to press Europe to share its role as self-appointed global policeman. For some years the alliance's consultative bodies have advocated 'serious consultation, coordination and planning' in regard to 'what type of action the Allies might be forced to take to protect national interests' out of the NATO area.[17] Nevertheless, 'recognizing the advantages of sharply delineated boundaries and unwilling to expand them, the alliance appears somewhat baffled about what to do about the global dimensions of security, beyond expressing concern and supporting bilateral or unilateral (in contrast to alliance) initiatives'.[18]

Just how confused the entire question of cooperation outside the NATO area has become was illustrated by the events surrounding the American bombing of Libya in April 1986. On the one hand the United States hoped to use the episode to enlist allied cooperation in the globalization of the Cold War to Libya and other potential Third World troublespots. The 'special relationship' with Britain was invoked to obtain Mrs Thatcher's agreement to the use of F-111 aircraft based in Britain, despite the fact that they were not militarily essential for the success of the raid.[19] And the Tokyo economic summit, held three weeks after the raid, was pressed into a strong statement endorsing joint measures against international terrorism. Yet on the other hand, the episode precipitated what Lord Carrington, the Secretary General of NATO, has called the worst crisis in relations between members of the alliance since World War II[20] (since Suez might have been more accurate). The raid was roundly condemned in Europe, with France and Spain refusing to allow the F-111s to use their airspace. At the same time the growing American propensity to go it alone was reinforced. A number of members of the American policy-making establishment (including Henry Kissinger and Richard Perle)[21] argued after the raid that the United States should be prepared to scale down its forces in Europe, if European governments were unwilling to support it outside the NATO area.

THE MECHANISM OF DOMINATION

If, to summarize the above, NATO has always functioned as a global alliance, how have members' interests been coordinated and superimposed upon the Third World? First, there is a complex tissue of relations between individual NATO members and the developing countries: their arms sales and transfers of military production technology; their proliferation of nuclear technology; their military training and assistance programmes; their bases and military 'facilities'; their navies and rapid deployment forces; and their interventions in Third World conflicts. In total, West European military activities in the Third World are not very much less than those of the United States.

Secondly, the shared interests of the United States and Western Europe in the prevailing relations between North and South have created the basis for an informal division of strategic labour among them. The military relationships which members of the alliance maintain with the developing countries cohere in a systematic manner as a *structure* – which cannot be explained as a simple aggregate of all their bilateral military relationships. They are complicated, however, by the interimperial rivalries already referred to, which are played out within an unstable equilibrium amongst the NATO powers.

Thirdly, alliance relationships with the Third World no longer (with a few limited but strategically important exceptions) involve direct physical and military control of Third World territory, as in the colonial era. For many years, especially during the period of detente, the Western powers have relied as much on the instruments of military diplomacy – arms transfers, military training programmes etc. – as upon the actual use of force. Their combined influence has been all the greater because their economic stranglehold in the developing South has scarcely been challenged by the socialist countries. Far from the two alliance systems enjoying rough parity, the Western bloc has always operated from a position of clear global advantage. Nevertheless, the past few years have seen a reversion by the Western powers to direct military intervention in the Third World: an apparent shift back from hegemony to domination, reminiscent of the colonial era, although outright conquest is no longer the goal.

Arms Transfers

Arms transfers are perhaps the most tangible European military connection with the Third World. Sales of major weapons by European members of the NATO alliance have increased steadily since the 1950s (figure 10.1). They rose most sharply when OPEC petrofunds were recycled during the 1970s and levelled off in the early 1980s, at a time when sales by the superpowers were actually falling. According to Stockholm International Peace Research Institute (SIPRI) figures, major weapons exports to the Third World by the five largest European exporters (France, Britain, Italy, West Germany and The Netherlands) were some 51 per cent of the total NATO transfers of major weapons to the Third World in the 1950s. They fell to 40 per cent in the 1960s and 37 per cent in the 1970s; but then rose again to 45 per cent between 1980 and 1984.

These arms transactions neatly illustrate the two-sided nature of the alliance: as a pact between the major capitalist powers against the socialist bloc; and as an institutional arrangement for the management of inter-imperial rivalries. Total NATO major weapons transfers to the Third World have generally exceeded those of the Soviet Union and Warsaw Pact countries, often by substantial margins. But whereas during the 1950s NATO major weapons exports exceeded those of the Warsaw Pact in a ratio of 3.8 to 1, in the 1960s this fell to 1.3 to 1. In the 1970s the ratio was 1.8 and between 1980 and 1984 it was 1.4 to 1. Europe's exports were all the more vital because from the 1960s Soviet arms transfers to the Third World have generally exceeded those of the United States – except in the late 1970s when the 'Nixon doctrine' of using arms to shore up client regimes in the Third World was implemented under the Ford and Carter administrations. European suppliers have often stepped in when the United States has run up against political restraints such as Congressional restrictions on sales to Arab governments. (It was such restrictions

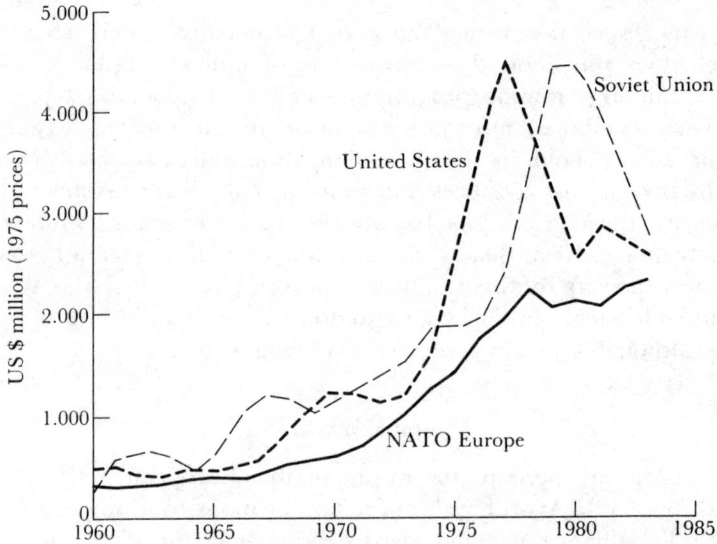

FIGURE 10.1 Exports of major weapons to the third world by NATO and Warsaw Pact alliances. Figures for Europe include only the largest five exporters (France, Britain, Italy, West Germany, The Netherlands).
Source: Stockholm International Peace Research Institute Yearbooks.

which, for example, cleared the way for Britain's recent sale of Tornado aircraft to Saudi Arabia in place of US F-15s.)

On the other hand, arms exports have also aggravated interimperial rivalries. Since the 1950s European suppliers have competed with *both* of the superpowers in Asia and the Middle East; and from the mid-1960s they began to make major inroads in Latin America, whose arms market was previously controlled by the United States. One of the main attractions of European weapons is that they enable Third World purchasers to escape dependence on the superpowers. France in particular has used its 'independent' defence policy and non-membership of the NATO command structure to good effect when pushing military sales. Currents of interimperial rivalry have also been stirred by the competition for market shares amongst European countries themselves. By the mid-1970s France had overtaken Britain – whose arms sales in the 1950s actually exceeded those of the Soviet Union and were two-thirds those of the Unites States – as the largest European supplier, and in the early 1980s she was selling more or less twice as many major weapons. Italy and West Germany have also emerged as major competitors.

Yet arms are a flawed instrument of influence. American arms and military assistance did not guarantee the survival of either the Emperor of

Ethiopia or the Shah of Iran; although arguably they have been crucial in preserving the Saudi monarchy, and in securing the continued adherence of Egypt to the Camp David agreement. French military aid has helped to hold a string of African client regimes (notably in Senegal, the Ivory Coast, Cameroun and Gabon) within a neocolonial protectorate; but it has not prevented the slide of others (like Chad) into anarchy; nor the installation of left-wing regimes in countries such as Benin, the Congo and Madagascar.

Nor has the unrestrained pursuit of Third World arms markets necessarily served the overall interests of the Western alliance. Rather, it has enlarged competition for spheres of influence, stimulated armed conflict and entrenched political instability. Third World imports of major weapons are presently five or six times larger in volume terms than twenty years ago, even after their relative decline in the early 1980s. The latter partly reflects a shift in emphasis in American strategy, from arms sales back to direct military intervention in the Third World (although European and Soviet exports have been less affected). More crucial, however, has been the impact of recession, which has dramatically increased the developing countries' debts[22] and reduced their ability to pay for weapons.

The danger of unrestrained competition for arms markets is recognized by Western governments. But few among them have observed unilateral restraint; and even these (notably West Germany,[23] Japan and Sweden) have become less enthusiastic about maintaining restrictions. The only major international negotiations to limit arms transfers since World War II took place during the Conventional Arms Transfer (CAT) talks held between the United States and the Soviet Union in 1977–8. However, these negotiations were torpedoed by the United States, partly because the US administration itself was divided about whether or not they should be used to extract concessions from the Soviet Union.[24] Even if they had succeeded, they still did not cover all the other major arms exporters, without whose participation bilateral restraint by the superpowers would almost certainly have failed.

Internationalization of Arms Production

Behind the competition of Third World military markets there have been powerful supply-side pressures, deriving from the mismatch between arms procurement and the military product cycle. In the United States procurement has also acquired an added cyclical momentum from the hegemonic cycles of the Cold War, described later in this chapter.

West European arms transfers have been less responsive than those of the United States to the cyclical pattern of the Cold War; but have been even more closely influenced by the commercial logic of arms manufacture. All European arms producers have difficulty recouping the heavy development costs of complex modern weapons systems from narrow domestic markets, although they face this problem in strikingly different ways. France and Britain have continued to develop and produce the full range of weapons systems, in order to support their claims to be global as well as European powers – France with more success than Britain, because arms manufacture has been harnessed to a coherent political and commercial strategy. Italy, on the other hand, has expanded its arms industry dramatically since the early 1970s, by acquiring foreign, mostly American, licences and components, thus holding down its own development costs. Through unrestrained selling of weapons to the Third World, it is now as large an exporter as Britain; and other European countries like Spain and Greece are following it into the market with similar commercial strategies. West Germany, on the other hand, has developed lines of military production (armoured vehicles, military electronics, tactical missiles) that are more closely integrated with its civilian industrial base, making it a formidable competitor in the high technology market. Smaller countries like Holland and Belgium produce narrower ranges of military products based on traditional specialisms (small arms in the case of Belgium), or linked to civilian lines of production, e.g. shipbuilding and electronics in Holland.

Despite such variations, most branches of West European arms production face severe structural crises, with ramifications for the intra-alliance division of labour and for relations with the Third World. Governments have tried to resolve these crises in a number of different ways, none of them satisfactory. Some have followed the logic of arms exports wherever it leads, which in the context of global competition has meant cut-throat competition with other producers, as well as substantial additions to Third World debt burdens. The best that can be said on behalf of such arms exports is that they have assured the survival of some national arms industries, thus preserving the pretensions of military power that can be constructed around an allegedly self-sufficient defence-industrial base. However, the available empirical evidence suggests that the countries that have specialized in the military sector have had less resources available for civilian investment and have enjoyed lower rates of non-military growth;[25] even though military spending may possibly have had a short-run pump-priming effect during the present recession. Moreover, the limits of export-led arms production have been reached, with a number of newly industrialized countries entering the international arms market at a time when most Third World countries cannot finance the same (let alone increased) imports of weapons.

A second solution has been to extend the military product cycle by selling components, parts and licences, and by participating in joint ventures with Third World arms manufacturers. European arms firms are less encumbered by political restrictions on the transfer of technology than are their American and still more their Soviet competitors. South America, South Asia and the Middle East have been their main areas of operation. In the latter they would have played a still more extensive role if plans for an Arab arms industry, based on the licensed production in Egypt of several weapons systems of mostly European origin, had not been aborted by the Camp David agreement. Yet the number of newly industrializing countries whose industrial base can support arms production and absorb military technology is too small to overcome the difficulties of the European defence industries.

The main alternative to transfers of arms and military technology is the rationalization of arms production within the NATO alliance or among its European members. Rationalization within NATO is not easy to reconcile with the United States' hegemonic position in the alliance. In a few cases European arms manufacturers have sold licences to the United States or have entered into coproduction agreements – as with the Harrier VTOL aircraft or Euromissile's tactical missiles – but only when European firms possess clear technological advantages which the United States has wanted to recapture. The 'one-way street' in American sales of weapons and military technology to Europe is still the predominant pattern. Transfers of technology, moreover, are hedged with restrictions, administered bilaterally and through the machinery of COCOM (the organization charged with monitoring transfers of technology by the members of the alliance and Japan to the Communist bloc). Such restrictions have been enforced with increasing stringency and have been extended to cover an ever broader ranger of 'dual-use' technologies (for instance computer software as well as computers and microprocessors themselves). The hegemonic intention of technology is clearly illustrated in the Reagan administration's offer to subcontract some of the 'Star Wars' research and development to European members of the alliance. This is intended both to draw the sting from European criticism of the Strategic Defense Initiative and to make use of European know-how within a framework organized and controlled by the United States.

Intra-European cooperation in arms and aerospace production dates back to the 1960s, when it coincided with (and was informally linked to) Britain's negotiations for membership of the EEC. Since then, several major collaborative ventures have been pushed through. Nevertheless, such production has never been centrally planned at a European level despite the elaborate consultative machinery described earlier. Rather, it has been organized through a series of ad hoc joint ventures negotiated between two or more national defence manufacturers. Moreover, the economics of coproduction have remained a matter of dispute, as for instance in the case of the high cost Tornado fighter bomber produced by the Anglo-German-Italian consortium Panavia. The recent controversy over the design of the proposed successor to Tornado, the European Fighter Aircraft (EFA) illustrates how longstanding political and economic rivalries among the Europeans themselves can obstruct cooperation, with France in the end deciding not to participate.

More to the point for the present discussion, there is little evidence that the rationalization of arms production, either within Europe or within NATO, has reduced the drive to export. Some of the products of joint ventures – like the Franco-British Jaguar aircraft, the Franco-German Alphajet (where coproduction allowed West Germany to obtain access to markets in countries it was unable to sell to directly) or Euromissile's Hot and Roland tactical missiles – have been widely marketed in the Third World. European coproduction may actually keep alive the pressure to export weapons, when it rescues defence enterprises which would otherwise have gone out of business, or spreads the burden of the subsidies required for complex weapons systems to compete in international markets. (Interestingly, the failure of the negotiations between France and other prospective partners in the EFA consortium turned upon the former's desire to produce a lighter, less complex aircraft suitable for the export market.) In sum, the development, production and export of complex conventional weapons will continue – both on a national and a cooperative basis – so long as European countries base their *own* defence on the large-scale deployment of indigenously developed conventional armaments.

The Nuclearization of the Third World

Nuclear proliferation as such falls outside the scope of this discussion. However, the transfer of 'civilian' nuclear technology by European suppliers has almost inevitably responded to the desire of Third World recipients to develop their own nuclear weapons capability.[26] Israel, South Africa and India are the only countries outside the two military blocs believed to have developed nuclear explosives, although all these deny (with varying plausibility) that they possess nuclear weapons. A number of other countries (most notably Pakistan, Brazil, Argentina and Iraq) are taking steps to obtain the required technologies.

As with the transfer of arms, the overall interest of the Western powers in controlling proliferation has been complicated by interimperial rivalries. Efforts to establish international control under the complex procedures of the Non-Proliferation Treaty (NPT) have been systematically undermined by commercial competition. West European producers, with their relatively narrow domestic markets, have been under intense pressure to sell reactors and technological know-how in order to maintain their commercial viability. West Germany's Kraftwerk Union (KWU) and France's Framatome have been particularly active in Third World markets, although British, Italian and Dutch concerns, as well as transnational conglomerates (like the German/Dutch/British company URENCO) have also been pursuing Third World markets for the different elements in the nuclear fuel cycle. In so doing, they have often paid insufficient regard to safeguards and have sometimes indeed supplied non-signatories of the NPT. Particularly notorious examples are France's construction of 'civilian' nuclear reactors in South Africa and West Germany's 1975 so-called Master Treaty with Brazil, providing for the phased transfer of the entire nuclear fuel cycle (although the agreement has been only partly implemented and was heavily criticized in Brazil itself). Such transfers have been facilitated by a complex network of nuclear fuel sales and technology interchanges among members of the Western alliance themselves. Yet efforts to pressure members of the alliance to control nuclear sales to the Third World – such as the Carter administration's non-proliferation initiatives – have generally come to nothing.

Efforts at international control have also been undermined on the demand side by the desire of a number of Third World countries to acquire nuclear weapons technology. As more acquire it, this desire feeds on itself, with further countries aspiring to catch up with nuclear-capable neighbours – to the extent that one can almost talk of submerged nuclear arms races developing in South Asia, the Middle East and South America. Added to this there is the the risk that regional nuclear powers could carry out preemptive strikes upon the nuclear installations of their neighbours, such as Israel's 1981 airstrike against the Osiris research reactor being constructed by France in Iraq.

The NPT itself has been criticized in the Third World on the grounds that 'all it does is to disarm the disarmed' (to quote an Admiral who until recently headed the Argentinian energy authority).[27] The nuclear powers' failure to restrain the vertical proliferation of nuclear weapons within their own armouries has been a central point of contention at NPT Review Conferences.[28] Moreover, their nuclear weapons development still depends on Third World testing sites, notably the Pacific, used by the United States, the USSR, France and (in the past) Britain to test nuclear devices and their delivery systems.

Military Assistance and Cold War Ideology

The ideological basis for the incorporation of the Third World by the system of military blocs is established through a dense network of military assistance and training programmes. The United States alone has trained close to half a million Third World officers and men in its military training institutions since World War II. The former colonial powers have trained rather fewer but their role has been no less crucial – both in providing military education in the metropolis and in establishing academies and training establishments in their former colonies. Nowhere is this more so than in Africa. France still maintains an elaborate superstructure of military cooperation agreements, training facilities and bases in French-speaking countries.[29] Britain has given priority to the formation of the military elite, sending out teams to help establish staff colleges in Nigeria, Ghana, Kenya and Zimbabwe. In the latter it has also trained former guerillas to form the core of an integrated national army, and Britain is similarly retraining the former revolutionaries of Mozambique's armed forces. Even Belgium and Portugal maintain military assistance teams to their former colonies – the latter training forces which were originally created to wage a guerilla war against its own colonial army.

The influence of these training links is profound, though in its nature difficult to quantify. The ideologies such links disseminate tend to homogenize Third World armies around a single professional paradigm, a process aptly characterized by the members of the British military assistance team which trained Zimbabwe's former guerillas, as 'the sausage machine'.[30] Professionalism tends to reinforce capital-intensive modes of warfare and thus to stimulate arms imports. It also demobilizes Third World armies politically: not by removing them from the political arena, but by cutting them off from radical or grass-roots politics. Particularly crucial in this respect are the teaching of the theory and practice of 'national security', 'counterinsurgency' and 'counter-revolutionary war'. These doctrines emerged in the historical matrix of the early Cold War and of colonial wars in Malaya, Algeria and Vietnam. Having been refined in the staff colleges of the West, they were transferred to the military training institutions and battlefields of the Third World as well as to the West's own 'insurgencies' (for example Northern Ireland) and acquired further doctrinal refinements, such as the Latin American versions of National Security Doctrine.[31]

Not only has military assistance been used to cement ties with Third World military elites and to shape the dominant political consensus; it has also been consciously tied to particular strategies of international development. France's military aid to its former colonies is administered by the Ministry for Cooperation and Development. British military assistance, though separately administered by the Ministry of Defence, tends to be provided to countries in which Britain has historical ties, commercial interests or prospects of military sales. At the same time British civilian aid has been used to support political and strategic objectives (the Overseas Development Administration's behind-the-scenes support for American efforts to block IMF and World Bank credits to Nicaragua is a recent example). Under the Reagan administration the United States has greatly expanded its military assistance programmes, making up for the cuts in the post-Vietnam period. It is also making more explicit use of civilian aid as an instrument of national security policy, a trend endorsed in 1983 by the Commission on Security and Economic Assistance,[32] which carried out the first official review of American aid policy for over a decade. Thus the revival of the Cold War has been pursued in parallel with a reorientation of development policy, supporting market-based restructuring carried out by strong governments whose 'security' (and that of the strategies of development they impose) is underwritten by protecting foreign powers.

Intelligence and the Cosmology of Terrorism

The export of counterinsurgency to the Third World has been paralleled by a consolidation of the national security state domestically. In the United States the grip of the intelligence services has been re-established after Vietnam and Watergate, following a sustained political campaign on their behalf by right-wing political groups. Meanwhile, the technological conditions of intelligence-gathering have been transformed by computers, electronic signals intelligence (SIGINT) and satellite surveillance. The distribution and control of intelligence has become a powerful instrument of intra-alliance cohesion, illustrated by the United States' sharing of satellite intelligence with Britain during the Falklands/Malvinas conflict. France is the only European member of the alliance with a global military communications network that remotely compares with that of the United States; and even she has used US satellite intelligence, for instance during operations in Chad. This intelligence gives the United States and its partners immense military advantages relative even to Third World countries that deploy relatively advanced weapons systems, like Libya. It can also be shared on a selective basis with regional allies such as Israel, Egypt, Saudi Arabia and Morocco (where it has helped turn the tide against the Polisario guerillas in the Western Sahara).

Electronic data-gathering has by no means displaced the more traditional functions of the secret services: espionage, covert operations and 'low-intensity warfare'. US counterinsurgency on behalf of friendly governments and destabilization of foes has been re-established on a more systematic footing by the Reagan administration, with its support for the Contras in Central America, the Mujehadeen in Afghanistan, UNITA in Angola and similar groups in the Horn of Africa and South-East Asia. The specialized forms of force deployed by the United States in the Third World include not only the CIA, but also the military intelligence, anti-terrorist and unconventional warfare units of the regular armed forces, such as the Special Forces (the Green Berets) or the US Navy's SEALS and Delta Force, which have been expanded and reorganized under a New Joint Special Operations Agency established in 1984.[33] The fact that it is not only the United States but also its European partners that engage in such activities was dramatically revealed by the sabotage of the Greenpeace vessel *Rainbow Warrior* in New Zealand by operatives of the French DGSE (military intelligence) in 1985.

The globalization of the national security state is being legitimized by the current campaign against 'international terrorism', which was placed at the forefront of the international agenda by the bombing of Libya and the 1986 Tokyo economic summit. There is little doubt but that terrorists have killed and maimed innocent people; and that they coordinate loosely among themselves and with the states (such as Syria and Libya) that support them. Yet the damage they cause is small relative to the casualties of Western-supported insurgencies and, still more, by contrast with the immense destruction of four decades of continuous warfare in the Third World. It is difficult to escape the conclusion that terrorism has been given such priority because it strikes against the infrastructures of global capitalism (air transport, tourism) and of global military intervention (bases, overseas military personnel); and at the same time because it breaches the carefully constructed quarantine between permanent war in the Third World and unstable peace in Europe and Latin America. The threat of terrorism has been woven into the cosmology of intervention, supplementing the threat of Communism as a source of legitimacy for alliance cohesion and for the globalization of the Cold War.[34] Yet the 'surgical' military strikes by Israel against Lebanon in 1982 (Operation Peace in Galilee) and by the United States against Libya in 1986 (Operation El Dorado Canyon) were qualitative escalations beyond counter-insurgency: not only out of proportion to the alleged threat, but also sharpening the very conflicts they were supposed to suppress.

The Infrastructure of Intervention: Bases, Rapid Deployment and 'Peacekeeping' Forces

Before the 1980s the trend was for the members of the Western alliance to reduce their direct military presence in the Third World: the former colonial powers as part of decolonization and the United States consequent upon the debacle in Vietnam. With the benefit of hindsight, however, it appears that this retreat may simply have paved the way for a new infrastructure of global military power organized around metropolitan based intervention forces and naval task groups, purporting to be able to 'project power' over long distances. Developments in military satellite communication and long-range air transport have made such redeployment easier; although the Western powers cannot entirely dispense with Third World facilities.

In spite of the loss of Vietnam, the United States still maintains a formidable world-wide network of bases, most especially in East Asia, the Pacific and the Eastern Mediterranean. It has acquired base rights on the island of Diego Garcia from Britain and has made it the centre of its Indian Ocean operations. Following the Arab oil embargo of 1973 – 4 and the revolutions in Ethiopia and Iran – which exposed the West's vulnerability in the so-called 'arc of crisis' – the Carter administration established the Rapid Deployment Force (RDF) in 1980, and negotiated base facilities for it in Morocco, Egypt, Oman, Somalia and Kenya, in exchange for military and development assistance. US Central Command (USCENTCOM), as the RDF has now become, is an immense military apparatus of over a quarter of a million men, for the most part regrouping already existing military units, including four army divisions (two air-mobile and one mechanized), an air cavalry brigade, marine amphibious forces, seven tactical fighter wings, two strategic bomber squadrons, three aircraft carrier battle groups, a naval surface action group and five marine air patrol squadrons, backed up by major increases in long-range air and sea transport. Although specifically assigned to USCENTCOM, these forces can be used in other emergencies – as they were in the invasion of Grenada, off the coast of Lebanon and in the bombing of Libya. Only a small portion (a small headquarters and a carrier battle group) is permanently deployed near the Persian Gulf, but those forces can draw on the larger naval forces based in the Pacific and Eastern Mediterranean and upon troops and aircraft based in the United States.

France, Britain and, on a smaller scale, Italy are the only European members of the Western alliance with any pretensions to 'project power' on a global scale. The former still maintains a network of bases and facilities in sub-Saharan Africa, though it steadily reduced its troops from over 60,000 men in 1960 to less than 7,000 in 1981 and abandoned one major base, in Ndjamena, because of the civil wars in Chad. At the same time, however, it has built up its mobile intervention forces in metropolitan France. These were reorganized by the socialist government of M. Mitterand under unified command as the Forces d'Action Rapide (FAR), with 47,000 men and a dual role as a mobile force in Europe and an intervention force in the Third World. France's present military support of Hissan Habré's regime in Chad against Libyan-backed opponents is only the most recent in a string of interventions in Africa, which have had a decisive effect on the power balance in client African states.

Since its withdrawal from east of Suez, Britain has played a less visible military role than France. Nevertheless, British troops have continued to be stationed outside the NATO area (in Belize, Hong Kong, Brunei, Cyprus and the Falklands) supplemented by units of the quasi-mercenary Gurkha Rifles. British military teams have been supplied on contract to Third World governments to train their troops and in some cases (notably Oman) to organize actual military operations. And British naval units have been dispatched to 'show the flag' outside the NATO area. The 1982 Falklands/Malvinas war demonstrated decisively that Britain was still quite capable of fighting limited engagements in the Third World, and it also helped to rescue the Royal Navy from budget cuts. Not long after the conflict Britain formally constituted its own intervention force based on the 5th Airborne Brigade of Paratroops and the 3rd Commando Brigade of the Marines. Since 1985 Italy has established a small tri-service intervention force for use in the Mediterranean, based on the experience of the Italian contingent which participated in 'peacekeeping' in the Lebanon in 1983.[35]

The role of the Europeans has been especially crucial in sub-Saharan Africa, a region where aggregate French and British arms sales, training and military deployments have well exceeded those of the United States and have matched those of the Soviet Union. Elsewhere United States policy-makers have viewed their NATO allies mainly as part of the supporting cast. This is described by the US Secretary of Defense in his FY1986 Annual Report to Congress, when referring to South-West Asia (i.e the Middle East, Persian Gulf and Indian Ocean):

> Many of our friends and allies have long experience – and in some cases still maintain a presence in SWA. France, for example, has naval and tactical air facilities in Djibouti: that could keep the Bab el Mandeb strait open in a conflict. Similarly, the United Kingdom has provided military personnel to assist the Sultan of Oman's military forces and has made arrangements for our using and improving its facilities in Diego Garcia. France, Italy, the

> United Kingdom, the Netherlands and Norway have all participated in multinational peacekeeping forces in the Middle East. A number of the European allies have provided en route support to US forces deploying to SWA for exercises or other missions. Furthermore, the United Kingdom and France routinely deploy forces to the region. Depending on the situation, external allied support and cooperation could be very helpful to us in a crisis. We and our NATO allies are studying ways for them to compensate in Europe for any diversion of NATO-oriented US forces to SWA in the event of simultaneous conflicts in the two regions.[36]

NATO's military staff prepared a South-West Asia Impact Study in 1983 of the 'implications for NATO/Europe of deployment to Southwest Asia of US military assets also designated as European reinforcements'.[37] 'En route' support (refuelling and overflight) facilities for American forces deploying to the region have also been discussed. However, 'Southwest Asia is the only area so far for which NATO has developed a contingency plan. It is essential to note that no multinational alliance force is planned for intervention in the area, even in a worst-case scenario'.[38]

Nevertheless individual members of the alliance have already cooperated in multinational interventions in the Third World outside the formal framework of NATO. Among the most striking of these were the 1977–78 operations against rebels in the Shaba province of Zaire, combining American and French logistical support, French and Belgian paratroops (in 1978) and military units from Morocco and French-speaking African states. The rubric of 'peacekeeping' has sometimees been used to legitimize allied cooperation in the Third World. This was the formula under which the United States secured the participation of European and Third World military contingents in the Multinational Force and Observers (MFO) policing the handover of the Sinai under the 1979 Egypt–Israel Peace Treaty in support of the Camp David Agreement. Similarly, it persuaded France, Italy and Britain to join in 'keeping the peace' in the Lebanon after Israel's 1982 invasion. The crucial fact about such peacekeeping forces, however, is that they are orchestrated by the Western powers. They have little or no connection to the peacekeeping machinery of the United Nations, to whose atrophy they may indeed have contributed.

Maritime Strategy: the New Gunboat Diplomacy

During their retreat from empire the European powers, notably Britain, have withdrawn their navies to the North Atlantic and the Mediterranean. Naval control of the world's oceans has passed to the superpowers, especially the United States, whose navy was already before World War II almost as much a Pacific as an Atlantic force. The United States has abandoned its former 'swing strategy' under which ships in the Pacific could be diverted to the Atlantic in periods of crisis. Instead, under its new Maritime Strategy[39] it is consciously pursuing naval superiority world wide, harking back to the geopolitical conceptions of sea power popularized in the late nineteenth century by Captain Alfred Thayer Mahan.[40] As John F. Lehman jun., the US Secretary of State of the Navy, put it when justifying the enlarged '600-ship navy':

> We need a strategy at once *global, forward deployed* and *superior* to our probable opponents. Global, because our interests, allies and opponents are global; forward deployed because to protect those interests and allies we must be where they are; superior, because if deterrence fails, it is better to win than to lose.[41]

Some 80 per cent of the 250 instances of the 'peacetime' employment of US military forces between 1946 and 1982 involved the navy. The US navy's operating tempo is presently 20 per cent higher than it was during the Vietnam War.[42] The crucial symbolic function of projecting power belongs to its fifteen carrier battle groups and four battleship surface action groups, the latter based on recommissioned World War II vessels. Carriers from these groups were involved in the invasion of Grenada and the bombing of Libya. The first military engagement of a battleship group was the shelling of the Lebanon in support of the US 'peacekeeping' force.

These increases are intended to counterbalance the Soviet Union's development of a 'blue water' navy. The Soviet navy has regularly deployed in the Mediterranean since 1963 and in the Indian Ocean since 1968, and has acquired its first fully developed overseas facilities, at the former American base at Cam Ranh Bay, Vietnam. Nevertheless the United States' pursuit of naval superiority is not simply a response to the 'Soviet threat', it is an adjunct of broader American escalation control and war-fighting strategies:

> Should war come, the Soviets would prefer to use their massive ground force advantage against Europe without having to concern themselves with a global conflict or with actions on their flanks. It is this preferred Soviet strategy the United States must counter. The key to doing so is to ensure that they will have to face the prospect of prolonged global conflict. Maritime forces have a major role to play in this regard.[43]

These new strategies also rationalize the increased deployment of sea-based nuclear weapons systems outside the North Atlantic, including submarine-launched ballistic missiles (whose increased range allows them to strike targets in the Soviet Union from a greater number of ocean firing sites), nuclear depth charges, carrier-based nuclear-capable aircraft and the sea-launched cruise missiles which are capable of being equipped with nuclear warheads. Such deployment makes the frontiers of deterrence in Third World conflicts still more ambiguous, since no government can be certain that the naval task forces off its coastline do not carry tactical nuclear weapons. Moreover, not only the two superpowers but also France and Britain – as was revealed during the Falklands/Malvinas war – deploy sea-launched nuclear systems ouside the NATO area.

The Maritime Strategy also explicitly builds the Third World into US naval planning, both because 'a fundamental component of the nation's success in deterring war with the Soviet Union depends upon our ability to stabilize and control escalation in Third World crises' and because 'our economy and security require oil from the Persian Gulf and Caribbean, and strategic minerals from Southern Africa. Our trade with nations of the Pacific Basin now surpasses that with Europe.'[44]

Although the Maritime Strategy is official American rather than alliance doctrine, the United States is making every effort to enlist the cooperation of its NATO allies and of its partners in other regional security pacts (like ANZUS and the US–Japan Mutual Security Treaty). It makes naval calls upon its allies, uses their naval facilities and has visited its displeasure upon those, like New Zealand, which have closed their ports to vessels that might be carrying nuclear weapons. Joint manoeuvres are another crucial instrument of collaboration. In 1984, for instance, the US navy and Marine Corps visited no less than 108 countries and held joint exercises with 55.[45] The 1986 Rimpac manoeuvres – with US, British, Japanese, Canadian and Australian ships participating – involved the largest naval force to assemble in the Pacific since World War II.

Britain – besides participating in these Pacific exercises – regularly sends naval task forces to show the flag in the Indian Ocean. The capacity of its naval forces to fight limited naval engagements outside the North Atlantic was demonstrated in the Falklands/Malvinas war, which helped to rehabilitate the use of sea power, not just by Britain but also within the alliance. France retains a substantial maritime capability, with permanent naval facilities in Djibouti and its Pacific and Caribbean territories, charged with the defence of the large maritime 'zones d'intérêt économique' to which it lays claim under the International Law of the Sea (figure 10.2). With the United States, it strongly opposes the denuclearization of the Pacific.

A Global Battlefield?

Thus, to summarize, strategic planning for war in Europe and 'outside the NATO area' in the Third World have become interconnected; and in both arenas there is an erosion of the threshold between nuclear and non-nuclear weapons. Instead of planning to be able to fight one and a half wars simultaneously (one in Europe and a low intensity war in the Third World) as under the Nixon doctrine, the United States now claims, under the Reagan doctrine, to be prepared for at least two and a half wars. It must be said that this claim contains more than a touch of fantasy; but if so, the fantasy is being transformed into weapons and force deployments with frightening speed.

The military infrastructures of members of the alliance incorporate this interdependence between Third World intervention and European defence. Both rapid deployment forces and naval task forces, as we have seen, are trained and equipped to operate within and outside the NATO area. The United States cannot easily 'project power' in the Gulf and Middle East without transporting US forces and matériel through Europe, or at the very least obtaining European agreement to their diversion from the European theatre. This has already been a source of conflict within the alliance, as for instance during the 1973 Arab–Israel War or at the time of the 1986 bombing raid on Libya.

Equally, however, European members of the alliance would not find it easy to embark on major military operations of their own outside the NATO area without the acquiescence of the United States, if not its active support. It is well known, for example, that the success of Britain's Falklands/Malvinas campaign depended on American and West European diplomatic support, on the (admittedly imperfect) arms embargoes imposed on Argentina and above all upon US satellite intelligence and military aid.

Technological developments have further interlinked Third World intervention with NATO defence.[46] Space technologies, for instance, have already begun to shift the balance of advantage in wars in the Third World. The United States' new Global-Positioning System, based on high altitude NAVSTAR satellites, enables the United States together with the allies with whom it shares information to monitor its own worldwide ship, aircraft and ground force movements with great accuracy. Moreover, it provides a cheap and efficient alternative to TERCOM (terrain contour matching) guidance for cruise missiles deployed outside the NATO area – despite being considered less suitable for strategic and nuclear roles in Europe because it may eventually become vulnerable to anti-satellite

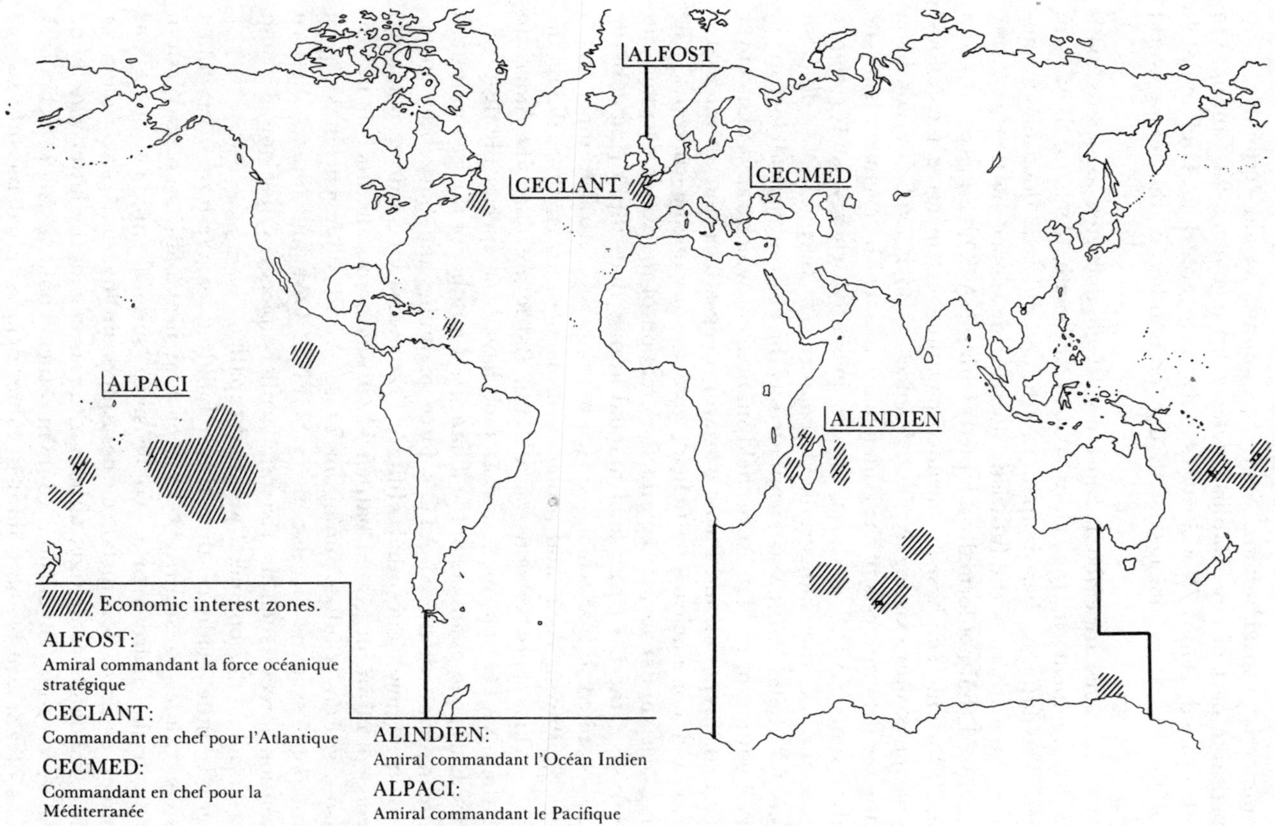

FIGURE 10.2 French maritime 'economic interest zones' and naval commands.
Source: Ministère de la Défense, Service d'Information et de Relations Publiques des Armées, *La Programmation Militaire 1984–8*, Dossier d'Information No 72 (Paris 1983).

attack. European space programmes are partly motivated by the desire of European governments for strategic alternatives to US systems as well as by commercial considerations. Such programmes would certainly be an indispensable part of any 'Gaullist' defence arrangements for Europe. On the other hand, Third World states only have access to satellite intelligence through their linkages with one or another of the major world powers.

Further linkages are embodied in the strategic doctrines associated with 'Rapid Deployment' in the Third World, and with 'AirLand Battle' in Europe. The latter is based upon two rather different doctrinal formulations.[47] First, there is the futuristic doctrine developed by the US Army and discussed (but not formally adopted) within NATO, known as AirLand Battle 2000. This emphasizes the incorporation of 'emerging technology' (ET) weapons into existing NATO defences. Also it explicitly considers that 'the security interests of the Alliance are affected by events outside the boundaries of NATO' because of the increased energy and resource requirements of the industrialized countries.[48] Secondly, a different version of AirLand Battle was formulated as the basis of tactical doctrine in the 1982 edition of the US Army field manual, in which rapid manoeuvre (rather than firepower and linear warfare), deep attack and an integrated (nuclear and non-nuclear) battlefield were the organizing concepts. The thinking was similar to that behind the creation of the Rapid Deployment Force. Indeed the US Army field manual argues that 'the AirLand Battle doctrine is suited to that which we face not only in Central Europe, but in Korea, Southwest Asia and other contingency areas throughout the world'.[49] Whilst both versions of AirLand Battle are officially American rather than NATO doctrine – and as such have been specifically disowned by some European members of the alliance – a number of their assumptions are already embodied in NATO's force planning and have been incorporated in its new Conceptual Military Framework for strategic planning. The concept of an integrated battlefield cutting across the nuclear threshold also carries over into planning for Third World contingencies. Many of the weapons systems in use by USCENTCOM and other Western intervention forces (such as 155 mm artillery pieces, cruise missiles and carrier-borne fighter bombers) are dual-capable.

There is little evidence that this rebuilding of Western intervention forces contributes to 'security' – or even that it actually protects Western interests in the Third World. To be sure, 'surgical' military operations sometimes succeed, for instance the American invasion of Grenada or Britain's Falklands campaign, although the success of the latter was by no means a foregone conclusion. But in other conflicts high technology methods of war are of more limited value, demonstrated recently by the

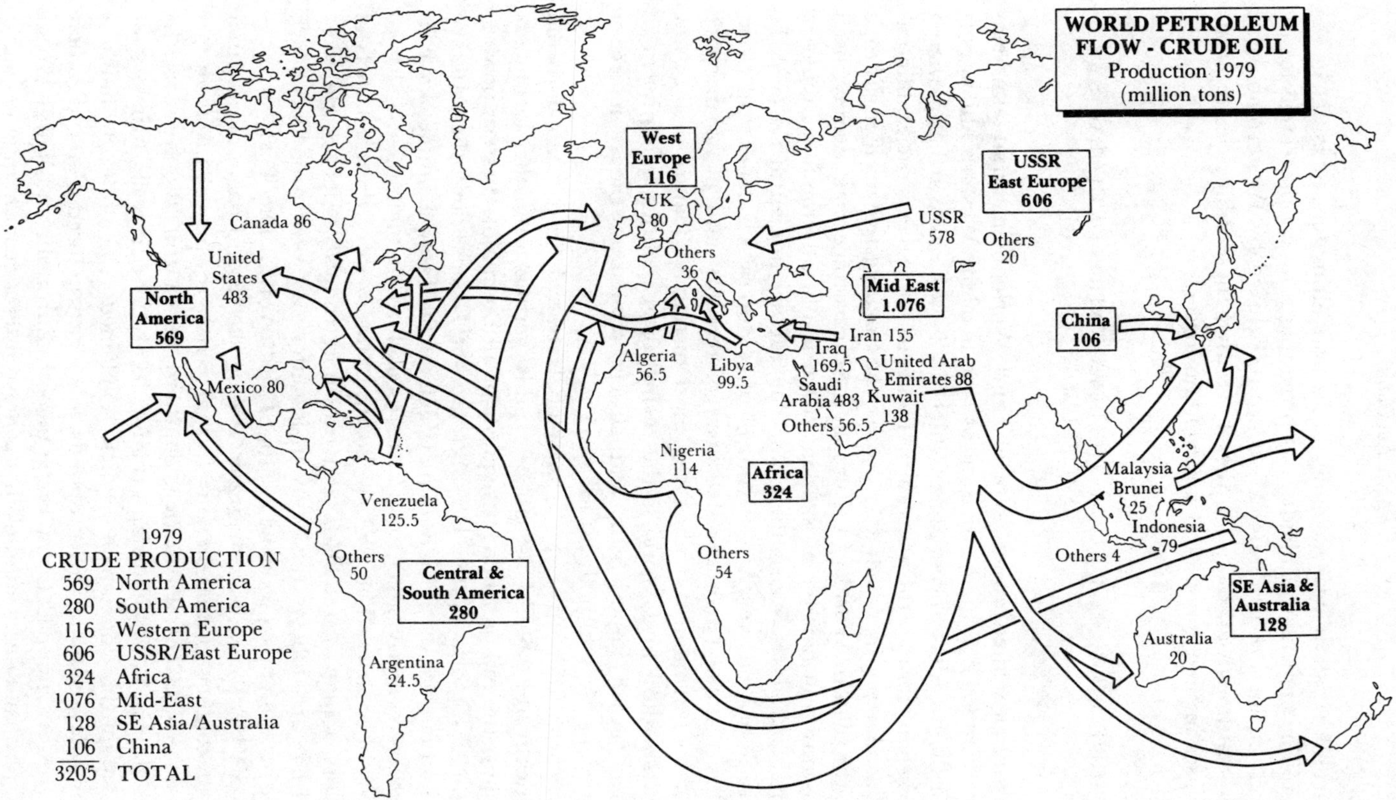

FIGURE 10.3 World petroleum flow according to the Pentagon.
Source: Organization of the Joint Chiefs of Staff, *United States Military Posture FY1982* (Washington, DC, 1981), p. 2.

impotence of Western peacekeeping forces and ultimately of Israel in the Lebanon. The enormous difficulties of providing military protection for oil fields and sea lines of communication are recognized by Western strategic planners – although all too often they have used these difficulties to argue for increases in their navies and intervention forces.

HEGEMONIC CYCLES AND THE REVALUATION OF GLOBAL REAL ESTATE

The picture presented above is of a Third World being gradually reincorporated into the strategic division of labour of the Western alliance. It is part of the broader process under which the New Cold War has gathered pace and reinvigorated the arms race. There are, however, crucial differences in the manner in which this process has manifested itself in Europe and in the Third World. In Europe the arms race has mainly been commensurated in balance of weapons (even if officially the objective is to deter territorial attack across the Cold War fracture in central Europe). In the Third World, however, it is control of resources, sea lanes and client states that counts. There is a fetishism of territory and of ocean space rather than of armaments. Thus, the most distinctive feature of the New Cold War in the Third World is the revival of geopolitics, reminiscent of an earlier age of imperialism; and closely related to the structure of Western economic and political interests.

Another way of putting it is that global strategic real estate is being systematically revalued. This can be readily verified from the documents that support the military budget requests of all the major Western powers. The Annual Reports of the US Secretary of Defense and the Military Posture Statements of the US Joint Chiefs of Staff, for example, have in recent years regularly given a quarter to a third of their page space to Third World security. The FY1982 Posture Statement of the US Chiefs of Staff prints a map of oil fields and transport routes on its second page (figure 10.3) and follows this with an inventory of American dependence on strategic minerals produced in the Third World. The Posture Statement for FY1985 provides a diagram (also on the second page) of potential sources of conflict located in four 'resource-rich regions of instability' – South-East Asia, Central America, Southern Africa and 'the area stretching from Libya to Afghanistan' (figure 10.4). The French Ministry of Defence publicity document which explained the 1984–8 military programme–law summarizes proposals for a restructured Force d'Action Rapide (FAR) equipped to intervene in both European and Third World conflicts, and contains a map of the 'zones d'intérêt économique' defended

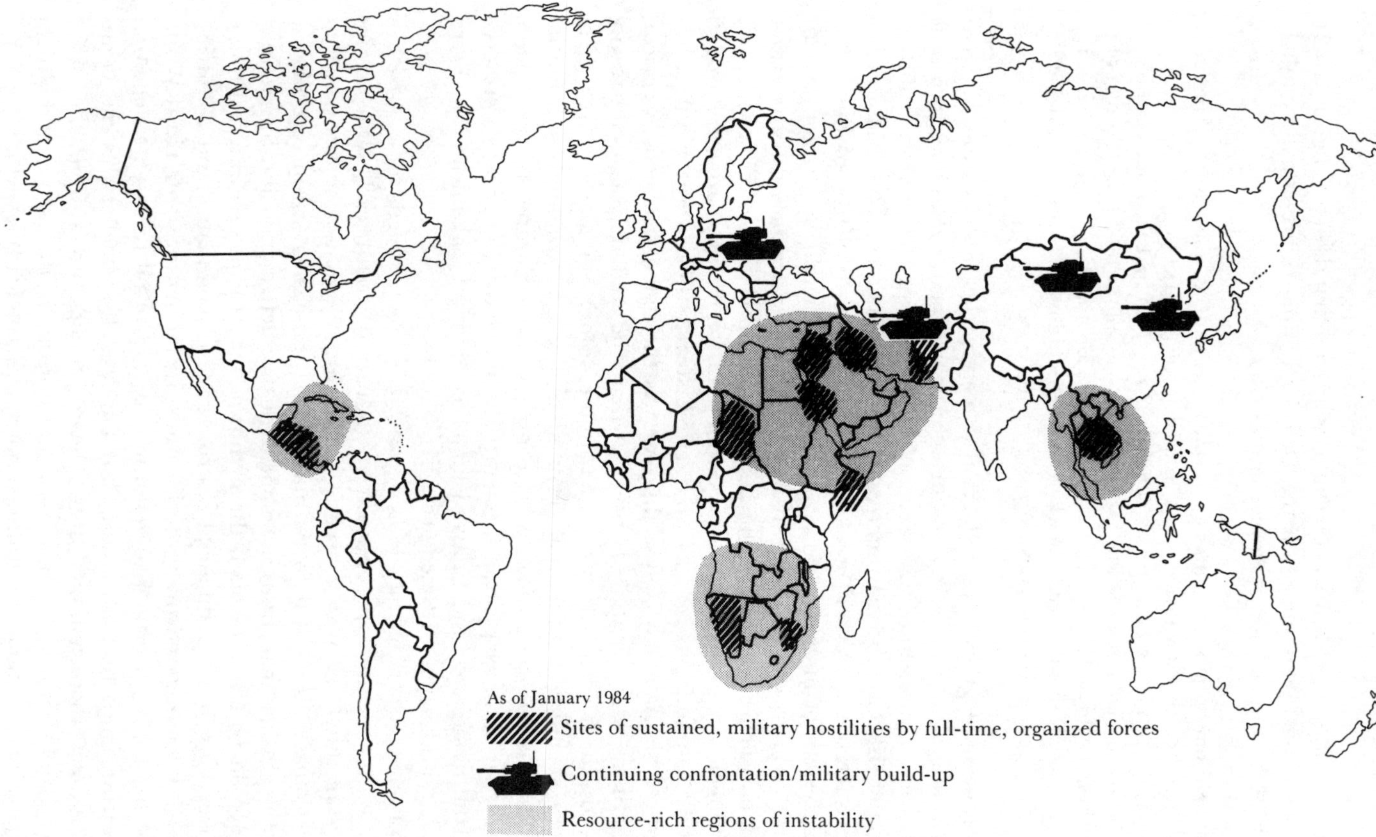

FIGURE 10.4 Potential sources of conflict according to the Pentagon.
Source: Organisation of the Joint Chiefs of Staff, *United States Military Posture FY1985* (Washington, DC, 1984), p.2.

by its Pacific and Indian Ocean naval commands (see figure 10.2). Britain's annual Statements on the Defence Estimates are equally explicit. The 1984 Statement, for example, argues that:

> Though our primary commitment must remain to the North Atlantic Alliance, the threat we face is not limited to the NATO area defined in the Treaty . . . An escalation of the conflict between Iran and Iraq, for example, resulting in interference with the passage of oil through the Straits of Hormuz could seriously affect the Western economies; nor can we remain unconcerned about events elsewhere in the Middle East which could have profound implications for East/West relations.[50]

This revival of geopolitics reflects not merely the prolongation of East/West conflict but also the restructuring of North/South relations. In a time of economic recession, the structures of strategic, of political and of economic risk have become increasingly interconnected. The situation has been exacerbated by the breakdown since the early 1970s of the established system of international economic management (the Bretton Woods system), which was based upon fixed exchange rates between the major world currencies and upon the supremacy of the dollar. Following this breakdown, international relations could no longer be managed through the dull compulsions of the market. Instead, they were in effect restructured through the New Cold War. As the dollar declined, American imperialism was revitalized. Even when the dollar was temporarily restored (in the mid-1980s) it was in the context of major increases in military spending (stimulating demand in the US economy), substantial trade deficits and consequently high interest rates. European governments were prepared under protest to tolerate the imbalance, in order to preserve the Atlantic alliance and to avoid major economic breakdown. The Third World, however, had little choice.

Economic restructuring, moreover, was closely allied to a crisis in accumulation within the advanced industrial countries.[51] One major feature of this crisis was a decline in the rate of profit. Another was that such profits as were still to be made came increasingly from speculative activities, rather than from investment in productive capacity. Speculative gains could be made through the manipulation of exchange rates; through takeover bids and the financial restructuring of companies and countries; from bank lending and high interest rates, including those on Third World debts; from rents accruing to governments and to oil firms entrenched on oil-bearing land; from the 'non-tariff barriers' by which industrial countries protect their markets from cheap manufacturers from the NICs (Newly-Industrialized Countries); and through the sale of political technologies (weapons, communications equipment and 'white-elephant' industrial projects) to Third World governments.

These speculative gains have been extremely volatile, enhancing the element of risk in international economic relations. They have also been *political* to the extent that they have been extracted because powerful governments like that of the United States can influence interest and international exchange rates, restrict trade, control the supply of technology and armaments and influence the level of global demand through military spending and budget deficits. Broadly speaking, the costs of recession have been imposed on organized labour, the beneficiaries of social services and the unemployed in the industrial countries; and on the poorest countries in the Third World. In both groups of countries this has caused social unrest, adding further hazards to the calculus of risk. To be sure, transformations in the global economy opened up opportunities for some of the more prosperous Third World countries: including NICs that expanded their share of global industrial exports; countries with good credit ratings able to finance expansion by borrowing at a time when (in the late 1970s) real interest rates were temporarily negative; and the oil-producing countries. However, as the crisis gathered momentum, the major borrowers were caught out by rises in interest rates, and the speculative gains of OPEC were wiped out by inflation and stagnating oil prices. Only the Asian NICs have continued to expand, building on their competitive advantages as low-cost producers of manufactured goods.

The strategic value attached to the Third World has thus increased in a complex interaction between rises in natural resource rents, changes in the spread of economic risk, and military and political considerations. One piece of real estate after another has been revalued. Five main criteria of valuation have evolved during this process:

1 Firstly, there are the valuations directly represented by the rents accruing to oil-bearing land. The rises in oil rents during the 1970s partly stemmed from changes in energy demand, partly from the oil producers' assertion of sovereignty over their resources and partly from the OPEC cartel. Some of the surplus thereby generated was reinvested in weapons and thus in further additions to state power.

For their part, the Western powers sought to reappropriate a share of these rents and of the enhanced sovereignty OPEC member states had used them to buy. They achieved this mainly by selling arms and by establishing political alliances with the ruling classes of the Middle East and Persian Gulf. When these alliances in turn began to fall apart – especially after the overturn of the Shah of Iran in 1978–9 – the United States began constructing its own security framework in the Middle East and the Gulf. The Carter Doctrine of 1980, under which the former president of the United States proclaimed that 'any attempt by any outside force to gain control of the Persian Gulf region will be regarded as an assault on the vital interests of the United States of America and such an assault will be repelled by any means necessary, including military force', represented, in the words of his National Security Adviser, 'a formal recognition of a centrally important reality: that America's security had become interdependent with the security of three central and interrelated strategic zones consisting of Western Europe, the Far East, and the Middle East–Persian Gulf area'.[52]

No clearer statement could be made of the relation between the revaluation of oil-bearing lands in the Middle East and Gulf and the wider purposes of American power. Note, however, that the security framework thus imposed was consolidated under the Reagan administration, despite a *decline* in oil rents in the first part of the 1980s – and even though few serious strategic analysts believed that the vast apparatus of USCENTCOM could actually protect oil installations in a crisis, or even save the governments of crucial regional allies, like Saudi Arabia. In other words, the rise in oil rents on its own cannot explain the revaluation of strategic real estate.

2 A second criterion is access to 'strategic minerals', now emphasized almost as frequently by strategic planners as oil and energy.[53] This criterion has brought new areas within the ambit of the Cold War, notably Southern Africa. The latter's minerals are held to be crucial for American and Western defence production; and its precious metals (despite the demonetization of gold) still help lubricate the circuits of the international economy. The crucial consideration, however, is not so much the rent extracted by producers from mineral-bearing land as security of access to it, allegedly threatened by 'Soviet expansion'. The latter in reality is a code for the inexorable southwards shift of the struggle against white rule. Outright inclusion of white-controlled South Africa within the Western security framework is impossible, due to international political sensitivities. Instead, there has emerged an uneasy informal alliance between South Africa and the West, blessed by the Reagan administration's policy of 'constructive engagement'.

Note again, however, that strategic minerals are 'strategic' only in the light of the Western powers' own defence production requirements. Many of them are stockpiled, even if the adequacy of such stocks is hotly debated. In any case, the Soviet Union would hardly risk interrupting their supply in peacetime. The supply of strategic raw materials has only reemerged as a serious problem because American and Western strategy has been reformulated in terms of ability to 'win' a protracted global conflict.

3 Values are also assigned in proportion to international financial flows and government credit ratings. This criterion has acquired significance because of the massive build-up in bank lending to Third World governments which took place from the latter part of the 1970s (partly making up for a relative decline in concessional aid and indirect investment by transnational firms). Some of this borrowing derives from purchases of armaments. There exist no direct estimates of military borrowing, although SIPRI has estimated indirectly that the debt burden of developing countries might be some 15 per cent smaller if they had refrained from purchasing arms. The risk of default on this accumulated debt suddenly increased in the early 1980s due to the onset of recession, to sharp rises of interest rates and to the drying up of new lending when it became clear that creditors would have problems collecting existing obligations.

Yet, it is not entirely clear how the risk of financial default has translated into the calculus of strategy. In some Third World countries, to be sure, financial restabilization and foreign military intervention have gone in hand, as in Chile during and after the 1973 coup, or in Zaire during and after the 1977–8 Shaba uprisings. However, major debtors, like Brazil, Mexico or Nigeria, cannot be kept in line by military force. Indeed they possess a certain amount of 'debtor power'; but it is their close integration into the circuits of the global economy, and the willingness of international financial institutions to renegotiate debts, which have so far prevented default.

4 In the calculus of geostrategy there are many Third World countries and regions whose value resides not in their own resources and relation to the global economy; but instead in their geographical proximity to such resources, to trade routes and to strategic lines of communication. Such is the case, for example, of the Horn of Africa, of Central America, of the Caribbean and of the South Pacific. They acquire aid, weapons and other forms of support for their ruling classes from the major world powers, having little to exchange in return, except their territory, harbours and airspace, whose strategic value is enhanced by the military and naval deployments of the major powers.

The strategic revaluation of these territories and of the oceans surrounding them during the New Cold War has in some ways resembled the bringing of marginal land under cultivation when agricultural prices rise. Competition between the blocs for bases and military facilities raises the strategic stakes, encourages the local states to invest in weaponry and states to invest in weaponry and feeds regional arms races. The most striking example is the Horn of Africa, where the countries of the region do not (with the potential exception of the Sudan), possess energy and resources on a scale that would make them a strategic priority. Instead, it is their geographical position adjacent to the Red Sea, the Indian Ocean and the Persian Gulf that is crucial. In order to obtain weapons and military support, they have surrendered portions of their sovereignty, by supplying military facilities to the United States, France and the Soviet Union. The region has become the point of accumulation for vast quantities of weapons. In the process the global arms race has been superimposed upon regional power struggles which have deep roots in the area's historical past.[54] The strategic advantages secured by the powers are in the final analysis ephemeral, being to a large extent vitiated by the rivalries among them.

5 Some of the global real estate which is fought over or garrisoned has little intrinsic economic or strategic value of its own. The Falklands/Malvinas are one example and Grenada another.[55] It seems that the revaluation of such territories has been primarily symbolic. They provide arenas for low cost demonstrations of military power and political resolve. Of course, the Falklands war was a gamble and has placed major burdens upon the British economy. However, one can think of few other places in the Third World where Britain could have launched a similar venture with any prospect of success. In this sense, it was imperialism on the cheap.

In sum, many of the strategic rationales for military intervention in the Third World belong within the realm of myth – even when more substantial interests such as oil, finance and sea routes are ostensibly at stake. One must look behind them to uncover the taproots of military expansion. Not only has global real estate been revalued in the manner suggested above. This revaluation has followed a distinct cyclical momentum. And it has led to the revaluation of one piece of Third World strategic real estate after another, following upon transformations in global power relations. The most crucial element in this cyclical pattern is the behaviour of the United States, which has alternated between bursts of Cold War reassertion and periods of relative quiescence (as during the period of detente in the early 1970s). US military expenditures peaked during the Korean War; rose once again during the so-called 'missile gap' of the 1960s and even more sharply during the Vietnam War; and accelerated sharply again during the early 1980s (see figure 10.5). This time, however, these rises have taken place in '*peacetime*' conditions. A number of explanations for the cyclical pattern suggest themselves:

1 First, it is sometimes argued that these hegemonic cycles are produced by long waves and/or technological cycles in the major capitalist economies.[56] In particular, they have been linked to the introduction

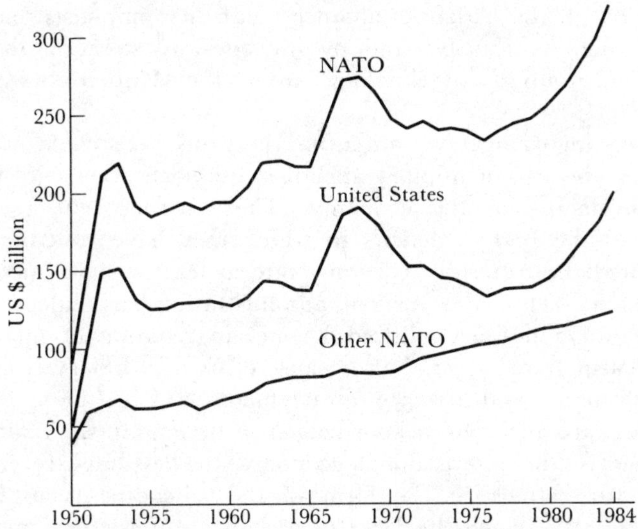

FIGURE 10.5 NATO military expenditure 1950–84 (at 1980 prices and exchange rates).

Source: Stockholm International Peace Research Institute Yearbook 1985, p. 229.

(through military innovation) of new technologies such as the microprocessor and the computer. Such technologies are at the heart of the present restructuring of the global economy. They are also the technological basis of present American rearmament, making possible the introduction of whole new families of weapons systems such as cruise missiles, ET (emerging technology) conventional armaments and the Strategic Defense Initiative (Star Wars). However, the US has been less successful than its competitors in making productive use of the new technologies for civilian output, this being a major factor in its relative economic decline since World War II.[57] Nor (except indirectly) could long waves be considered responsible for the Korean and Vietnam Wars, the two previous peaks in the United States' hegemonic cycle.

2 Another hypothesis is that the United States has periodically reasserted its military power and its hegemony within the Western alliance to compensate for the long-run decline of its economy relative to Europe, Japan and the NICs. This decline has almost certainly been hastened by its military spending, and yet the military sector is one of the few sectors in which the United States (like the Soviet Union)[58] still retains a clear comparative advantage. It can only enjoy this advantage in periods of global tension, when the military spending of its main rivals is

also on the increase. Moreover, it is an advantage which is enhanced by the structure of the Atlantic alliance, with its emphasis on military 'burden-sharing' by Europe, and by the one-way street in the transfer of arms and military technology from the United States to its allies.

3 Shorter-run cyclical variations in the arms race could possibly be explained by the use of military spending by governments to counteract cyclical movements in the economy. Thus, the present US military increases and the budget deficits to which they have contributed, have arguably lifted the American economy into at least a short-term recovery from recession. Yet if the Reagan administration has indeed stumbled backwards into a military-induced Keynesian reflation of the economy, this has been in spite rather than because of its own monetarist economic policies. US fiscal and balance of payments deficits, along with high interest rates, are generally acknowledged to be among the major sources of imbalance in the international economy.[59] They have recently come under domestic attack in the form of the amendments to budgetary legislation through which the US Congress has imposed automatic limits on all forms of government (including military) spending.

4 Another hypothesis is that aggressive foreign and military policies have been drummed up to 'manage' the political dissent created by economic recession. As we have already seen, it is at least superficially plausible to regard Britain's Falklands campaign and the American invasion of Grenada as forms of political theatre aimed at the domestic electorate, as much as at the international community. The same could well be said of the bombing of Libya in April 1986, that country being regarded as the 'softest' target among the countries (Syria, Iran and Libya) that are said to sponsor international terrorism.

5 Lastly, it may be argued that hegemonic cycles have been linked to cyclical movements, not so much in the overall economy, as within defence production itself (even though trends in the latter remain influenced by broader cyclical movements). Thus the origins of the present US military expansion can be traced back to the post-Vietnam cutbacks, when military procurement was temporarily reduced to around a third of its previous level.[60] The continued development of new weapons (military research and development having been cut by much less than procurement) generated immense pressures from the defence industry and the military establishment to manufacture and deploy them. These in turn were legitimized by the reassertion of American global military interests. Further pressure has been added by major increases in spending on military R&D under the Reagan administration (figure 10.6). This seems to have acquired a political momentum all of its own. Rapid deployment

forces and carrier battle groups etc., have created supplementary 'missions' for the conventional military forces of the United States and of the other Western powers, legitimizing their procurement of new weapons systems. In this manner they have supplemented and indeed partly replaced arms exports, through which earlier structural crises of the arms industry had been resolved.

Military intervention and the arming of Third World governments have also been crucial for the reproduction of the military sector in another way. Since the greater part of the major powers' own conventional arsenals are locked up in the Cold War stalemate in Europe, warfare outside the NATO area has been almost the only way of testing the effectiveness or use-value of these weapons. This was demonstrated with special clarity during the Falklands episode, which was regarded by the strategic community as a vital test of the doctrine and practice of high-technology war; and by the arms manufacturers as a useful adjunct to their advertising campaigns. It was also a factor in American military operations against Libya in 1986, which were regarded as an opportunity to test equipment such as the HARM radar-seeking missiles and the navigation radar-jamming and target-finding equipment on the F-111 fighter bombers sent into action from British airfields. The use of the latter had the added advantage of providing the US Air Force with a 'piece of the action', helping to moderate inter-service rivalries.[61] Thus the Third World, it may be argued, provides political and territorial space for solving the realization crises of the arms industry.

The hegemonic cycle followed by the United States has been superimposed over the declining hegemonies of the European members of the alliance. Their military spending has not had the same cyclical momentum as that of the United States and their arms sales have been dominated by commercial rather than territorial imperatives. Britain in particular, though sharing the centre of the world stage with the two superpowers at the end of World War II, cannot be said to have developed a coherent strategy for the management of its decline since. Instead it jettisoned its special relations with the Commonwealth when it joined the EEC; withdrew from east of Suez; and in spite of maintaining a theoretically 'independent' deterrent, fell back for its security upon the United States and the Atlantic alliance.

France, in contrast, has consciously used its Third World connections to sustain its status as a global power, following the 'project' for defence, foreign policy and nationally planned capitalism developed by General de Gaulle and his successors. Not only did it withdraw from the NATO command structure, it also developed its own nuclear armoury (rather

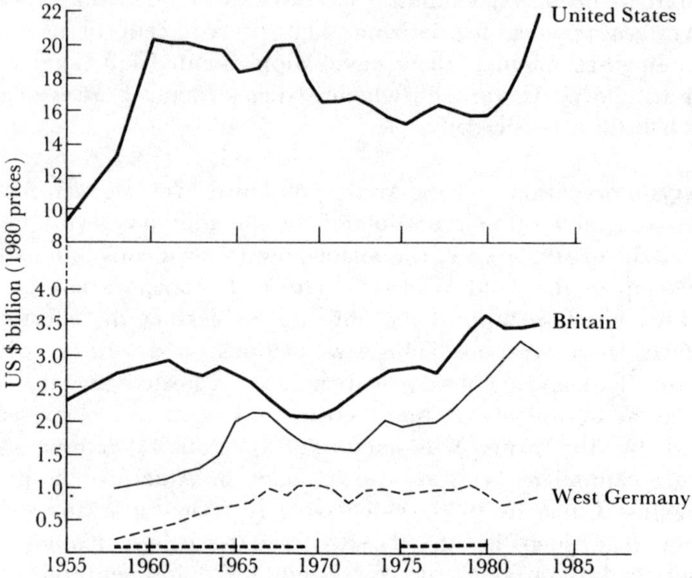

FIGURE 10.6 Military research and development trends in Western countries.

Source: Philip Gummett, 'Controlling Military R&D', *ADIU Report*, 8 (May–June 1986).

than acquiring it, like Britain, from the United States) and elaborated its own strategic doctrines (like the concept of 'du faible au fort') to support it. It promoted high technology sectors of the French economy, including the defence industries. It aggressively pursued markets for arms, nuclear technology and other political goods in the Third World. It established a dense network of ties with former French colonies in Africa. And France's well publicized support for Third World causes – such as the New International Economic Order, the International Law of the Sea, the proposal for an International Disarmament Fund for Development and (under the Mitterand government) economic sanctions against South Africa – has been crucial for its international credibility.

CRISIS IN THE ALLIANCE: AN OPPORTUNITY FOR DEALIGNMENT?

The Western alliance has begun to disintegrate under the weight of its accumulated contradictions. Fewer and fewer Europeans believe that it guarantees their security. Added to this there are the dangers of the new cycle of US global interventionism just described. The latter seems all the more dangerous because it has arisen in the context of a long-run decline of the American economy, which it seeks to reverse.

There is another factor which has not been dealt with directly in this chapter, although it is implicit in the analysis: that the hegemony of the Western powers in general and the United States in particular has been constantly under challenge from the Third World itself. No matter that decolonization has failed in most cases to make an impact on underdevelopment. No matter that the great anti-imperial revolutions – in Cuba, Vietnam, Ethiopia, Iran, Southern Africa etc. – have brought further suffering in their wake. No matter that OPEC's challenge to Western economic control has brought only limited economic gains to the oil producers; and that demands for a New International Economic Order have come to nothing. The fact is that the inability of the major world powers to control events in the Third World has been time and again decisively demonstrated. Hence, there is a surreal quality about their creation of vast military apparatuses for Third World intervention. These add to the influence of the major powers only so long as they are confined to minor or symbolic engagements in which there is little risk of failure. But the more such apparatuses are built up, the greater is the temptation to ignore such limitations and risk the escalation of conflict beyond the major powers' capacity to control it.

Yet the restoration of the fragmented Pax Americana is precisely what many Western and in particular US policy-makers hope to achieve by their new security framework outside the NATO area. This framework parallels and in certain respects supports attempts to restore the discipline of the market through the 'structural adjustment' programmes insisted on by Western aid donors and international financial organizations as the price of aid and the renegotiation of debt. It also connects, as argued earlier, to the new military doctrines and technologies being introduced in Western Europe. Other chapters in this volume argue that the technological fixes embodied in such doctrines have failed to dampen the growing chorus of dissent within the alliance. Broadly, the same is true of military solutions to the problems of the Third World.

Powerful currents of isolationism have developed on both sides of the Atlantic. In Europe there has occurred a complex interaction between different national 'projects' (right- and left-wing Gaullism in France, Thatcherism in Britain, Ostpolitik in West Germany, etc.) and the broader project of a European bloc with a self-sufficient defence industrial base, its own nuclear deterrent(s) and an independent defence policy. This vision of Fortress Western Europe bristles with difficulties. In the first place, Europe is deeply embedded at every level in the alliance division of labour. Hence the more cautious exponents of a European-based defence argue for a stronger European pillar of the alliance, still within rather than outside of NATO. Added to this, however, there are the notorious difficulties of achieving agreement between European governments in the EEC and in the still nebulous framework of European political and defence cooperation. Nor would a broader European project necessarily inherit the more progressive features of French Gaullism, one of whose alleged advantages is that it has allowed France to take a more independent, non-aligned, role in the Third World. It would be just as liable as the latter to be influenced by military–industrial pressures for high-technology defence in Europe and for arms sales and intervention in the Third World.

Even an isolationist United States would hardly welcome the emergence of a more assertive Europe – all the more so if it began casting aside the restraints of the Atlantic relationship. This would aggravate existing American impatience with the alliance, speed the shift in the United States' centre of strategic gravity towards the Pacific rim and Persian Gulf, and perhaps even reinforce American determination to intervene militarily in the Third World – with or without the help of its NATO partners. Committed Atlanticists have tended, therefore, to argue that Europe should stay in the alliance in order to restrain the United States. The historical record, however, hardly suggests they have had much success.

Yet is dealignment, as proposed in this book, any more likely to rescue Europe from the catastrophe of the arms race? It is conceivable that a merely neutral Europe, opting out of the blocs without considering what should replace them, might have even less chance of moderating the struggle between the superpowers; whilst shifting this struggle's focus even more decisively in the direction of the Third World. Dealignment (unlike neutrality) not only requires strategies for removing the sources of tension in Europe, it must also seek ways of influencing the superpowers outside the existing system of blocs. This cannot be done without addressing the exploitative relations between the industrial North and the developing South protected by the NATO and Warsaw Treaty alliances (especially, but not only, the former).

The question remains how such strategies could be turned into practical politics. The political forces that would be ranged against any tampering, however marginal, with the existing alliances would be formidable. This can only be overcome, as other contributors to this book suggest, by mobilizing public opinion and democratizing decisions concerning foreign policy and defence. The task can be made easier by diagnosing and harnessing the contradictions already present within the Western alliance. (Similar democratization would also be needed in the Eastern bloc, even though the process of transformation may be harder to initiate than in the West.)

If it is true, as I have argued, that the Cold War has acquired cyclical momentum from the military sector itself, it follows that deconstruction of the latter – by curbing military R&D, planning for conversion from arms production, developing alternative *defence* policies etc. – would necessarily accompany any dealignment from the blocs. Dismantling the technologies, doctrines and force structures that have linked the defence of Europe to arms transfers and military intervention outside the NATO area, could also help transform relations with the Third World. Disarmament, and not just the Cold War, can be globalized.

Dealignment would also facilitate the construction of alternative security arrangements in the Third World, implementing the principles of non-alignment and mutual security. Such arrangements began to emerge very tentatively and incompletely during the period of detente. They included a variety of proposals for nuclear-weapons-free zones (like that declared by the 1967 Treaty of Tlatelolco in Latin America); for zones of peace (as proposed in the Indian Ocean); for regional arms limitation accords (like the 1974 Ayacucho Agreement under which Latin American governments committed themselves to restrain international purchases of arms and to ban especially destructive weapons); for regional peacekeeping forces (like the ad hoc forces of the Organization of African Unity); and for regionally based mutual defence and non-aggression pacts (like that linking members of the Economic Community of West African States). Such proposals were broadly endorsed at the 1978 and 1982 United Nations Special Sessions on Disarmament. They would be greatly strengthened by a reinforcement of the UN's own peacekeeping machinery which has often been hampered by the difficulties of securing agreement among UN member governments.

That such initiatives have up to now failed almost totally to restrain conflict and prevent external military intervention in the Third World is partly due to internal disagreements among developing countries themselves. Even more, it is because of the indifference or active hostility of the major world powers. A particularly salient example is the fate of the proposal to declare the Indian Ocean a 'zone of peace', which is still officially on the international agenda, but has been fatally undermined by the breakdown of talks between the superpowers and the subsequent escalation of naval deployments. A dealigned Europe would be in a much better position to lend its support to disarmament initiatives in the Third World.

Like the dismantling of the blocs in Europe, however, dealignment in the Third World would be actively opposed by the superpowers. Political alliances would need to be built in order to resist such pressures; and indeed to apply influence in reverse to secure changes in superpower behaviour. An example of such reverse pressure is the informal six-nation group (of Argentina, Mexico, Tanzania, Sweden, India and Greece) formed in May 1984 to coordinate the efforts of non-nuclear countries against the arms race. As Singham and Hune point out in chapter 9, the Non-Aligned Movement has at least managed to keep non-alignment on the agenda of world politics. It is time that Europe too began to globalize peace.

NOTES

1 Useful summaries of the arguments and evidence on these questions are contained in the report of the UN Group of Governmental Experts (the Thorsson Report), *Study on the Relationship between Disarmament and Development. Report of the Secretary General* (New York: United Nations A/36/356, 5 October 1981) and in Saadet Deger and Ron Smith, 'Military Expenditure and Development: the Economic Linkages', *IDS Bulletin* 16, (September 1985). The same issue of the *IDS Bulletin* contains articles (notably David Evans, 'Back to Benoit?' and Hans-Henrik Holm, 'Brandt, Palme and Thorsson: a Strategy that Does Not Work?') that are more critical of the received wisdom that military spending harms development. For analyses of how military spending may be related to particular *types* of development, see Robin Luckham, 'Militarism and International Dependence' and Mary Kaldor, 'The Military in Third World Development', in Mac Graham, Richard Jolly and Chris Smith (eds), *Disarmament and World Development* (Oxford: Pergamon Press, revised ed. 1986).

2 One of the more sophisticated characterizations of the Soviet Union's 'thrust toward globalism' is to be found in a Report Prepared for the Committee on Foreign Affairs, US House of Representatives, by the Congressional Research Service, Library of Congress, *Soviet Policy and United States Response in the Third World*, 97th Congress, 1st Session, 1981 (Washington: USGPO).

3 Zbigniew Brzezinski, *Power and Principle, Memoirs of the National Security Adviser, 1977–1981* (New York: Farrar, Straus, Giroux, 1983), p. 447.

4 Talk to the Council on Foreign Relations, quoted in Michael Klare, 'Reagan's Global Strategy', *The Mobiliser* (Summer 1984).

5 *Observer*, 15 June, 1986.

6 See especially Miroslav Nincic, *How War Might Spread to Europe* (London: Taylor and Francis for the Stockholm International Peace Research Institute, 1985).

7 Istvan Kende, 'Local Wars 1945–1976' in Asbjorn Eide and Marek Thee (eds),

Problems of Contemporary Militarism (London: Croom Helm, 1980).
8 Brzezinski, *Power and Principle*, p. 189.
9 Francis J. West, former Assistant Secretary of Defense for International Security Affairs, 'Defense and Security Beyond Europe', *Defense 83* (May 1983).
10 Quoted in Alfred Grosser, *The Western Alliance. European–American Relations Since 1945* (London: Macmillan, 1980), p. 187.
11 Communiqué of the October 1984 meeting of the foreign and defence ministers of the WEU, quoted in Stanley R. Sloan, *NATO's Future: Toward a New Translantic Bargain* (Washington, DC: National Defense University Press, 1985).
12 See the analyses of French defence policy in Jolyon Howorth and Patricia Chilton, *Defence and Dissent in Contemporary France* (Beckenham: Croom Helm, 1984), chs 1, 2 and 4.
13 North Atlantic Assembly, Political Committee, *Interim Report of the Sub-Committee on Out of Area Security Challenges to the Alliance*, AA200PC/OA(83)7, November 1983, p. 2.
14 Christopher Coker, *NATO, the Warsaw Pact and Africa* (London: Macmillan for RUSI, 1985), chs 1 and 2.
15 This communiqué is reprinted in North Atlantic Assembly, Political Committee, *Interim Report*, Appendix, p. 1.
16 See Christopher Coker, 'The Western Alliance and Africa, 1949–81', *African Affairs*, 81 (July 1982).
17 North Atlantic Assembly, Political Committee, *Interim Report*, p. 2.
18 Ibid., p. 7.
19 See Malcolm Spaven, 'A Piece of the Action: the Use of US Bases in Britain', in Mary Kaldor and Paul Anderson (eds), *Mad Dogs. The US Raids on Libya* (London: Pluto Press, 1986).
20 *Guardian*, April 1986.
21 Henry Kissinger, 'Bring the F-111s Back Home', *Observer*, 11 May 1986, p. 10 and report of a special briefing by Richard Perle, *Guardian*, 21 May 1986, p. 7.
22 *SIPRI Yearbook 1985*, ch. 12.
23 See Michael Lucas, 'West Germany: Can Arms Save the Export Giant?' *ADIU Report*, 7 (August 1985).
24 See Barry M. Blechman, Janne E. Nolan and Alan Platt, 'Pushing Arms', *Foreign Policy*, 46 (Spring 1982).
25 Dan Smith and Ron Smith, *The Economics of Militarism* (London: Pluto Press, 1983) ch. 4, is a good general discussion of the effects of military spending in the industrial countries, based partly on detailed empirical studies by R. P. Smith, 'Military Expenditure and Capitalism', *Cambridge Journal of Economics*, March 1977, pp. 61–76 and 'Military Expenditure and Investment in OECD Countries', *Journal of Comparative Economics*, March 1980.
26 A useful set of case studies of the acquisition by Third World countries of nuclear weapons capability is Joseph A. Yager, *Nonproliferation and US Foreign Policy* (Washington, DC: Brookings, 1980).
27 Quoted in Thijs de la Court et al., *The Nuclear Fix. A Guide to Nuclear Activities in*

the Third World (Amsterdam: World Information Service on Energy, 1982).

28 The background of the 1985 Conference is described in John Simpson, *Ploughshares into Swords? The International Nuclear Non-Proliferation Network and the 1985 NPT Review Conference*, Faraday Discussion Paper No.4 (London: Council for Arms Control, 1985).

29 Robin Luckham, 'French Militarism in Africa', *Review of African Political Economy*, 24 (May–August 1982).

30 Interview with the author, March 1982.

31 See Armand Matteland, 'Notes on the Ideology of the Military State', in Armand Matteland and Seth Siegelaub (eds), *Communication and Class Struggle 1. Capitalism, Imperialism* (New York and Paris: International General and IMMRC, 1979).

32 The Commission on Security and Economic Assistance, *A Report to the Secretary of State* (Washington, DC, 1983).

33 The Organisation of the Joint Chiefs of Staff, *United States Military Posture FY1986* (Washington, DC, 1985), pp. 67–8.

34 Mary Kaldor, 'Introduction', in Kaldor and Anderson, *Mad Dogs*, pp. 8–10.

35 Ben Lowe, 'Libya and NATO's Out of Area Role', in Kaldor and Anderson, *Mad Dogs*, pp. 84–5. The decision to create a special force was taken somewhat earlier, in 1981.

36 Caspar W. Weinberger, Secretary of Defense, *Annual Report to the Congress Fiscal Year 1986* (Washington, DC: Department of Defense, 1985), pp. 236–7.

37 North Atlantic Assembly, Political Committee. *Interim Report of the Sub-Committee on Out-of-Area Security Challenges to the Alliance*, AC182PC/OA(85)2, October 1985, p. 8.

38 Ibid., p. 9.

39 *The Maritime Strategy*, US Naval Institute, January 1986. This is claimed by the Institute's Director (p. 2) to be 'the nearest thing to a British White Paper – that is, an official statement of policy – that we are likely to encounter in the American political system'.

40 Ibid., pp. 15–16.

41 Ibid., p. 36.

42 Ibid., p. 8 and p. 5.

43 Ibid., p. 8.

44 Ibid., pp. 5–6.

45 Ibid., p. 8.

46 For some examples, see Richard Burt 'Local Conflicts in the Third World', in Richard K. Betts (ed.), *Cruise Missiles: Technology, Strategy, Politics* (Washington, DC: Brookings, 1981).

47 A concise summary is provided by Rik Coolsaet, 'Nato Strategy: Under Different Influences', *ADIU Report*, 6 (November–December 1984).

48 Summary of the 'AirLand Battle 2000' document in Diana Johnstone, *The Politics of Euromissiles* (London: Verso, 1984), pp. 198–9.

49 1982 edition of the US Army field manual (FM100–5) quoted in Coolsaet, 'Nato Strategy', p. 5.

50 UK *Statement on the Defence Estimates 1984*, 1 Cmnd 9227–1 (London: HMSO,

1984), p. 7.

51 The extent of this crisis and the reasons for it are still a matter of controversy. A number of different interpretations are discussed in two special issues of the *IDS Bulletin*: *Slowdown or Crisis? Restructuring in the 1980s*, 16 (January 1985); and *The Western Hemisphere in the World Crisis*, 16 (April 1985).

52 Brzezinski, *Power and Principle*, p. 443.

53 Michael Klare, *Beyond the 'Vietnam Syndrome': US Interventionism in the 1980s* (Washington, DC: Institute of Policy Studies, 1981), ch. 4.

54 Robin Luckham and Dawit Bekele, 'Foreign Powers and Militarism in the Horn of Africa', *Review of African Political Economy*, 30, 31 (September, December 1984).

55 Eldon Kenworthy, 'Grenada as Theater', *World Policy Journal*, 1 (Spring 1984).

56 Mary Kaldor, *The Baroque Arsenal* (London: André Deutsch, 1982), pp. 3–4. See also Andrew Brody, 'Growth, Cycles, Crisis' and Carlota Perez, 'Long Waves and Changes in Socioeconomic Organisation', in *IDS Bulletin*, 16 (January 1985); the former points out that technological cycles are analytically distinct from long waves.

57 Raphael Kaplinsky, 'Guns and/or Butter: The Relationship between the Economy and the Military', *IDS Bulletin*, 16 (September 1985).

58 Robin Luckham, 'Soviet Arms and African Militarization', in Robert Cassen (ed.), *Soviet Interests in the Third World* (London: Sage for Royal Institute of International Affairs, 1985), pp. 103–6.

59 See, for example, the World Bank, *World Development Report, 1985* (Washington, DC, 1985), pp. 35–7.

60 Jacques Gansler, *The Defense Industry* (Cambridge, Mass.: MIT Press, 1980), p. 12–28.

61 Spaven, 'A Piece of the Action'.

INDEX